CONTEMPORARY CHINESE LITERATURE

An East Gate Book

CONTEMPORARY CHINESE LITERATURE

An Anthology of Post-Mao Fiction and Poetry

Edited with introductions by
Michael S. Duke for the
Bulletin of Concerned Asian Scholars

M. E. SHARPE, INC., ARMONK, NEW YORK/LONDON

East Gate Books are edited by Douglas Merwin
120 Buena Vista Drive, White Plains, New York 10603

Copyright © 1984, 1985 by the *Bulletin of Concerned Asian Scholars*

All rights reserved. No part of this book may be reproduced
in any form without written permission from the *Bulletin of
Concerned Asian Scholars*.

First published in the United States in 1985 by M. E. Sharpe, Inc.
80 Business Park Drive, Armonk, New York 10504

Available in the United Kingdom and Europe from
M. E. Sharpe, Publishers, 3 Henrietta Street, London WC2E 8LU

Contemporary Chinese Literature is an expanded version of the
Bulletin of Concerned Asian Scholars (Vol. 16, No. 3, 1984).

Library of Congress Cataloging in Publication Data

    1. Chinese literature—Translations into English.
2. English literature—Translations from Chinese. I. Duke, Michael S.
II. Bulletin of concerned Asian scholars.
PL2658.E1C66   1985   895.1′08′005   85-10866
ISBN 0-87332-339-4
ISBN 0-87332-340-8 (pbk)

Printed in the United States of America

Contents

Michael S. Duke	3	Chinese Literature in the Post-Mao Era: The Return of "Critical Realism"

Ruins

Wan Zhi (Chen Maiping)	9	Open Ground/*translated by Bonnie S. McDougall*
Shi Mo (Zhao Zhenkai)	11	The Homecoming Stranger/*translated by Susette Cooke*

History

Shi Tiesheng	19	Blacky/*translated by Michael S. Duke*
Dai Houying	25	Father's Milk Is Also Blood Transformed *translated by Jeannette L. Faurot*
Zhu Lin	30	Downpour on a Leaky Roof/*translated by Richard King*
Yang Zhenwen	35	Fu Da Regains His Wife/*translated by Ping Yen and Michael S. Duke*

A World of Their Own

Bei Dao (Zhao Zhenkai)	41	Poems/*translated by Bonnie S. McDougall*
Gu Cheng	47	Poems/*translated by Shiao-ling Yu and Bonnie S. McDougall*
Shu Ting	52	Poems/*translated by Shiao-ling Yu*
Xie Ye, Jiang Wenyan, and Zhang Zhen	55	Poems/*translated by Bonnie S. McDougall*

Intellectual Youth in Quest of Light and Truth

Li Ping	59	Autumn/*translated by Daniel Bryant*
Li Chao	80	Spring Chill/*translated by Laifong Leung*

Women Then and Now

Zhang Xian	91	The Widow/*translated by Howard Goldblatt and Ellen L. Yeung*
Zhang Kangkang and Mei Jin	98	The Tolling of a Distant Bell *translated by Daniel Bryant*

The System

Dai Qing	109	No!/*translated by Dale R. Johnson*
Qiao Shi	115	Providing a Meal/*translated by Wendy Larson*
Shen Rong	120	Troubled Sunday/*translated by Vivian Hsu*

Marginal Lives

Shi Tiesheng	129	One Winter's Evening/*translated by Alison Bailey*
Shi Tiesheng	134	Lunch Break/*translated by Alison Bailey*
	137	About the Translators

CONTEMPORARY CHINESE LITERATURE

Photo by Saundra Sturdevant

Chinese Literature in the Post-Mao Era: The Return of "Critical Realism"

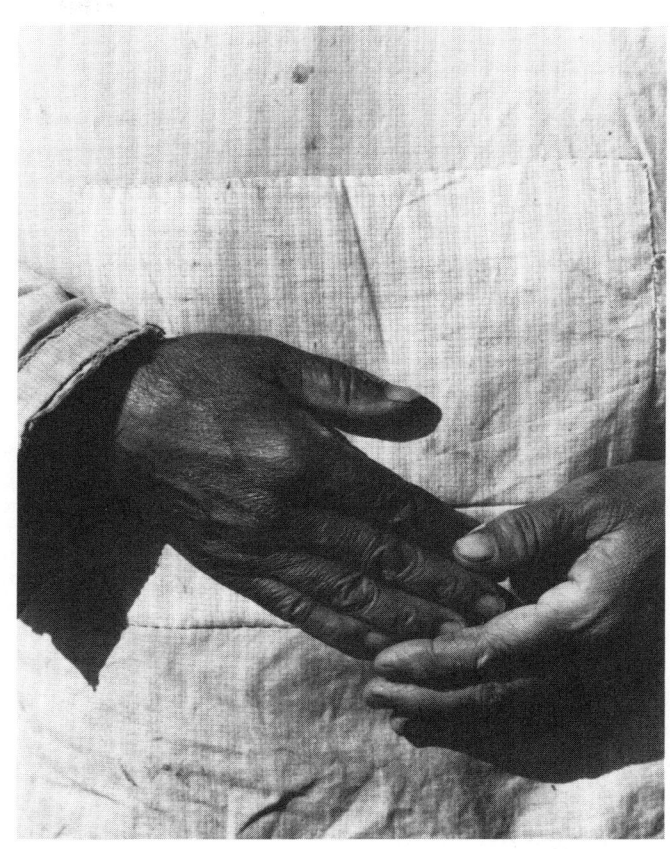

Photo by Saundra Sturdevant

by Michael S. Duke

> *To my mind, however, though all literature is propaganda, not all propaganda is literature. . . . In addition to slogans, posters, proclamations, telegrams, textbooks and so forth, the revolution needs literature—just because it is literature.*
>
> —Lu Xun, 1928[1]

The mainstream of modern Chinese literature during the pre-communist era was a form of realism that fits very well Rene Wellek's definition of realism as a regulative idea in European literature;[2] namely, it aims at

> . . . "the objective representation of contemporary social reality." It claims to be all-inclusive in subject matter and aims to be objective in method, even though this objectivity is hardly ever achieved in practice. Realism is didactic, moralistic, reformist. Without realizing the difference between description and prescription it tries to reconcile the two in the concept of "type." In some

writers, but not all, realism becomes historistic: it grasps social reality as dynamic evolution.

Such a tradition of realist fiction—didactic, moralistic, reformist—grew up in China through a combination of serious concern for society and principled demand for social justice that was characteristic of the finest products of traditional Chinese literature and the more individualistic humanitarianism of predominantly nineteenth-century European literature. It flourished during the period from the May Fourth Movement (1919) to the end of the Civil War between the Communist Party and the Kuomintang and the establishment of the People's Republic (1949). Under the influence of a narrow-minded Maoist interpretation of the function of literature in society, it lost its critical edge and humanistic thrust and became the handmaiden of the Party.

The works presented in this anthology are ample proof that the tradition of critical realism did not die. Chinese writers consider themselves to be intellectuals and are so regarded by society in general. As intellectuals they feel a serious responsibility to comment on and influence society. Accordingly, the majority of Chinese writers in the immediate post-Mao era, like their May Fourth predecessors, endeavored to use "critical realism" once more to ameliorate social ills by

---

1. Lu Xun, "Literature and Revolution," written 4 April 1928, in *Selected Works*, 3rd. edition (Peking: Foreign Language Press, 1980), Vol. III, p. 27.
2. Rene Wellek, *Concepts of Criticism* (New Haven: Yale University Press, 1963), pp. 252-253.

probing and criticizing injustices in the immediate past as well as the present.[3] After a decade of nearly complete suppression of literature in any meaningful sense of the term, a decade during which scores of writers and other intellectuals were hounded to death, the serious moral purpose of the bulk of Chinese literature in the immediate post-Mao era was to analyze and expose the systematic injustices created or exacerbated by the increasingly dictatorial and disastrous policies of the Maoist regime, from the Anti-Rightist Campaign (1957) and the Great Leap Forward (1958) through the Cultural Revolution (1966–1976). These writers were determined to "tell the truth" about society as they saw it and never again to lie to themselves and to others. Tang Dacheng put their credo most forcefully at a literary conference sponsored by the Anhui branch of the Chinese Writers Association in July 1980.[4]

> For a long time now it has been forbidden to write the truth, forbidden to truthfully reflect the people's lives, the people's loves and hates, forbidden for writers to base their works on their own observations and feelings about life and to express their own opinions. We could only write campaign literature or footnote literature. As a result we've been unable to produce true works. . . . This has been a tragic and shameful page in our nation's literary history. We must not under any circumstances ever again write lying or vainglorious literature.

In order to understand contemporary Chinese literature and its relationship to contemporary Chinese society, then, we should keep the following two points in mind:

• Chinese literature of the immediate post-Mao era is an outgrowth of May Fourth literature and is related to contemporary Chinese society in ways that parallel the relationship of May Fourth literature to the society of that era.

• Post-Mao literature reflects the changes that have occurred in Chinese society since 1949, the changing attitudes toward those events since the death of Chairman Mao, and the new regime's increasing emphasis on economic modernization as the overriding goal of the Chinese revolution.

During the decade of the Cultural Revolution, an ever more narrow application of the literary principles laid down in Mao's *Talks at the Yan'an Forum on Literature and Art*[5] had created a situation in which "critical realism" had been completely replaced by "Revolutionary Romanticism,"[6] an abject servant of each and every minor twist and turn of Party Central's day-to-day political policies. Nearly everything that had characterized May Fourth literature and even the previously acceptable "revolutionary" literature of the first seventeen years of the People's Republic was then forbidden. Gone were objective truth or common sense factuality, having been denounced as "naturalism" or "critical realism." Psychological exploration of character, one of the key elements that made modern Chinese literature modern, was denounced as a "bourgeois" indulgence. Universally applicable humanistic concern was forbidden because it detracted attention from the "essential class relations" (however prescriptive these had become since the elimination of the landlord gentry and bourgeois classes) said to determine all human behavior. Romantic love unrelated to interests of state or class solidarity was an unacceptable theme, as was the depiction of so-called middle characters as yet uncertain of their ideological commitment to the communist revolution. Finally, no spontaneous resistance to social injustice not led by the Communist Party, even in a historical context, could be presented in fiction.

This situation changed dramatically from late 1977 until the middle of 1981, as a result of liberalized literary policies pursued by the Deng Xiaoping reform faction during its power struggle with a faction predominantly composed of Maoist diehards, or "leftists," the former advocates of Jiang Qing's literary line. The relaxation culminated in Deng and Zhou Yang[7] extending personal promises, at the Fourth Congress of Writers and Artists in late 1979, that the Party would continue to let literature be free from "the issuing of executive orders." Although Deng and Zhou both outlined an agenda for writers to follow, their basic premise, proclaimed by Deng, was that "the sole criterion for deciding the correctness of all work should be whether that work is helpful or harmful to the accomplishment of the Four Modernizations." As a result of this open invitation from the highest Party leadership, the years 1979 and 1980 witnessed an unprecedented outpouring of critical realism that went far beyond anything written during the brief Hundred Flowers Campaign of 1956–57 or the previous two post-Mao years.

These works, harsh, satirical, or ironic, exposed such dark sides of contemporary Chinese life as rural poverty and the often cruel treatment of the peasantry by rural cadres; the venality and special privileges of older "revolutionary cadres" who had been attacked during the Cultural Revolution but were now getting even at the expense of society; corruption and degeneracy in the officer corps of the once sacrosanct People's Liberation Army; endemic bureaucratic corruption among

---

3. "Critical realism" is a term given great currency in literary criticism by Georg Lukács in his 1956 essay "Critical Realism and Socialist Realism." For a variety of personal, artistic, and perhaps political reasons, many contemporary PRC writers do not characterize their works as "critical realism" and some scholars of contemporary Chinese literature do not use the term. Nonetheless, I am hard put to find a better term for this literature. Except for the so-called obscure poetry (*menglongshi*) and possibly "One Winter's Evening," which is critical of a certain universal species of human insensitivity or cruelty, the fiction and a good part of the poetry in this book seem to me to be both realistic in Wellek's sense and critical in Lukács's sense. As Lukács wrote:

> The critical realist, following tradition, analyses the contradictions in the disintegrating old order and the emerging new order. But he does not only see them as contradictions in the outside world, he feels them to be contradictions within himself; though he tends—again following tradition—to emphasize the contradictions rather than the forces working for reconciliation. (Georg Lukács, *The Meaning of Contemporary Realism*, London: Merlin Press, 1963, p. 114)

I understand that contemporary Chinese writers, especially the younger ones, would like to go beyond realism, but I don't believe very many of them have succeeded in doing so to date. I certainly hope more knowledgeable readers will correct me if I am in error on this point.

4. "Bujian baodao de yici wenyi zuotanhui—ji Huangshan bihui" (An Unreported Literature and Art Discussion Meeting—Report on the Huangshan Writers' Conference), *Qishi niandai* (*The Seventies*), January 1981, p. 102.

5. Bonnie S. McDougall, *Mao Zedong's "Talks at the Yan'an Conference on Literature and Art": A Translation of the 1943 Text with Commentary* (Ann Arbor: University of Michigan Center for Chinese Studies, 1980).

6. This term was created for Mao by Zhou Yang in 1958 to replace "Socialist Realism" after the Sino-Soviet split, and was greatly elaborated by Jiang Qing and Yao Wenyuan during the Cultural Revolution.

7. Former Minister of Culture who was purged by Mao and rehabilitated by Deng as Vice-Chairman of the Chinese Writers Association.

economic cadres so bad that nothing can be produced without going through an incredible extra-legal network of bribery and gift-giving; embezzlement by high level officials; moral corruption and nihilism among a segment of the younger generation, often the children of high cadres; and the physical exhaustion of middle-aged intellectuals and professional cadres. These works also contained a number of technical "innovations," reintroductions, or rediscoveries from the pre-communist era of modern Chinese literature as well as from western fiction. Among the more notable of these were structural irony combined with allegory, ironic undercutting of accepted Party interpretations of reality through the playful manipulation of socialist rhetoric, the presentation of morally flawed characters as protagonists, settings involving high-ranking cadres in compromising positions, and the use of "stream-of-consciousness" and "internal monologue" aimed at revealing or even confessing a character's inner thoughts, feelings, and motivations.

As Deng's reform faction became increasingly secure politically throughout 1980 and 1981, they began to narrow the scope of what was artistically permissible. At a Drama Forum held in Peking in January and February of 1980, Hu Yaobang delivered a six-hour speech outlining precisely how the Party leadership wanted writers to treat nearly every conceivable literary topic. The immediate result of this speech was that the satiric drama *What If I Really Were?* (*Jiaru wo shi zhende*, 1979) was refused permission for open performance unless objectionable passages were revised. The leadership was particularly unhappy with the play's implication that the Party is a bastion of privilege that lords it over the general population. This was said to be an inaccurate presentation of the true relationship between the Party and the masses. Also unacceptable was the great sympathy shown to a young man who impersonates the son of a high cadre in order to wangle a transfer from the countryside back to the city where he can marry his already pregnant girlfriend. The authors refused to revise the play, but they did go on subsequently to tone down their criticisms and write safer, less objectionable, and less interesting plays.

The speech had a chilling effect on both writers and editors who had always been confused about the limits of the new freedoms and were afraid of overstepping those limits. There were some exceptions. Zhao Dan, a sixty-five-year old film star, denounced Hu's speech from his deathbed as another instance of the kind of "wanton interference" with literature that had always led to its stagnation in the PRC. Although his speech was printed in the *People's Daily*, Party policies towards literature grew continually more repressive.

From April to November 1981, the playwright Bai Hua was criticized for his supposedly anti-Party, anti-socialist film script *Bitter Love* (*Kulian*). It had been written in 1979, was then well received by critics, and hence made into a film in 1980–81, one destined never to be released. It was Hu Yaobang who took over the anti-Bai Hua campaign. It had been initiated by Deng's "leftist" opponents, but he made it the prototype for a late 1981 media blitz against "bourgeois liberalization," which Deng Xiaoping said was in essence "opposition to Party leadership." In late November Bai Hua finally submitted a letter of self-criticism. He confessed to having been ideologically confused when he wrote *Bitter Love* and reaffirmed his faith in the Party and the literary principles of Mao's *Yan'an Talks*. He went on the following year to write another historical play that appeared to be critical of Mao Zedong's last ten years. It was very popular with theatre audiences, and was also criticized in the press; but not to anything like the same degree that *Bitter Love* had been. This was probably because the later play adhered very closely to the dominant party faction's view of Mao and "ultra-leftism" as the main problem in recent Chinese history while *Bitter Love* implied an overall criticism of Communist Party policies since at least 1957.

Throughout 1982 the CCP conducted a campaign in favor of the building of a "socialist spiritual civilization" the most important aspect of which was said to be the education of the populace in communist ideology. By 1982 the great wave of critical realism with its open attacks on contemporary social problems had subsided. Many fiction writers continued to examine personal problems and employ modernist narrative techniques. Their works touched on the overall social situation, but were less obviously critical of the current regime. Meanwhile many young poets, despite being attacked as "obscure" and "nihilistic" by their elders, continued to experiment with the use of private symbolism. They advocated writing as a means of self-expression as much as social commentary. Indeed, many writers both young and old went on trying to produce works that emphasized technical artistry at least as much as, if never more than, theme.

Further insecurities were to affect Chinese literature late in 1983, after Zhou Yang himself tentatively suggested, following the young Marx of the *Economic and Philosophical Manuscripts* then in favor among some Chinese Communist Party theoreticians, that there could be Marxist-style "alienation" from labor, from political power, and from self and society in contemporary China. This opening quickly closed, though, when a shakeup took place in inner Party propaganda offices. A short-lived media campaign was carried on against these and other ideas grouped together as "spiritual pollution," meaning the pollution of China's revolutionary communist ideology by the importation of Western ideas and practices. The latter now included "bourgeois individualism," views of writing as self-expression, modernist literary techniques, "bourgeois humanism," alienation, the profit motive, sexual promiscuity, and others. A number of writers were publicly criticized and continued to be under a cloud into 1984, but many of those who were criticized by name refused to write self-criticisms. The Deng-Hu-Zhao Ziyang leadership, anxious not to alienate the intellectuals and professionals whose labors they took to be the key to modernization, did not vigorously pursue the campaign.

The literary situation in 1984 was one of general stability under a paternalistic system of literary control. Over thirty official journals churned out a vast amount of generally unremarkable material, but a few gifted writers consistently continued to turn out readable works. Now and again a particularly bright gem would be spotted by alert readers, receive national attention (perhaps official government condemnation, possibly the surest way to increased public notice and popularity), and be eagerly sought out by readers and scholars of Chinese literature abroad.

The present anthology was collected and translated with the readers of English language literature in mind. It is intended to introduce them to some artistically excellent examples of the genre of "critical realism" from the immediate post-Mao era in China. Most of the writers and all of the selections appear here for the first time in English. I do not maintain that these particular works are either the most popular inside the PRC or the most representative of the literally thousands of works published there from 1979 through 1982. What I do affirm is that each of the stories and all of the poetry in this volume was chosen for its intrinsic literary merit; not merely for its readability, but for its re-readability. There is no doubt much to be learned about the problematic areas of contemporary Chinese society from these works, but they are presented here as technically successful works of literary art worth reading and studying, in Lu Xun's words, as "literature—just because it is literature."[8]

★

---

8. I would like to thank Jeffrey Kinkley of St. John's University for his "labor of love" as both an outside reader and a strong supporter of this entire manuscript before it went to press. The poetic epigrams that precede each thematic section below were translated by Bonnie S. McDougall (Bei Dao) and Shiao-ling Yu (Gu Cheng and Shu Ting). I would like to give my thanks to Saundra Sturdevant who took the fine photos of China that grace this volume and chose them carefully to complement the themes of the selections.

RUINS

Everywhere are ruined walls and broken ramparts
how can the road extend beneath our feet
—Bei Dao

The most important of the unofficial literary magazines that sprang up during the "Peking Spring" of December 1978 to March 1979 was *Jintian* (*Today*). First appearing as a big-character poster on the walls of the Peking Ministry of Culture, *Jintian* published some 29 short stories, 87 poems, and other miscellaneous items before being closed down by the Public Security Bureau in August 1980. Its best known young writers included in this volume are Zhao Zhenkai (pseud. Shi Mo and Bei Dao), Chen Maiping (pseud. Wan Zhi), and Shu Ting. The writers in *Jintian* attempted to avoid blatantly tendentious literature because they believed "that literature should reflect the uniqueness of the individual human being; should present the author's individual vision of life; should express genuine emotions through the beauty and artistry of skillfully employed imagery, metaphors, and symbols; and, above all, should be autonomous and free from the direct restraints of politics."*

The "literature of the ruins" (*feixu wenxue*) is a term applied by Hong Kong critics to a group of stories like Shi Mo's "On the Ruins" (*Zai feixu shang*, *Jintian*, no. 1) that bear witness to the personal and cultural ruination caused by the Cultural Revolution years. The writer's intention, which is often compared to that of post-war German literature, is to provoke thought about the deeper significance of a terrible decade.

Wan Zhi's "Open Ground" (*Kaikuo di*) is one of those very short "ruins" stories dealing with the tragic irony of twentieth-century Chinese history, symbolized in a battleground where "ignorant armies," impelled perhaps by Fate, "clashed by night." Ironically, history comes full circle when the same Americans who once fought against the communist led PLA forces are now invited back to assist the present communist government in building a modern economy for China. Through his inner musings a nameless old ex-Kuomintang army officer asks but cannot answer the ultimate question—what was it all for?

Zhao Zhenkai is primarily a poet (pseud. Bei Dao) but his story "The Homecoming Stranger" (*Guilaide moshengren*)* evokes the pathos of the many lives and families ruined by Maoist policies, from the Anti-Rightist Campaign to the Cultural Revolution. The most poignant and fearful line in the story is that spoken by the young woman Lanlan, who has been deprived of her father's care by the state and betrayed by her mother for political reasons. Her mother says she will understand "a mother's suffering" when she marries and has children, but she replies, "We don't want children if we can't be responsible for their future." The "literature of the ruins" digs up the ruins of the past in order to prepare for a future that must never again suffer a holocaust like the Cultural Revolution. ★

---

* Michael S. Duke, *Blooming and Contending: Chinese Literature in the Post-Mao Era* (Bloomington: Indiana Univ. Press, forthcoming).

* The Chinese University Press of The Chinese University of Hong Kong has given its kind permission for the inclusion of "The Homecoming Stranger" by Shi Mo (Zhao Zhenkai) in this collection.

Open Ground

Photo by Saundra Sturdevant

by Wan Zhi (Chen Maiping)

The open ground lay ahead. Night still lingered there, no moon, but the sky was light and the stars were shining, so the ground looked vaster, darker. The murky shapes of several blockhouses loomed up in the twilight.

He walked over. There was no road, but he walked straight toward the dark shapes of the blockhouses, his feet from time to time tumbling over a stone. Once he even fell, skinning his palms, but he kept pressing forward in great haste.

He did not really want to go there at all. He felt afraid, and the hand that gripped the iron shovel was trembling involuntarily. It seemed as if someone was pursuing him from behind, and he often stopped still in alarm, turned and looked back, but apart from the lights at the small station there was not a soul in sight. As he had crossed the river, he had startled a pair of young lovers who had crossed the small bridge and were heading for the small slope over there, into the pine forest below the memorial. They had certainly not bothered speculating about what the old man with the shovel was up to.

What lay ahead? He did not know what the answer was either. It seemed there was a voice calling him, which seemed to come both from outside and from within himself. The voice was indistinct, and he could not make out the words which rose and fell, receded and returned in his mind, in rhythm with his pounding heart and coursing blood. It seemed like an invisible wind sobbing low. Driven on by the voice, he finally arrived.

Now he stood in front of the blockhouses. Constructed out of reinforced concrete, they had weathered the storms of thirty years, and were overgrown with wild artemisia. It was a grave, in which were buried a battle, a crime and worthless lives. The blockhouses stood in a row; the open ground had become a graveyard. He stood facing them: they were the past, the past was death, and death was what he remembered.

Yes, he had fought here. He had stood guard in this blockhouse, with American-style carbines and machine-guns, and with a brain that an American drill sergeant had given him . . . He had fought very well, and the open ground had helped him; he remained on guard until the last batch of people retreating south pulled out from the station. But here he had also become a prisoner.

The machinery of his memory had long since ceased revolving and was covered with a thick layer of dust. He had forgotten the past, he had even forgotten his memories. Now he had two rough hands, a wooden face, two lackluster eyes, seven false teeth and a heart that beat sixty times a minute.

This machine, however, could suddenly be set in motion again. If someone pressed the button, the motor would start throbbing. He did not know who had pressed the button, but now he began to recall the past. He could still count the growth rings on the tree of his life, remembering his childhood, his time at high school, his life at the military academy, his wife, their honeymoon, and the scented oak in front of the old cottage. He also remembered the prison camp, and the certificate of release when he had served his term . . .

It was not a dream, nor a story, but his memories had become so elusive, so confused.

Perhaps "it" was what had pressed the button. "It" was fate, "it" was the low voice that drove him on! Life was like a circle that "it" had drawn, starting out at a certain point and coming to an end at the same point. He had come here earlier in an American truck to build the blockhouses, but although he hadn't come in an American truck this time he had come to build an American-equipped factory and to demolish the blockhouses.

The blockhouse embrasures were staring at him. He felt afraid. The night air was cold and he was shivering from head to foot. The open ground was silent, full of the smell of death. A piercing whistle. He looked toward the station, where a train was just pulling in. The bright white gleam of the headlamps breached the darkness, stinging his eyes and casting his huge shadow over the open ground.

He withdrew in alarm into the shadow of the blockhouses.

The shovel struck against the reinforced concrete of the blockhouses and the sharp sound made him tremble with fear, his legs and feet numbed. He did not know why he was so afraid. Perhaps it was just instinct. The last few decades had worn away the luster of courage in his life, leaving behind a dingy color, the color of rust, the color of ice.

Nevertheless he set to work again. The shovel struck into the loose, soft mound of earth they had dug out during the day with a thud that spread out over the open ground. Startled by the noise, he stopped and turned around. Everything was terribly still, but the very stillness frightened him. He felt as if there was someone peering at him from inside the blockhouse. Staring at the pitch-black embrasures, he involuntarily crouched down, shrinking into himself, feeling safer in this position.

He decided not to use the shovel, and began digging up the earth with both hands. Grabbing a handful of moist earth, he felt the chill of the mud on his palms. This was earth that had been stained with blood. Perhaps there were still some molecules of blood, or had they already disappeared? They had evaporated in the sunlight and then been scattered in the wind, cast to the far corners and then to the open country beyond. Life comes and goes, but its material components always remain.

He continued groping, digging through the loose, soft earth, searching in the darkness. He felt himself touching something long and thin and pulled it out of the earth. Soon afterwards, a long piece, two long pieces, a short piece, two short pieces. He piled up the things from the mud under the blockhouse wall.

It was an accumulation of death, because these insubstantial objects were the bones of dead men—thigh bones, ribs, vertebrae, long and short, thick and thin. Perhaps they were one man's; more likely, two or three men's . . .

During the day, he and the workmen had been digging the foundations of a future factory here, and the white bones were dug up then. In the beginning, when they had dug up the first bone, no one had minded very much; anything can be dug up on a worksite. The young men threw the bone up into the air, their way of mocking him, an old KMT officer. Like him, they were former convicts who had stayed on after their release. They had committed all kinds of major and minor crimes, theft, robbery and rape, but they still had the right to mock him, since his crime was war and defeat. It was then that he had begun to recall his memories.

He did not tell the others that he had fought here; the past was over and gone. He had looked at the white bones, blankly shaking his head. When the bones increased in number as they dug, however, even these young men who boasted that blood and death held no terrors for them, felt the dry, lackluster bones gradually seizing their hearts; this accumulation of white bones was a concrete representation of death. The skulls and teeth, having experienced the taste of life in this world, now revealed the hideous smile of Death.

Now he started piling the bones up again. There was no doubt it was them, the people who had stubbornly held out in these blockhouses with him. When the gunfire had abated, the bodies of the victors were carried away and the victors buried over there—under the memorial, where glory stood guard over them, and they stood guard over peace, tranquility and happiness! But the bodies of the defeated were buried here, beside the blockhouses, crime stood guard over them, and they stood for death, disgrace and disaster!

Of course, there was still him, he was not buried here, not one of these bones was his; he had been taken prisoner, he was still alive. And yet he touched them as if touching himself, his own decaying teeth and empty eyesockets . . . He could well have been buried here too.

Human forms which would never return again to their original shapes were once attached to these bones. In his blurred memories he still seemed able to tell whose bones they were. This one with two big incisors was the machine-gunner's, he gnawed on other bones with these teeth, getting a box on the ear from him; this big thigh-bone, he could tell from its length who it had belonged to, a man who had liked to drink, and who cried at night thinking of his wife . . . None of them could be brought back into existence. Why had they died? When had their lives lost their value? No, he had no answer. He had ordered them about and told them off; why had he done that? Didn't he still not understand even today?

He had committed a crime, but why? Through trusting too readily in the Americans? Or was it fate? Or his own ignorance?

He knelt on the open ground, as if praying, but there were no words of prayer in his breast, no desires for the future; it was still the voice that drove him on sounding close by.

He had a sack with him. He put the bones into the sack, slung it over his shoulder and started on his way back. The sack was not at all heavy, but his legs felt very weak. A wind blew across the small river, a cold wind, a desolate autumn wind. The moon was rising, its silver light rippling over the river. He stopped by the side of the river and stood there in silence for a while. Then he took down the sack and with great care threw it into the water. The water splashed up, startling a pair of birds in the reeds opposite. They flew up abruptly, over his head, over the wide stretch of open ground, and disappeared behind the dark shadow of the blockhouses.

The moon cast a solemn shadow from the memorial on the hillside opposite. It looked very much like a sentry on night watch, staring at the open ground. Very soon, a modernized factory would be built on this piece of ground. ★

Originally published in *Jintian (Today)*, no. 5, 1979.

Translated by Bonnie S. McDougall

The Homecoming Stranger

by Shi Mo (Zhao Zhenkai)

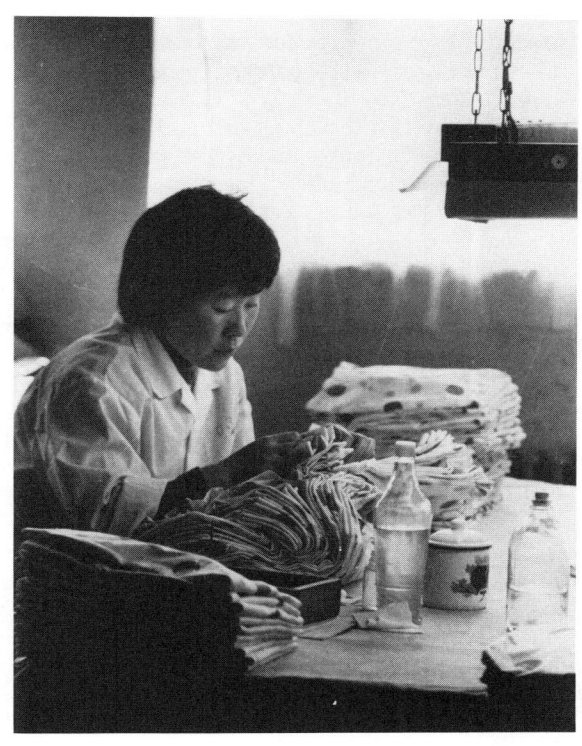

Photo by Saundra Sturdevant

1

Papa was back.

After exactly twenty years of reform through labor, which took him from the North-East to Shanxi, and then from Shanxi to Gansu, he was just like a sailor who, swept overboard by a wave, struggles blindly against the undertow until miraculously another wave tosses him back onto the same deck.

The verdict was: it was entirely a misjudgment, and he has been granted complete rehabilitation. That day, when the leaders of the Theater Association honored our humble home to announce the decision, I almost jumped up: when did you become so smart? Didn't the announcement that he was an offender against the people come out of your mouths too? It was Mama's eyes, those calm yet suffering eyes, that stopped me.

Next came the dress rehearsal for the celebration: we moved from a tiny pigeon-loft into a three-bedroom flat in a big building; sofas, bookcases, desks and chrome folding chairs appeared as if by magic (I kept saying half-jokingly to Mama that these were the troupe's props); relatives and friends came running in and out all day, until the lacquer doorknob was rubbed shiny by their hands, and even those uncles and aunts who hadn't shown up all those years rushed to offer congratulations . . . all right, cheer, sing, but what does all this have to do with me? My papa died a long time ago, he died twenty years ago, just when a little four or five year old girl needed a father's love—that's what Mama, the school, some kind-hearted souls and my whole social upbringing, starting from birth, told me. Not only this, you even wanted me to hate him, curse him, it's even possible you'd have given me a whip so I could lash him viciously! Now it's the other way round, you're wearing a different face. What do you want me to do? Cry, or laugh?

Yesterday at dinner time, Mama was even more considerate than usual, endlessly filling my bowl with food. After the meal, she drew a telegram from the drawer and handed it to me, showing not the slightest sign of emotion.

"Him?"

"He arrives tomorrow, at 4:50 in the afternoon."

I crumpled the telegram, staring numbly into Mama's eyes.

"Go and meet him, Lanlan." She avoided my gaze.

"I have a class tomorrow afternoon."

"Get someone to take it for you."

I turned towards my room. "I won't go."

"Lanlan." Mama raised her voice. "He is your father, after all!"

"Father?" I muttered, turning away fiercely, as if overcome with fear at the meaning of this word. From an irregular spasm in my heart, I realized that stitches from the old wound were splitting open one by one.

I closed the composition book spread in front of me: Zhang Xiaoxia, 2nd Class, 5th Year. A spirited girl, her head always slightly to one side in a challenging way, just like me as a child. Oh yes, childhood. For all of us life begins with those pale blue copybooks, with those words, sentences and punctuation marks smudged by erasures; or, to put it more precisely, it begins with a certain degree of deception. The teachers delineated life with halos, but which of them does not turn into a smoke ring or an iron hoop?

Shadows flowed in from the long old-fashioned windows, brightly illuminating the opaque glass desk-top. The entire staff-room was steeped in drowsy tranquility. I sighed, tidied my things, locked the door and, crossing the deserted school grounds, walked towards home.

The apartment block with its glittering lights was like a huge television screen, the unlit windows composing an elusive image. After a little while some of the windows lit up, and some went dark again. But the three windows on the seventh floor remained as they were: one bright, two dark. I paced up and down for a long time in the vacant lot piled with white lime and fir-tree poles. On a crooked, broken signboard were the words: "Safety First."

Strange, why is it that in all the world's languages, this particular word comes out sounding the same: papa. Fathers of different colors, temperaments and status all derive the same satisfaction from this sound. Yet I still can't say it. What do I know about him? Except for a few surviving old photographs retaining a childhood dream (perhaps every little girl has such dreams), . . . him, sitting on an elephant like an Arab sheik, a white cloth wound round his head, a resplendent mat on the elephant's back, golden tassels dangling to the ground . . . there were only some plays that once created a sensation and a thick book on dramatic theory which I happened to see at the waste-paper salvage station. What else was there? Yes, add those unlucky letters, as punctual and drab as a clock; stuck in those brown-paper envelopes with their red frames, they were just like death notices, suffocating me. I never wrote back, and afterwards, I threw them into the fire without even looking at them. Once, a dear little duckling was printed on the snow-white envelope, but when I tore it open and looked, I was utterly crushed. I was so upset I cursed all ugly ducklings, counting up their vices one by one: greed, pettiness, slovenliness . . . because they hadn't brought me good luck. But what luck did I deserve?

The elevator was already shut down for the day, and I had to climb all the way up. I stopped outside the door to our place and listened, holding my breath. From inside came the sounds of the television humming, and the clichés of an old film. God, give me courage!

As soon as I opened the door, I heard my younger brother's gruff voice: "Sis's back." He rushed up as if making an assault on the enemy, helping me to take off my coat. He was almost twenty, but still full of childish attachment to me, probably because I had given him the maternal love which had seemed too heavy a burden for Mama in those years.

The corridor was very dark and the light from the kitchen split the darkness into two. He was standing in the doorway of the room opposite, standing in the other half of the darkness, and next to him was Mama. The reflection from the television screen flickered behind their shoulders.

A moment of dead silence.

Finally, he walked over, across the river of light. The light, the deathly-white light, slipped swiftly over his wrinkled and mottled neck and face. I was struck dumb: was he this shriveled little old man? Father. I leaned weakly against the door.

He hesitated a moment and put out his hand. My little hand disappeared in his stiff, big-jointed one. These hands didn't match his body at all.

"Lanlan." His voice was very low, and trembled a little.

Silence.

"Lanlan," he said again, his voice becoming a little more positive, as if he were waiting eagerly for something.

But what could I say?

"You're back very late. Have you had dinner?" said Mama.

"Mm." My voice was so weak.

"Why is everyone standing? Come inside," said Mama.

He took me by the hand. I followed obediently. Mama turned on the light and switched off the television with a click. We sat down on the sofa. He was still clutching my hand tightly, staring at me intently. I evaded his eyes, and let my gaze fall on the blown-up plastic doll on the window-sill.

An unbearable silence.

"Lanlan," he called once again.

I was really afraid the doll might explode, sending brightly-colored fragments flying all over the room.

"Have you had your dinner?"

I nodded vigorously.

"Is it cold outside?"

"No." Everything was so normal, the doll wouldn't burst. Perhaps it would fly away suddenly like a hydrogen balloon, out the window, above the houses full of voices, light and warmth, and go off to search for the stars and moon.

"Lanlan." His voice was full of compassion and pleading.

All of a sudden, my just-established confidence swiftly collapsed. I felt a spasm of alarm. Blood pounded at my temples. Fiercely I pulled back my hand, rushed out the door into my own room and flung myself head-first onto the bed. I really felt like bursting into tears.

The door opened softly; it was Mama. She came up to the bed, sat down in the darkness and stroked my head, neck and shoulders. Involuntarily my whole body began to tremble as if with cold.

"Don't cry, Lanlan."

Cry? Mama, if I could still cry the tears would surely be red, they'd be blood.

She patted me on the back. "Go to sleep, Lanlan, everything will pass."

Mama left.

Everything will pass. Huh, it's so easily said, but can twenty years be written off at one stroke? People are not reeds, or leeches, but oysters, and the sands of memory will flow with time changing into a part of the body itself, teardrops that will never run dry.

. . . a basement. Mosquitoes thudded against the searing light bulb. An old man covered with cuts and bruises was tied up on the pommell horse, his head bowed, moaning hoarsely. I lay in the corner sobbing. My knees were cut to ribbons by the broken glass; blood and mud mixed together . . .

I was then only about twelve years old. One night, when Mama couldn't sleep, she suddenly hugged me and told me that Papa was a good man who had been wrongly accused. At these words hope flared up in the child's heart: for the first time she might be able to enjoy the same rights as other children. So I ran all around, to the school, the Theater Association, the neighborhood committee and the Red Guard headquarters, to prove Papa's innocence to them. Disaster was upon us, and those louts savagely took me home for investigation. I didn't know what was wrong with Mama, but she repudiated all her words in front of her daughter. All the blame fell on my small shoulders. Mama repented, begged, wished herself dead, but what was the use? I was struggled against, given heavy labor and punished by being made to kneel on broken glass.

. . . the old man raised his bloody face. "Give me some water, water, water!" Staring with frightened eyes, I forgot the pain, as I huddled tightly in the corner. When dawn came and the old man breathed his last, I fainted with fright too. The blood congealed on my knees . . .

Can I blame Mama for this?

2

The sky was so blue it dazzled the eyes, its intense

reflections shining on the ground. I was clutching a butterfly net, holding a small empty bamboo basket and standing amidst the dense waist-high grass. Suddenly, from the jungle opposite appeared an elephant. The tassels of the mat on its back were dangling to the ground; Papa sat proudly on top, a white turban on his head. The elephant's trunk waved to and fro, and with a snort it curled round me and placed me up in front of Papa. We marched forward, across the coconut grove streaked with leaping sunlight, across the hills and gullies gurgling with springs. I suddenly turned my head and cried out in alarm. A little old man was sitting behind me, his face blurred with blood; he was wearing convict clothes and on his chest were printed the words "Reform Through Labor." He was moaning hoarsely, "Give me some water, water, water . . ."

I woke up in fright.

It was five o'clock, and outside it was still dark. I stretched out my hand and pulled out the drawer of the bedside cupboard, fumbled for cigarettes and lit one. I drew back fiercely and felt more relaxed. The white cloud of smoke spread through the darkness and finally floated out through the small open-shuttered window. The glow from the cigarette alternately brightened and dimmed as I strained to see clearly into the depths of my heart, but other than the ubiquitous silence, the relaxation induced by the cigarette, and the vague emptiness left by the nightmare, there was nothing.

I switched on the desk lamp, put on my clothes and opened the door quietly. There was a light on in the kitchen and a rustling noise. Who was up so early? Who?

Under the light, wearing a black cotton-padded vest, he was crouching over the waste-paper basket with his back towards me, meticulously picking through everything; spread out beside him were such spoils as vegetable leaves, trimmings and fish heads.

I coughed.

He jumped and looked round in alarm, his face deathly-white, gazing in panic towards me.

The fluorescent light hummed.

He stood up slowly, one hand behind his back, making an effort to smile. "Lanlan, I woke you up."

"What are you doing?"

"Oh, nothing, nothing." He was flustered, and kept wiping his trousers with his free hand.

I put out my hand. "Let me see."

After some hesitation he handed the thing over. It was just an ordinary cigarette packet, with nothing odd about it except that it was soiled in one corner.

I lifted my head, staring at him in bewilderment.

"Oh, Lanlan," beads of sweat started from his balding head, "yesterday I forgot to examine this cigarette packet when I threw it away, just in case I wrote something on it; it would be terrible if the Team Leader saw it."

"Team Leader?" I was even more baffled. "Who's the Team Leader?"

"The people who oversee us prisoners are called Team Leaders." He fished out a handkerchief and wiped the sweat away. "Of course, I know, it's beyond their reach, but better to find it just in case . . ."

My head began to buzz. "All right, that's enough."

He closed his mouth tightly, as if he had bitten out his tongue. I really hadn't expected our conversation would begin like this. For the first time I looked carefully at him. He seemed even older and paler than yesterday, with a short greyish stubble over his sunken cheeks, wrinkles around his lackluster eyes that seemed to have been carved by a knife, and an ugly sarcoma on the tip of his right ear. I could not help feeling some compassion for him.

"Was it very hard there?"

"It was all right, you get used to it."

Get used to it! A cold shiver passed through me. Dignity. Wire netting. Guns. Hurried footsteps. Dejected ranks. Death. I crumpled up the cigarette packet and tossed it into the waste-paper basket. "Go back to sleep, it's still early."

"I've had enough sleep, reveille's at 5:30." He turned to tidy up the scattered rubbish.

Back in my room, I pressed my face against the ice-cold wall. It was quite unbearable, to begin like this, what should I do next? Wasn't he a man of great integrity before? Ah, Hand of Time, you're so cruel and indifferent, to knead a man like putty; you destroyed a father before his daughter could remember his real face clearly . . . eventually I calmed down, packed my things into my bag and put on my overcoat.

Passing through the kitchen, I came to a standstill. He was at the sink, scrubbing his big hands with a small brush, the green soap froth dripping down like sap.

"I'm going to work."

"So early?" He was so absorbed he did not even raise his head.

"I'm used to it."

I did not turn on the light as I went down along the darkness, along each flight of stairs.

3

For several days in a row I came home very late. When Mama asked why, I always offered the excuse that I was busy at school. As soon as I got home, I would dodge into the kitchen and hurriedly rake up a few leftovers, then bore straight into my own little nest. I seldom ran into him, and even when we did meet I would hardly say a word. Yet it seemed his silence contained enormous compunction, as if to apologize for that morning, for his unexpected arrival, for my unhappy childhood, these twenty years and my whole life.

My brother was always running in like a spy to report on the situation, saying things like, "He's planted a pot of peculiar dried-up herbs," "All afternoon he stared at the fish in the tank," "He's burned a note again. . . ." I would listen without any reaction. As far as I was concerned, it was all just a continuation of that morning, not worth making a fuss about. It was my brother who was strange, talking about such things so flatly, not tinged by any emotion at all, not feeling any heavy burden on his mind. It was no wonder; since the day he was born Papa had already flown far away, and besides, in those years he was brought up in his Grandma's home, and with Mama's wings and mine in turn hovering over Grandma's little window as well, he never saw the ominous sky.

One evening, as I lay on the bed smoking, someone knocked at the door. I hurriedly stuffed the cigarette butt into a small tin box, as Mama came in.

"Smoking again, Lanlan?"

As if nothing had happened I turned over the pages of a novel beside my pillow.

"The place smells of smoke, open a window."

Thank heavens, she hadn't come to nag. But then I realized that there was something strange in her manner. She sat down beside the small desk, absently picked up the ceramic camel pen-rack and examined it for a moment before returning it to its original place. How would one put it in diplomatic language? Talks, yes, formal talks . . .

"Lanlan, you're not a child anymore." Mama was weighing her words.

It had started; I listened with respectful attention.

"I know you've resented me since you were little, and you've also resented him and resented everyone else in the world, because you've had enough suffering . . . but Lanlan, it isn't only you who's suffered."

"Yes, Mama."

"When you marry Jianping, and have children, you'll understand a mother's suffering . . ."

"We don't want children if we can't be responsible for their future."

"You're blaming us, Lanlan," Mama said painfully.

"No, not blaming. I'm grateful to you, Mama, it wasn't easy for you in those years . . ."

"Do you think it was easy for him?"

"Him?" I paused. "I don't know, and I don't want to know either. As a person, I respect his past . . ."

"Don't you respect his present? You should realize, Lanlan, he showed great courage in staying alive!"

"That's not the problem, Mama. You say this because you lived together for many years, but I, I can't make a false display of affection . . ."

"What are you saying!" Mama grew angry and raised her voice. "At least one should fulfill ones own duties and obligations!"

"Duties? Obligations?" I started to laugh, but it was more painful than crying. "I heard a lot about them during those years. I don't want to lose any more, Mama."

"But what have you gained?"

"The truth."

"It's a cold and unfeeling truth!"

"I can't help it," I spread out my hands, "that's how life is."

"You're too selfish!" Mama struck the desk with her hand and got up, the loose flesh on her face trembling. She stared furiously at me for a moment, then left, shutting the door heavily.

Selfish, I admit it. In those years, selfishness was a kind of instinct, a means of self-defense. What could I rely on except this? Perhaps I shouldn't have provoked Mama's anger, perhaps I should really be a good girl and love Papa, Mama, my brother, life, and myself.

4

During the break between classes, I went into the reception office and rang Jianping.

"Hello, Jianping, come over this evening."

"What's up? Lanlan?" He was shouting over the clatter of the machines. His voice sounded hoarse and weary.

"He's back."

"Who? Your father?"

"Clever one, come over and help; it's an absolutely awful situation."

He started to laugh.

"Huh, if you laugh, just watch out!" I clenched my fists and slammed down the receiver.

It's true, Jianping has the ability to head off disaster. The year when the production brigade chief withheld the grain ration from us educated youth, it was he who led the whole bunch of us to snatch it all back. Although I normally appear quite sharp-witted, I always have to hide behind his broad shoulders whenever there's a crisis.

That afternoon I had no classes and hurried home early. Mama had left a note on the table, saying that she and Papa had gone to call on some old friends and that they would eat when they returned. I kneaded some dough, minced the meat filling, and got everything ready to wrap the dumplings.

Jianping arrived. He brought with him a breath of freshness and cold, his cheeks flushed red, brimming with healthy vitality. I snuggled up against him at once, my forehead pressed against the cold buttons on his chest, like a child who feels wronged but has nowhere to pour out her woes. I didn't say anything. What could I say?

We kissed and hugged for a while, then sat down and wrapped dumplings, talking and joking as we worked. I was almost on the verge of tears from the gratitude, relaxation and the vast sleepiness that follows affection.

When my brother returned, he threw off his work clothes, drank a mouthful of water, and flew off like a whirlwind.

It was nearly eight when they got home. As they came in, it gave them quite a shock to see us. Mama could not then conceal a conciliatory and motherly smile of victory; Papa's expression was much more complicated. Apart from the apologetic look of the last few days, he also seemed to feel an irrepressible pleasure at this surprise, as well as a precautionary fear.

"This is Jianping, this is . . ." My face was suffocated with red.

"This is Lanlan's father," Mama filled in.

Jianping held out his hand and boomed, "How do you do, Uncle!"

Papa grasped Jianping's hand, his lips trembling for a long time. "So you're, so you're Jianping, fine, fine . . ."

Delivering the appropriate courtesies, Jianping gave the old man such happiness he was at a loss for what to do. It was quite clear to me that his happiness had nothing to do with these remarks, but came from feeling that at last he'd found a bridge between him and me, a strong and reliable bridge.

At dinner, everyone seemed to be on very friendly terms, or at least that's how it appeared on the surface. Several awkward silences were covered over by Jianping's jokes. His conversation was so witty and lively that it even took me by surprise. After dinner, Papa took some Zhonghua cigarettes from his tin cigarette case and offered them to Jianping. This set them talking about the English method of drying tobacco and then on to things like soil salinization, the insect pests of peanuts and vine-grafting. I sat bolt upright beside them, smiling like a mannequin in a shop window.

Suddenly, my smile began to vanish. Surely this was a scene from a play? Jianping was the protagonist—a clever son-in-law, while I, I was the meek and mild new bride. For reasons only the devil could tell, everyone was acting to the hilt, striving to forget something in this scene. Acting out happiness, acting calmness, acting out glossed-over suffering. I suddenly felt that Jianping was an outsider to the fragmented, shattered suffering of this family.

I began to consider Jianping in a different light. His tone, his gestures, even his appearance, all had an unfamiliar flavor. This wasn't real, this wasn't his old self. Could strangeness be contagious? How frightening.

Jianping hastily threw me an enquiring glance, as if expecting me to repay the role he was playing with a commending smile. This made me feel even more disgusted. I was disgusted with him, and with myself, disgusted with everything the world was made of, happiness and sorrow, reality and sham, good and evil.

Guessing this, he wound up the conversation. He looked at his watch, said a few thoroughly polite bits of nonsense, and got to his feet.

As usual, I accompanied him to the bus-stop. But I said not a single word along the way, and kept a fair distance from him. He dejectedly thrust his hands in his pockets and kicked at stones.

An apartment block ahead hid the night. I felt alone. I longed to know how human beings survived behind these countless containers of suffering and broken families. Yet in these containers, memory is too frightening. It can only deepen the suffering and divide every family until everything turns to powder.

When we reached the bus-stop, he stood with his back to me, gazing at the distant lights. "Lanlan, do I still need to explain?"

"There's no need."

He leaped onto the bus. Its red tail-lights flickering, it disappeared round the corner.

5

Today there was a sports meet at the school, but I didn't feel like it at all. Yesterday afternoon, Zhang Xiaoxia kept pestering me to come and watch her in the 100 meter dash. I just smiled, without promising anything. She pursed her little mouth and, fanning her sweaty forehead with a handkerchief, stared out the window in a huff. I put my hands on her shoulders and turned her around, "I'll go then, all right?" Her face broadening into dimples, she struggled free of me in embarrassment and ran off. How easy it is to deceive a child.

I stretched, and started to get dressed. The winter sunlight seeped through the fogged-up window, making everything seem dim and quiet, like an extension of sleep and dreams. When I came out of my room, it was quiet and still; evidently everyone had gone out. I washed my hair and put my washing in to soak, dashing busily to and fro. When everything was done, I sat down to eat breakfast. Suddenly I sensed that someone was standing behind me, and when I looked round it was Papa, standing stiffly in the kitchen doorway and staring at me blankly.

"Didn't you go out?" I asked.

"Oh, no, no, I was on the balcony. You're not going to school today?"

"No. What is it?"

"I thought," he hesitated, "we might go for a walk in the park, what do you think?" There was an imploring note in his voice.

"All right." Although I didn't turn round, I could feel that his eyes had brightened.

It was a warm day, but the morning mist had still not faded altogether. It lingered around the eaves and treetops. Along the way, we said almost nothing. But when we entered the park, he pointed at the tall white poplars by the side of the road. "The last time I brought you here, they'd just been planted." But I didn't remember it at all.

After walking along the avenue for a while, we sat down on a bench beside the lake. On the cement platform in front of us, several old wooden boats, corroded by wind and rain, were lying upside down, dirt and dry leaves forming a layer over them. The ice melting in the water crackled from time to time.

He lit a cigarette.

"Those same boats," he said pensively.

"Oh?"

"There're still the same boats. You used to like sitting in the stern, splashing with your bare feet and shouting, "Motor-boat! Motor-boat!" The shred of a smile of memory appeared on his face. "Everyone said you were like a boy . . ."

"Really?"

"You liked swords and guns; whenever you went into a toyshop you'd always want to come out with a whole array of weapons."

"Because I didn't know what they were used for."

All at once, a shadow covered his face and his eyes darkened. "You were still a child then . . ."

Silence, a long silence. The boats lying on the bank were turned upside down here. They were covering a little girl's silly cries, a father's carefree smile, soft drink bottle-tops, blue hairclips, children's books and toy guns, the taste of earth in the four seasons, the passage of twenty years . . .

"Lanlan," he said suddenly, his voice very low and trembling, "I, I beg you to forgive me."

My whole body began to quiver.

"When your mother spoke of your life in these years, it was as if my heart was cut with a knife. What is a child guilty of?" His hand clutched at the air and came to rest against his chest.

"Don't talk about these things," I said quietly.

"To tell you the truth, it was for you that I lived in those years. I thought if I paid for my crime myself, perhaps life would be a bit better for my child, but. . . ," he choked with sobs, "you can blame me, Lanlan, I didn't have the ability to protect you, I'm not worthy to be your father. . . ."

"No, don't, don't. . . ." I was trembling, my whole body went weak, all I could do was shake my hands. How selfish I was! I thought only of myself, immersed myself only in my own sufferings, even making suffering a kind of pleasure and a wall of defense against others. But how did he live? For you, for your selfishness, for your heartlessness! Can the call of blood be so feeble? Can what is called human nature have completely died out in my heart?

" . . . twenty years ago, the day I left the house, it was a Sunday. I took an afternoon train, but I left at dawn; I didn't want you to remember that scene. Standing by your little bed, the tears streaming down, I thought to myself: "Little Lanlan, shall we ever meet again?" You were sleeping so soundly and sweetly, with your little round dimples, . . . the evening before, as you were going to bed, you hugged me by the neck and said in a soft voice, 'Papa, will you take me out tomorrow?' 'Papa's busy tomorrow.' You went into a sulk and pouted unhappily. I had to promise. Then you asked again, 'Can we go rowing?' 'Yes, we'll go rowing.' And so you went to sleep quite satisfied. But I deceived you, Lanlan. When you woke up the next day, what could you think. . . ."

"Papa!" I blurted out, flinging myself on his shoulder and crying bitterly.

With trembling hands he stroke my head. "Lanlan, my child."

"Forgive me, Papa," I said, choked with sobs. "I'm still your little Lanlan, always . . ."

"My little Lanlan, always."

A bird whose name I don't know hovered over the lake, crying strangely, adding an even deeper layer of desolation to this bleak winter scene.

I lay crying against Papa's shoulder for a long time. My tears seeped drop by drop into the coarse wool of his overcoat. I seemed to smell the pungent scent of tobacco mingling with the smell of mud and sweat. I seemed to see him during the breaks between heavy labor, leaning wearily against the pile of dirt and rolling a cigarette, staring into the distance through the fork between the guard's legs. He was pulling a cart, struggling forward on the miry road, the cart wheels screeching, churning up black clods of mud. The guard's legs. He was digging the earth shovelful after shovelful, straining himself to fling it towards the pit side. The guard's legs. He is carrying his bowl, greedily draining the last mouthful of vegetable soup. The guard's legs . . . I dared not think any more, I dared not. My power to imagine suffering was limited after all. But he actually lived in a place beyond the powers of human imagination. Minute after minute, day after day, oh God, a full twenty years . . . No, amidst suffering, people should be in communication with one another, for suffering can link people's souls even more than happiness, even if the soul is already numb, already exhausted . . .

"Lanlan, look," he drew a beautiful green necklace from his pocket, "I made this from old toothbrush handles just before I left there. I wanted to give you a kind of present, but then I was afraid you wouldn't want this crude toy . . ."

"No, I like it." I took the necklace, moving the beads lightly to and fro with my finger, each of these wounded hearts . . .

On the way back, Papa suddenly bent over and picked up a piece of paper, turning it over and over in his hand. Impulsively I pulled up his arm and laid my head on his shoulder. In my heart I understood that this was because of a new strangeness, and an attempt to resist this strangeness.

Here on the avenue, I seemed to see a scene from twenty years earlier. A little girl with blue hairclips, both fists outstretched, totters along the edge of the muddy road. Beside her walks a middle-aged man relaxed and at ease. A row of little newly-planted poplars separates them. And these little trees, as they swiftly swell and spread, change into a row of huge insurmountable bars. Symbolizing this are twenty years of irregular growth rings.

"Papa, let's go."

He tossed away the piece of paper and wiped his hand carefully on his handkerchief. We walked on again.

Suddenly I thought of Zhang Xiaoxia. At this moment, she'll actually be in the race. Behind rises a puff of white smoke from the starting gun and amid countless faces and shrill cries falling away behind her, she dashed against the white finishing tape. ★

Originally published in *Jintian* (*Today*), no. 1, 1979.

Translated by Susette Cooke

HISTORY

I was obliged to do battle with history and at knife-point formed a family alliance with idols, . . .
—Bei Dao

In the immediate post-Mao era many writers attempted to come to grips with the enormity of the events of the past decade as well to probe more than ever before into all of the problematic areas of the stormy, first thirty years of the People's Republic. Without being outspokenly political, "Blacky" (*Heihei*), by the talented young Peking writer Shi Tiesheng, combines realism and allegory in its moving presentation of rural poverty "in that age now past." The "good dog" Blacky may be seen as a powerful symbol for the trusting and long-suffering Chinese peasants during the Great Leap Forward and the Cultural Revolution. They were a people who "joyfully" followed their master's orders. But before they "had time to realize what had happened," as Günter Grass would say, their master turned out to be the hangman.

Dai Houying's 1980 novel *Ren a, ren!* is the most ambitious attempt yet to fathom the existential meaning of the Maoist era from 1957 to the 1970s. It is a plotless work in the conventional sense of plot as story line. In it the author employs the western, modernist technique of multiple first-person narration combined with internal monologues and non-linear time sequences to explore the problematic areas of individual responsibility, the relation of the individual to history, and the fate of individual human nature in a mass state. The novel immediately gained great popularity and became the subject of ideological controversy, a controversy that was renewed in the 1983–84 campaign against "spiritual pollution."

The autobiographical female protagonist, Sun Yue, was once in love with He Jingfu, but abandoned him for another man when he was branded as a "Rightist" in 1957. She "gave her heart to the Party" at that time and turned away from her natural inclination to seek personal happiness. Her husband betrayed her during the Cultural Revolution and entered into a liaison with a "rebel faction" woman of dubious moral character. Sun and her husband have a daughter Hanhan who is greatly troubled by her parents' separation and who wants very much to understand the father she has never known. Sun Yue is torn between her daughter's desire to meet her father, He Jingfu's renewed courtship and the possibility of happiness it holds, her former husband's attempts at reconciliation, and her fear of what the Party and society in general would think of her if she agrees to marry He Jingfu. The working out of her problems, never fully resolved, amounts to a confession of political and moral failure and an affirmation of faith in a future wherein the individual will not be sacrificed on the altar of social necessity or political expediency.

The male protagonist, He Jingfu, whose internal monologue is presented here, embodies the most insistent theme of the novel—the possibility of reconciling Marxism and humanism. He sees a unity between the two in their respect for the dignity and worth of the individual human personality, and their defense of independent ideas and opinions. Theory aside, much of his humanism is actually derived from the example of his father's simple goodness and dignity in the face of oppression, starvation, and death. This chapter represents the finest writing in the novel as well as one of the most poignant scenes in all of post-Mao literature.

"Downpour on a Leaky Roof" (*Yukuang wulou*) is a self-contained section from the young writer Zhu Lin's 1979 novel *The Path of Life* (*Shenghuo de lu*).* Based on personal experience, the novel tells the tragic story of an urban youth, Tan Juanjuan, who is "sent down" (*xiafang*) to the Anhui countryside in the late 1960s. There she is shocked and disillusioned by the peasants' extreme poverty and the rural cadres' cruelty and corruption. She commits suicide after being raped by the Party Secretary of her work unit.

This brief section compresses the inexorable cycle of rural deprivation, betrayal, beggary, and death into one day in the life of the old peasant Louwa. The title comes from an aphorism meaning that disaster strikes hardest at those least able to protect themselves.

"Fu Da Regains His Wife" (*Fu Da jieqin*), by the forty-four year old professional writer Yang Zhenwen, might be more reasonably titled "Fu Da Regains Himself." Although quite obviously in favor of the current reforms in agricultural economic policy—Yuegui and her new husband can now sell privately raised pigs for private profit and have money to travel—the heart of Yang's story is his delineation of the simple and sincere inner thoughts and recollections of the once obedient peasant Fu Da ("Lucky"). He gradually comes to rejoice in his ex-wife's good fortune and, more importantly, overcomes his subservient attitude toward the once all-powerful Revolutionary Committee Chairman Qin. ★

---

* Richard King, the translator, is now working on a doctoral dissertation in which this novel figures prominently. My thanks to him for his assistance with this passage.

Blacky

by Shi Tiesheng

Photo by Saundra Sturdevant

It is necessary to explain at the outset that this is something that happened in that age now past.

1

At that time I really was prepared to kill myself, but then I thought why not go and take a look at the old home I had been parted from for so long and then die? I was being sent back anyway and didn't need to arrange anything.

I wrote a last letter to my ex-wife and boarded the train west all alone. The letter was quite simple: "At a time when everyone is competing to sing bright songs, anyone who reveals the darkness will come face to face with an endless darkness—I don't know if this in itself is good or evil." At any rate I had decided upon suicide and wasn't afraid of having another line added to my dossier: "utterly incorrigible." No, I was no hero. Aren't heroes all courageous and far-sighted, full of unbounded confidence, with never the slightest feeling of pessimism, depression, or sadness? And me? To tell you the truth all I *could* feel was pessimism, depression, and sadness. My bedroll bounced from side to side on the overhead luggage rack; tied around it was a good strong rope . . .

2

The hills and streams of my old home were the same, but all of the people there were strangers. There were a few older people that I could still recognize, but they could not for the life of them remember me. All I could do was smile at them and recall a line from an ancient poem: "I left home as a youth and return an old man. . . ,"* but I still felt pretty silly. Only the yellow earth of my old home gave me some comfort; it would probably be quite satisfying to be buried underneath it.

A young Brigade Leader led me up the hill. The broad clear river flowed by in front of the village sounding just like the blind storyteller's zither I remembered from my childhood; but I recalled He Jingzhi's folksongs:* the lambs they were nursing and eyeing their mother, millet gruel nourished me as I grew up. . . . As I entered the village I saw a child picking weeds and chewing on a dumpling made from chaff.

The young Brigade Leader kept looking me up and down. His attitude wasn't really very stern, in fact he was so kind he was almost humble. That was probably because I was wearing a uniform and, although my shoes were worn, they were *leather* shoes nevertheless. On the road from the commune to the village, we ran into an old man herding sheep and the Brigade Leader struck up an animated conversation with him. "Huh? He didn't think it was good enough to be a cadre in Peking? He must've done something wrong!" That was the old man's sadly commiserative voice. Perhaps a wanderer's greatest sadness is to be misunderstood by his loving mother.

At the top of the hill there were two dilapidated cave dwellings surrounded by a courtyard wall made of piled up rocks. My heart skipped a beat. Mother will never again stand by the millstone in the front yard and call me home for dinner. Right there was where my cradle used to sit.

"It's this one on the right," the Brigade Leader said.

I never imagined this would also be my grave, I thought.

"When your Pa died, this dwelling was given to Zhang Shan's family. You know Zhang Shan? You don't know him, Zhang Shiyou's son?"

---

*This is the first line of a famous quatrain by the Tang dynasty poet He Zhizhang (Ho Chih-chang, 659–744).

*He Jingzhi (1924–) is a famous poet, author of many popular ballads employing the Northern Chinese folk song style *shun-tian-you* ("follow the drift of the singer") as well as co-author of the opera *White Haired Girl* (1945).

"Cre-e-e-ek," the courtyard gate swang open and suddenly a dog barked. I stepped back instinctively.

"Don't be afraid," said the Brigade Leader, "Blacky doesn't have the strength to bite anybody."

Blacky!? I thought I was seeing a ghost: a dog was lying in front of that cave dwelling on the left. I had a black dog when I was little. I even hated that black dog once when I heard the blind man tell the story of "Creating Great Havoc in the Heavenly Palace."* But one time when I was tending the sheep and ran into a wolf, if it hadn't been for that strong, healthy black dog, never mind about the sheep, even I wouldn't be here today. It may sound funny, but from that time on I always believed that Erlang's dog was brown. Children have their own kind of logic for solving problems; they can't think of any better way to explain undeniable contradictions, but they're very anxious to arrange things according to their own imagination in order to achieve psychological harmony.

This was not a ghost. There really was a black dog lying in front of that cave dwelling on the left. Her lusterless black fur could no longer hide her rib bones; her two thigh bones stuck out sharply on either side of her shriveled up stomach, and the ends of the bones looked like they might pierce through the skin at any time. She stared at me with eyes full of enmity, but she didn't move; she just kept on barking every once in a while. That was when I finally realized that her bark was so weak it resembled nothing more than the last gasps of someone who was wasting away in isolation.

That dog at least aroused my interest, stirred up my feelings for my old home. I walked over towards Blacky.

Blacky struggled to her feet, gnashed her teeth together, and emitted a hoarse growl from her throat.

"Don't tease her, Blacky's not long for this world." The Brigade Leader's voice was full of empathy and pity.

I broke off a piece of leftover *mantou* and threw it to Blacky, but she remained on her guard, staring at me without even looking at it. Now that's a good dog! My childhood experience taught me that. I even felt that she must be that very same black dog that saved my life, or else its offspring. That black dog of mine died a long time ago; it had finally been killed by a wolf. My father had its skin made into a rug and sent it to me; I brought it back with me.

"Eat it Blacky! That's good steamed bread, stupid Blacky!" A boy of eleven or twelve stood on the roof of the cave dwelling and yelled at Blacky.

"Come on down and let her eat," I shouted at the boy.

The boy came down to the front of the cave and hugged Blacky's head. Although Blacky's eyes still looked fierce, she just lay there in the boy's arms and barked in a most peculiar manner, like a freezing hen emitting a long drawn out cry. I understood that sound; she was complaining about the insult she had just suffered. From the looks of it, that boy was the one person she trusted most.

Suddenly I had a malicious thought: what would happen if at this moment that boy were to give Blacky a terrible beating . . .

---

*"Creating Havoc in the Heavenly Palace" is a popular storyteller's account of episodes from chapters 5 and 6 of the novel *Journey to the West*. In it the Monkey King Sun Wukong has a terrible fight with several emissaries of the Jade Emperor and is finally subdued by the Immortal Master Erlang with the aid of a small black hound. See pages 134-165 of Anthony C. Yu's translation, volume 1, University of Chicago Press, 1977.

3

I lived in the eastern cave dwelling while Blacky guarded the western cave dwelling. Ever since Zhang Shan disappeared, a big brass lock hung on the door to that western cave dwelling and the yellowing window paper was completely splattered with muddy rain drops. Blacky was on guard against me for fear that I would invade her territory, and I was on guard against other people; no telling when they might drag me out for a criticism session. Blacky could hardly pay me any mind: she was hungry. And I was in no state to think about her: I wanted to die. We both kept to our thoughts and left each other in peace. Occasionally, when the boy came by and gave Blacky half a ladle of pig slop or a handful of sweet potato peelings, Blacky would wolf them down in a hurry, lick the boy's hand a couple of times, sprawl out in front of the cave like before, and continue guarding her territory. Many villagers would often stand at the courtyard entrance on their way by and look in, mostly to get a look at the man from Peking; but they would always compliment Blacky before they moved on. "*Ai*, his young wife took the kids and left! But Zhang Shan raised such a good dog. . . ," they all said.

There were two reasons why I had not yet used that rope: one was because the cave dwelling didn't have any roof beams, and the other was because I had not yet seen enough of the mountains and rivers of my old home. But then again, perhaps neither of these was the true reason. It could be counted my good fortune that the people had no time to pay me any mind. They were in bondage to famine and thus I gained my freedom. I wandered around on the little paths between the paddyfields, watching the dewy buckwheat flowers bursting into bloom and listening to swarms of bees working noisily away. I walked slowly and quietly into the depths of the jujube groves. I was moved at the sight of new shoots springing up from the roots of the old trees and sighed at the birds' busy pursuit of life. Evenings I watched the moon from the threshing ground and was touched by the old cow nursing her calf. Late nights when my nightmares kept me from sleep, I was awakened by the calls of wild animals in the fields . . . All of nature's myriad creatures instinctively resist death, and how much more should man! But only man sometimes thinks of suicide. Where, then, is man's superiority?

In July a thunderstorm brought on a mountain flood. That tame little river in front of the village suddenly grew angry; with thunderous waves and rolling white waters leaping up to the sky, it roared as it uprooted the old trees on the hillside and swept them along on the crests of its waves or tossed the slow moving herds of sheep down into its swift flowing valley . . . I ran down the hill to the river bank. Usually the waters, which barely deserved to be called a river, just managed to cover my knees, but at that time the river was several meters wide. The hills on the other side were lost in the rain and mist, just as if this yellow water made a solid mass with the sky; the heavens too were a yellowish-brown color, brightened every so often by a fiery flash of lightning, after which the thunder rumbled on for some time. I thought of a picture I'd seen once, of force-nine waves. That was on the ocean, but I still imagined that if I had an old sailboat, this water would be strong enough to lift it off; of course it would be strong enough to capsize it too . . . I was stupefied by the mighty rush of this distant offspring of the Yellow River, I could not recall a similar situation, probably because at that time the hills had not yet been as thoroughly cultivated or as completely denuded of trees as they were today.

"Look! Blacky is over there going crazy again!" Someone was yelling.

I looked up at the top of the cliff. It was Blacky. She was standing on the edge of the cliff, stretching out her neck and barking wildly as if she were just about to jump down into the roiling torrent. Every bit of her fur was matted down strand by strand on her emaciated body. The sound of the thunder and the water was too loud, but just from Blacky's appearance I could tell that her bark was angry and hoarse, full of fear and resentment.

"That Zhang Shan certainly raised a good dog!" everyone said once more.

I walked up to the top of the ridge. The boy was leaning against the courtyard wall with an empty gunnysack thrown over his shoulders,

"What's the matter with Blacky," I asked him.

"She's feeling bad."

"Why?"

"On account of her conscience."

"Conscience?"

"Look at how sadly she's barking."

Blacky crouched down at the edge of the cliff, then she lay down, put her head to the ground and held her nose between her front paws. Rather than say she was panting it would be better to say she was trembling. I walked up close to her, but she didn't seem to notice; her bark was now only a whimper. Blacky was certainly acting strange.

"She's crying," said the boy.

"Crying? Why?"

"For Zhang Shan. When Zhang Shan was dragged away that day, Blacky wasn't at home. If she had been, she would have been able to follow them; but a mountain flood came down just as she was returning home and cut off her road. Every time there's a big rain storm, Blacky starts to cry, she's so sorry...."

"Zhang Shan was taken away? What for?"

The boy stared straight ahead; I asked him again, but he said nothing.

Blacky ran down to the front of the western cave dwelling as if she had suddenly awakened from slumber. She walked back and forth inspecting her territory, looking over the cave door with the brass lock, the rain soaked window paper, and the cobweb covered door lintel before she lay down, seemingly relieved, in front of the door. Her bark changed again to a steady "woo woo woo . . . ," as though she had converted her grief into strength.

Zhang Shan was a mystery.

While hoeing in the fields I employed every sort of verbal stratagem and circumlocution I could think of to try to learn something about Zhang Shan from the local villagers, but everyone's lips were sealed up like a wine jug. Or else they'd just say, "You'll understand by and by." From the way they sighed, shook their heads, and looked away lost in thought, I could gather that they all felt great sympathy for Zhang Shan and also seemed to have a guilty conscience on his account. Sometimes I even felt that the villagers had great respect for Zhang Shan. When they were quietly lost in thought, puffing away on their long stemmed pipes, they were probably praying to Heaven for Zhang Shan's sake.

4

I made a sincere effort to make friends with Blacky. Those who are alone and helpless should be drawn together by mutual concern for their common fate, I thought.

I put a piece of sweet potato on the ground and called out for Blacky.

Blacky didn't even pay any attention to it. I picked up the sweet potato and edged over closer to her. She struggled to stand up and let out a weak "woo-loo woo-loo" sort of bark.

"You like Blacky too?" The boy appeared once again on top of the cave dwelling.

I tried to explain myself with a laugh, "But she's even less sympathetic than I am."

The boy didn't understand my remark. He replied, "Blacky understands people and she's loyal too! But she's afraid of your leather shoes."

"She can recognize leather shoes?"

"Of course she can; those men wore them too!"

"Who?"

The boy realized he'd said too much already and didn't answer.

I changed into a pair of sneakers and once more kicked that piece of sweet potato over toward Blacky in an effort to express my desire for friendship.

Blacky still paid no attention.

"You hide first," the boy motioned me away.

Oh, right, I had to let Blacky know that my offering was completely good intentioned and didn't harbor even the least bit of hidden danger. I walked nonchalantly into my cave dwelling, shut the door, and watched Blacky through a crack in the door.

Blacky was really sharp. She put on an air of nonchalance too, kept on barking to make it clear that her anger had not yet dissipated, and seemed to be saying, "Don't try to pull anything on me!" But she was very hungry after all. After looking to the left and the right, she let down her guard, stopped barking, and hurriedly gulped down the sweet potato. She wolfed it down fast and furiously, all the while casting anxious glances over at my cave door. *Ai*, that pitiful look in her eyes was very nearly human. I threw out another piece of sweet potato from behind the door; Blacky hesitated a moment, but having had a taste of something good her reason had become a prisoner of her appetite and she started right in eating again.

It was quite amazing! From then on whenever Blacky saw me again, although her ears twitched constantly to express her lingering fear, still she didn't bark anymore, she only stared imploringly at me, and when I threw her a morsel of food she ate it right up in full acceptance of her abject status. Nevertheless she absolutely refused to allow me anywhere near the door to her cave dwelling.

One time I used some vegetables that had been sautéed in oil to lure her aside, and then quietly approached the door of that cave dwelling. When Blacky noticed she rushed at me, roaring like a lion. We were friends, but that guaranteed only that she wouldn't bite me; she roared at me insistently, both as a reprimand and a warning to stay away. I suddenly had a mystical feeling about that cave dwelling—perhaps it was the dog's sacred altar? Perhaps Blacky's idol was inside?

That summer's tempest of rain and hail and the consequent flooding brought on a great calamity. The wheat, for which there was no time to harvest, simply rotted in the fields; the corn and sorghum that were just putting forth buds and tassels were crushed and scattered around the hillside. The purple color of the roots and stems all exposed to view predicted the harshness of life in the fall and winter to come. Every family started to eat only chaff and husks; the children went up the hills with little baskets to look for edible wild grasses; and everyone stored away what little good grain still remained, more carefully than ever, in order to prepare for next spring's famine conditions—they could not be without food in the spring, that's the season when they need their strength.

Who could pay any mind to Blacky? Although she was a dog with almost human feelings, still the chaff and husks were eaten by the people and the sweet potato peelings, slops, and so forth were just enough to feed the hogs. When the little boy was scolded by his family, he ran over empty-handed to hug Blacky as well as to console himself. What about me? Every night I dreamed of visiting famous restaurants like the House of Virtue, Eastern Ease, and Prosperity Gardens, and every day I woke up to ravenously wolf down sourdough pancakes made from chaff and bitter yams left over from last year. Blacky continued stubbornly guarding her cave dwelling, not searching for food and not stealing anything. When she felt that her territory was absolutely secure, she would nose around quietly and find some human excrement to consume and redigest.

I was somewhat disgusted with Blacky. I felt that her actions embodied a sort of disgraceful practice that was contrary to nature. I don't mean simply because she ate excrement, but rather because she insisted on guarding her sacred altar.

"A good dog, she's really a good dog," the passers-by always said.

"If my place was threatened by wolves, I'd just take Blacky home with me," someone else affirmed.

"Blacky wouldn't go home with you. A good dog doesn't care if his home is poor; a good dog can't be led away!" still another passer-by insisted.

"Oh Blacky! It's really hard; seems like only a willingness to suffer repeated hardships can make you a good dog."

From Blacky's case I went on to think about myself: why hadn't I committed suicide yet? Was this earth simply the sacred altar that *I* was stubbornly guarding? Was the humiliation and repression my spirit had suffered any more savory than excrement? Who knows whether or not when our souls leave their flesh and blood outer shells, they are able to find truth, freedom, and happiness in another realm?

All that night I heard Blacky barking in the courtyard. That time the sound of her bark was of a sort I'd never heard before: first it was long and drawn out like a sigh, then it was a deep moan, as if she were suffering from some sort of inner turmoil. Did Blacky feel empty too? I wondered as I laughed bitterly to myself and began to fiddle with that long untouched luggage rope of mine. Maybe hanging it on the lintel of the door would accomplish my purpose . . . I unconsciously pushed the door open and hung the rope up over the door . . .

Suddenly I realized that I couldn't hear Blacky's bark any longer. Huh!? Blacky had disappeared. This seemed like a most interesting development. I sat down on the doorstep and stared at that empty patch of Blacky's territory; I only hoped she had not gone to eat excrement again. Then I suddenly felt like a miracle was about to take place. I looked forward to the appearance of some sort of miracle. When a person reaches the nadir of emptiness, any small, slightly out of the ordinary occurrence in his life is sufficient to arouse great interest. Thus I sat there on the doorstep until dawn. Hurray! She'd gone AWOL! Blacky, too, had come to her senses. She hadn't come home all night. I tossed my luggage rope into the corner again.

That morning the boy stood on top of the cave dwelling again.

"Oh! Blacky went looking for a mate!" he told me.

He laughed out loud. "Blacky wants to start a family!"

Suddenly it dawned on me. After so many years I'd actually forgotten such things. Blacky's bark last night was just like the complaints of a love-sick fool, but that sound also contained a kind of beautiful desire—Blacky had gone courting! Emotional needs and survival needs can cause any living thing to break out of the prison house of habit. This, then, is creativity; this is the reason for and the force behind creativity. No matter how ruthlessly the outside world ties one down, no matter how rigid the concepts of one's inner world, they are no match for the elemental forces of life itself.

Once more I forgot about dying. I was constantly picturing Blacky's happiness to myself. Where are you at this moment? Are you frolicking through the mountains and fields with your sweetheart, laughing in gay abandon? Rolling around in the tall grass, pouting and acting spoiled in the embrace of your sweetheart? Chasing and capturing your prey, experiencing the joy of creativity? Savoring raw flesh and blood as you joyfully devour your prey together? Caressing each other's fur, nuzzling, and enjoying the sweetness of love? Howling in the wilderness, giving vent to your primeval emotions? You sleep peacefully under the starlight with a completely reliable friend at your side to keep guard and ward off trouble for you. You murmur in your sleep, dreaming beautiful dreams. You bite him because he's not tender enough. You bark fiercely in a fit of temper because he doesn't understand you. You two keep your distance for a while in anger and then you make up again. You weep on each other's shoulders and then comfort each other's wounded heart. You tell each other everything without suspicion or defense . . . In the morning when the sun shines down on your den, the two of you sing to the sky, lift up your spirits, run forth into that boundless wild with your hearts full of new hopes and expectations . . . My heart followed Blacky, ran on in freedom, immersed in some sort of obscure hope.

5

Not long after that, however, Blacky returned from her "honeymoon."

She came back very quietly. At noontime, just as I was walking back and forth on Blacky's territory chewing on a piece of coarse-grain bread, she lightly pushed open the courtyard gate and came in. She didn't actually bark or demand that I get out of her territory immediately; she just sort of loped over to her "guard station" and lay down. The embarrassed expression on her face seemed to say: "This is not your fault, it's mine. It's a good thing it's only you and not some outsider."

Blacky did not seem the least bit interested in anything; she just lay there rolling her eyes and worrying about her situation. Was she exhausted from her travels? Was she longing for her "sweetheart"? Was she still wrapped up in her recent happiness? With your beautiful dreams in the tall grass, your words of love under the bright moon, and with a friend and equal to worry about you and treat you tenderly, what did you want to come home for? Lying there in front of this lonely cave dwelling . . . Oh, the wind in the mountains is very cold; but who's going to show you the least bit of warmth here?

While Blacky was on her "honeymoon," I had poked open the paper windows of that western cave dwelling: there was the musty smell of mildew; a discolored mat coverlet was draped over the adobe *kang*;* in the back of the room there were two empty rice bins; a long bench nearby was covered with dust and imprinted all over with rat tracks. That was all, just that much was all that Blacky had been guarding. My God! Habit is truly frightening! A dog really is a dog after all and a dog's nature is hard to change. I actually felt like beating her then; but as soon as I saw that sincere expression on Blacky's face, of one who is willing to bear gladly the work and the calumny of office, I could no longer bear to scold her. All the more so, given the state I myself was in, what right did I have to be overly critical of a dog?

An obvious change in Blacky since she returned this time was that she'd become extremely taciturn. For days on end she just lay there quietly, worrying, in front of the cave dwelling.

One day the little boy found a dead crow somewhere. "Blacky, here's a reward for you!" he called out; and then he stroked Blacky's stomach and yelled out with a laugh, "Blacky's going to be a Mama!"

Oh, so that's what she was worrying about. Of course, living alone is difficult enough—what would happen if she tried to raise a family? Would her future life be beautiful or hard and bitter? A man's inability to understand a dog is just like a dog's inability to understand a man—who could have known what Blacky was planning?

The boy brought over a willow basket which he had lined with a gunnysack and some straw. Blacky rubbed herself back and forth against the boy's pantleg to express her gratitude. "My pups will never forget your kindness." If she could speak, that is certainly what she would say. Mothers are completely unselfish and motherhood is most readily respected by others, most capable of arousing other people's sense of compassion. I brought that dog skin rug of mine over and wrapped it around the willow basket. Then I suddenly grew frightened, but Blacky just kept on rubbing back and forth all around me to express her gratitude—she was incapable of understanding where that pelt came from. At that same moment I felt once again the pride of being a human being; we are able to sum up the lessons of history. In my own case, for example, I spoke out about the reality of the darkness and corruption—and what a similarity there is between the beginnings of this darkness and so many other tragedies in history!—even though I was banished and lost my wife and children on that account . . .

Blacky's abdomen was growing bigger and bigger. As her time grew near she actually became very active. Was it her hopes of motherhood spurring her on? She stretched out regularly in the willow basket, inspecting to see if the straw and gunnysack were arranged properly, or else she'd jump in and try it out, straightening up here and there, all the while barking away softly. Perhaps she was practicing a lullaby. *Ai*, no matter what you say, the little lives forming in her belly knew nothing of the heat or cold of the outside world; as a mother she had to think out everything very carefully for their sake.

---

*A *kang* is a Northern Chinese bed made of adobe bricks under which a fire can be built.

Blacky began to go wrong. She regularly abandoned her post and she began to forage for food, began to wag her tail everywhere in an effort to gain sympathy. She began to fight with other hungry dogs, scrambling for a piece of sweet potato skin or a small amount of slop left behind in the hog trough.

Later on Blacky actually began to steal. The first couple of times she still felt ashamed. When I cursed her up and down after discovering that some rice soup left in my bowl had been licked clean, Blacky hid behind the willow basket, held her breath and didn't even dare to raise her head. When I kicked her a couple of times, she neither yelped nor ran away, but was perfectly willing to accept punishment. She did not, however, reform; she kept on stealing time after time. I was getting ready to teach her a lesson with a stick when the boy stopped me.

"Blacky's very worried!"

"You trying to defend her?"

"Haven't you noticed Blacky's teats? They're not swollen at all, but she's just about to give birth!"

I forgave that pitiful mother.

For her part Blacky became less and less able to gauge the seriousness of her crimes, and I had people coming to my door every day to settle a score with Blacky. She had stolen some provisions from this house; she had eaten up the pig slops at that house; she had broken down and chewed up the corn stalks on someone's private plot; she had dug up someone else's sweet potato field . . . The people angrily cursed her, "You rotten mut! You steal again and we'll skin you alive!" Some people pelted her with rocks and some people went after her brandishing their hoes while she tried to appease them and begged for help with her high pitched yelp. Fortunately the boy was Blacky's staunch protector.

"Keep your gate closed and don't let Blacky get out!" the Brigade Leader said. I was hoping, though, that her maternal nature might bring about some sudden change in Blacky, and so I left the gate open a crack.

On the very night that she gave birth Blacky came home dragging a badly battered leg behind her. She moaned and cried softly, "woo woo," while the boy tried to console her. "Can you blame them? They don't have anything to eat either; their kids don't have any milk either . . ."

That night Blacky dropped a big litter of pups.

As soon as her pups were born, her maternal heart was comforted; they squealed as they scrambled for her teats and as her milk dripped into their little mouths her own humiliations no longer counted for much. Blacky licked this one's head and kissed that one's eyes and sang a soft song while her own eyes were full of maternal love and satisfaction. Her place in front of that desolate cave dwelling was bursting with life.

Passers-by stopped once again in front of the yard, crowded around the willow basket to watch for a while, praising her once more as if they had forgotten Blacky's temporary lapse into bad behavior and remembered that she was a good dog.

"Hey, if you want to raise a dog, just take one of these pups home; they're guaranteed to keep good watch on your house, guaranteed!"

"Let Blacky nurse 'em a little longer, then the pups will grow a little big stronger."

"Blacky even caught a badger once."

"Those badger skins of Zhang Shan's were worth money!"

"One time a wolf forced open the Zhangs' pig pen, and Blacky fought for dear life . . ."

6

Blacky and her pups just rested there in the willow basket for a few days.

The little pups ate more every day, Blacky's teats were dry again, and once again she dragged her emaciated body around everywhere seeking food.

It was a famine year. The summer floods had destroyed the wheat, the autumn grain yield was practically nil, and every family was boiling thin rice gruel and steaming coarse dumplings. Blacky found absolutely nothing.

Having licked the trough until it shone brightly, the old sow could only grunt with hunger.

Human excrement was hard to find . . .

The little pups were barking and crying. They were not yet able to forage for themselves.

Blacky dragged her tired body out every day only to return with a feeling of defeat. When she thrust her dried up teats into her pups' waiting little mouths, they cried out again as if they had been cheated . . . Blacky had a glazed look in her eyes. Now she probably regretted her days of happiness in the wilds. Life was so much more difficult than she had imagined then.

For another month of dark and windy nights, Blacky once more ran around everywhere like before, with her stomach growling loudly. Every single family locked their outer gate. Blacky did not dare to come home and face her pups' reproach nor did she have the heart to try to fool them with those dried up teats of hers. She chased after a wild hare, but couldn't catch it. Then she went after a fox that was vainly attempting to steal some chickens, but was once again left behind, panting for breath and sore all over. A little later she spotted a hungry wolf that was greedily eying the sheepfold. She was too exhausted to be any match for it and the best she could do was to bark loudly; a dog derives power from association with human beings, however, so the wolf ran away as Blacky approached the sheepfold. I don't know if it was due to the urging of her lofty maternal nature or the rebirth of her primitive animal instincts, but she was so attracted by the prospect of eating flesh and blood that she momentarily forgot her proper role as a domestic dog. She was even surprised at herself for not discovering that sumptuous flavor sooner. That's probably what she felt. At any rate, although I don't know how she managed to become so clever, she finally forced open the tightly closed wattle gate and carried off a young lamb. If she had eaten the lamb right there on the spot and then licked the blood clean from her mouth, probably no one would have suspected that it was not the work of a wolf; but Blacky, overly proud of her own cleverness, closed the gate neatly behind her and carried the lamb home to make her pups happy. Perhaps she was already mentally prepared to be given a good beating, but didn't understand that this particular crime went far beyond the limits that human beings would tolerate.

The boy and I were both thrown into a panic as we hurriedly helped Blacky to cover up her crime—wiping the blood spots off the willow basket and tossing the leftover skin and bones into the river. After that I kicked her several times without mercy. Strangely enough Blacky then grew very peaceful, believing that since people understood her difficulties and were being lenient about her mistake, she could once again resume her role as a good dog.

The old shepherd's dog, however, had always been more intelligent than most dogs. That night as soon as he returned from chasing that hungry wolf, he immediately discovered he had been tricked by Blacky. The people very quickly discovered the real criminal.

The moment of Blacky's punishment had arrived, but she was not the least bit prepared as she continued to frolic happily with her pups.

The people gathered around her willow basket. Blacky had absolutely no inkling of the disaster to come. She thought that since she had already been beaten and granted clemency, this crowd of people could not possibly harbor evil intentions; but it was still necessary to ingratiate herself with them, so she wagged her tail at their approach.

"She used to be such a good dog," the people said.

Blacky did not understand the implication of the words "used to be," but, owing to its frequent use in the past, she did seem to understand the title "good dog." Thus she stretched out her front paws to greet the people.

When someone she knew well slapped her and sent her reeling she thought he was playing and romped back and forth all the more animatedly at his feet. And when someone else kicked her and sent her rolling she imagined that turning tricks that way was an even better way of expressing her sincere loyalty.

"Once she's eaten a lamb she'll always remember the taste of lamb meat and soon she'll be back for another one," the people said.

The little pups yelped shrilly, Blacky jumped into the willow basket, licking this one and that one. "There's nothing to be afraid of; after a while you will all go out with human beings and you must be good dogs." The look in Blacky's eyes was so calm and good-natured.

When the people slipped the rope around her neck, Blacky stretched her neck out joyfully. She thought it was a special prize; an extra special honor for being a good dog—didn't that fat city dog who could jump through rings of fire have a beautiful chain collar around his neck?

But the rope was pulled tight. As Blacky ran along with the man pulling the rope, she seemed to be somewhat surprised: why was the rope becoming tighter and tighter?

Blacky gradually felt that something was amiss: so many strangers were loitering by the door to her cave dwelling and sitting on the windowsill of her "sacred altar." She let out a shrill warning yelp.

The man pulling the rope threw the free end over a tree branch and pulled it hard. Blacky thought this joke was really being carried too far and she let out another shrill yelp of protest.

But the people didn't stop pulling; several of them pulled all at once. Blacky began to feel choked; but before she had time to realize what had happened, her body was already hanging in the air.

The look in Blacky's eyes in that last second left a deep impression on me—she looked so perplexed, so terrified, and so unjustly wronged.

The reason that I can tell you this story today with no fear of anyone pinning a bad label on me is precisely because humanity has triumphed over that dark age. But if we want to defeat it, we must first recognize it . . . ★

Originally published in the Beijing University student magazine *Chouxiaoya (The Ugly Duckling)*.

Translated by Michael S. Duke

Father's Milk Is Also Blood Transformed

Photo by Saundra Sturdevant

by Dai Houying

Sensing that Hanhan wanted him to leave, Xiwang turned to me and said, "I've got to go now. Hanhan, why don't you stay here a little longer?" Then he stood up and left, and Hanhan quickly went over and locked the door behind him.

I had her sit right next to me, and waited for her to speak, but for a long time she didn't say a word. I couldn't help asking, "Hanhan, was there something you wanted to talk to me about?"

"No," she said quickly, shaking her head. But her eyes told me she did have something on her mind. Her eyes were exactly like Sun Yue's, fine and bright. Usually they were gentle and mild, but when she had something on her mind they became agitated. She glanced for a moment at the letter in her hand, and then at me.

"Hanhan, can't you tell your Uncle what it is?" I made an effort to help her relax and say what was on her mind. A child's worries shouldn't be too serious.

She bit her lip, as though she were trying to decide something.

"I feel sorry for Papa," she said, looking at the letter in her hand.

"Yes, I sympathize with him too, in his present situation," I replied.

"Uncle He, do you think that after Mama has finished the road history has laid out for her, maybe . . . ?"

She stopped in midsentence, looked at me hesitantly, and did not go on.

"You hope Papa and Mama will get back together again, is that it?" I forced a smile as I asked this, suppressing the agitation in my own heart.

She glanced at me, but then quickly shook her head and said, "That'll never happen. He has that other woman now. Uncle He, do you think they will get a divorce? They'll never be able to get back together!"

"They might," I replied.

"What about little Huanhuan?" she asked.

"She will go with her Papa or Mama."

"I wish I had a little brother or sister. It's no fun being all alone," she said.

I understand the way children feel, and her wish was quite natural. If this family of three could get back together, and if someone like little Huanhuan were added too, maybe they could have a happy home once again. But what about me? What would my position be? Should I be out of the picture, or painted in? I felt as if someone had plucked out my heart. I wanted to go look at the long-stemmed pipe, but I made an effort to control myself. Hanhan was a sensitive child.

"Uncle He!" Suddenly Hanhan called out my name, and I gave a start, as if taken by surprise. I didn't want the child to know what was on my mind.

"Did Mama give you back that pipe herself, or did you ask her for it back?"

She was still on this topic. How should I answer? How did she hope I would answer? Sometimes it is hard to grasp a child's thinking. I didn't want my reply to hurt her, so I decided to try to find out exactly what was going through her mind. I deliberately smiled and said, "What would you guess?"

Her gaze swept back and forth across my face twice, and she asked hesitantly, "Mama gave it back to you, right? Mama said she would give it back when you got out of the hospital."

I nodded. I knew now what she hoped, and I did not want to disappoint her. I felt worse.

"Uncle He, don't feel bad." She pulled the stool closer to me, and leaned up next to me.

"Why should I feel bad?" I asked. My heart was suddenly thrown into a turmoil by this young girl. Did my voice sound a little strange? I didn't dare look directly at her, for fear I would begin to cry.

"I know you feel bad. Xiwang told me you loved my Mama. Is that true, Uncle He?" The sound of her voice was very faint, as if she were afraid someone else would hear. But to me, every word weighed heavily. And her eyes? Concerned, anxious, unsettled, sympathetic. How could such a young girl have such complex emotions?

"Is it true, Uncle He?" Why must you ask me this, Hanhan? If you already have a dim understanding of what love is, you probably detected the truth. Didn't you always take great pleasure in reporting all of your Mama's activities to me? The fact is, you have been trying all along to get me and your Mama together. But today you have to ask me, "Is it true, Uncle He?" I know that if I answer "No," you will be hurt, you will doubt me, you will think I have been deceiving you. But if I answer "Yes," what will you think? All right, Hanhan, in your presence I can only be a child too.

"Yes, Hanhan, it is true," I replied, looking at her, and my voice too was faint.

She crumpled the letter into a ball, and suddenly slumped down over the table and began to cry.

Child, child! What are you crying for? I have tied a cord to your little heart, and have pulled it so your heart aches, is that it? I understand, child! You love me, almost as much as you love your mother. You hope I will be happy. But now something has come up that blocks the happiness between the people you love . . .

Child, child! Don't cry! This is what it is like to be human. Life is always like this. Each person's heart is pulled in many different ways, and nothing can be done about it. You are still young. The net you live in—the network of social relationships—still has only a few threads, all clearly visible. Later on this network will become denser and more complex. Perhaps then you will stop crying, the way I have.

I lifted up Hanhan's head, wanting to wipe away her tears, but I could not wipe them dry.

"Hanhan! Uncle He doesn't like to see people cry." I wiped her tears again, urging her to stop crying.

"Uncle He, will we still be friends later on?" she asked, grasping my hand.

"Of course, Hanhan. We are best friends. Come on, 'Fingers hooked together, we'll be friends forever.'" I tried to get her to hook fingers with me, and she stopped crying and started to smile.

"You are so good, Uncle He! I'll keep on coming to see you."

"That's fine, Hanhan, you will always be welcome here."

Her mood was a little better. She started thumbing through the books on the table.

"Hanhan, it's time to go home. Your Mama will be worried about you," I reminded her. I thought Sun Yue might not know Hanhan had come over here.

Hanhan pulled my arm over and took a look at my wristwatch, then stuck out her tongue and said, "Oh, it's time to eat! I've got to go!"

"I have to go to the cafeteria too, so let's go together!" I picked up my ricebowl and went out with her.

"Should I let Mama read the letter?" she asked.

"Might as well let her read it. Hanhan, from now on you must be more understanding of your Mama, and gradually let her know how much you feel. She will listen to you. She loves you very much!" As I said this, I had an uncomfortable tight feeling in my throat. Fortunately we were almost to the cafeteria. I said to Hanhan, "I'm going to eat now, so you go on alone." She said goodbye to me, gave me a tender glance, and left.

When she had gone a certain distance I quickly turned and went back toward my room. I needed to rest. The past couple of days had really been tiring.

I bolted the door securely. No one must come! I wanted to lie down quietly by myself.

The case which had lasted more than twenty years has thus closed. It started from "nothing" and has ended in "nothing." A young fellow has turned into a middle-aged man. When he lies down, he is still the same length, and when he stands up he is just as tall as before. He comes and goes with no strings attached.

A tear fell from the corner of my eye, but I did not want to wipe it away. I have never enjoyed the pleasures of love; might I not at least express its pains? I did not want to wipe away the tears. From "nothing" to "nothing"? My hand once again touched the long-stemmed pipe under my pillow. There was a different tobacco pouch. This change meant "something." This was the only trace my long and unfulfilled love had left in my life. The tobacco pouch was hand sewn, stitch by stitch, exquisitely done. Each time the needle penetrated, Sun Yue, what were you thinking? Is it possible that you did not want the secrets of your heart to be revealed in these stitches? Is it possible you did not hope the seeds long buried in the earth would sprout, blossom, and bear fruit?

"My self-respect will not permit it." Is that really true, Sun Yue? Last night I thought about it all night and never came to a clear conclusion. Zhao Zhenhuan was tossing and turning. How I wanted to ask him about how he met you! How I wanted to know what impressions you have of each other! But I didn't say a word. That tattered photograph that Hanhan let me see is still suspended before my eyes. I see the torn places made whole, the images of three people once again distinct, complete, and tender.

"If there is a world to come. . . ," Sun Yue, would you still like to be united with me? If it really is a matter of your self-respect not permitting it, I still have some hope. Because someday you will come to understand that respecting one's own feelings is the only true self-respect. So then, Sun Yue, when you say that, are you hinting that I should wait? Not wait for a world to come, but wait for the future . . .

"Did Mama give you back that pipe herself, or did you ask for it back?" Let me think about that carefully. It seems like I asked for it back. Yes, I was the one who asked for it. "Let me have a smoke!" I had stretched out my hand toward her, and she gave it to me. When I left I didn't ask whether she wanted to keep it for me any longer, I just took it back with me, this token of love! How could I be so insensitive? Even Hanhan saw that this point was very important, but I didn't think about it at all. What a numbskull!

I ought to go to her and say: "My feelings have not changed. I am willing to wait, wait forever." I want to give her back the pipe and say, "Please keep this for me forever."

I got up. Went into the courtyard. The sky was full of stars. I walked forward. I could already see the window where she lived, the light glowing, brighter than any star in the sky. I stood still, facing this star.

Sun Yue, if you are standing at the window, can you see me walking toward you? Sun Yue, if you are a star, can you come out the window and fly into my embrace? "Uncle He, you are so good." I seem to hear Hanhan's voice again. The words "so good" carried a lot of meaning: when she said "I feel sorry for Papa," I sympathized with her; and when she said, "I hope Papa and Mama will get together again," I agreed with her. "I know you feel very bad"—this shows she approved of the sacrifice I would make for the sake of her family's unity. Today Hanhan judged me not only emotionally but also morally.

Is there a moral question here?

"If a person lives only for himself, he is not even as good as a barnyard animal. Even pigs and dogs know how to love their young!"

Father, my father, you are speaking to me. I should not continue on this path any longer. I will turn back, no matter how painful it may be. Sun Yue, will you suddenly discover me, fly after me in pursuit, and snatch away my pipe? I lengthen my stride and hurry back to my room. Close the door, lock it, lie down. Sun Yue didn't pursue me. She didn't see me. Or, she didn't want to come after me. That's all right too.

The case which had lasted more than twenty years has thus closed. It started from "nothing" and has ended in "nothing." No, it left me one trace, one memento—this tobacco pouch.

The two people I have loved most in my life—my father and Sun Yue—both left me the same memento, this pipe with the tobacco pouch hanging from it. Is that a coincidence?

From now on the pipe will become even dearer to me. Through it I can see two hearts: a father's and a lover's; a peasant's and a scholar's. How different these two hearts are! But both are equally filled with love. Both have trembled and moaned with pain, both have given rise to noble sentiments and sacrifices.

"My brother, you and I lost our parents when we were small. We grew up begging for food, hand in hand. That winter we could not get enough to eat, we could not bear the hunger, so we went hand in hand to throw ourselves into the river. We slowly made our way toward the middle of the river, I in front and you behind. The water was up to my stomach, up to your chest. You stood still and would not go on, you cried to me, 'Elder Brother, let's not die! The water is too cold!' . . . Then we made our way out again, hand in hand, you in front and I behind. We sold ourselves, sold ourselves to two families to be 'sons'; you became my 'uncle' and I your 'nephew'. After liberation we became brothers again. You even got to be a cadre. But then you ended up throwing yourself into the river after all. Oh my brother, weren't you afraid the water would be cold? Why didn't you say something to me?"

This halting lament made by my father as he stood before my uncle's corpse was probably the longest speech he ever made in his life. Each phrase, each word, is clear in my memory. Because from then on I saw something through my father that I had never seen before.

My uncle had "committed suicide to avoid punishment." He was accused of "wildly opposing the Three Red Banners." People were already starving in the countryside, but the papers were still urging everyone to "continue to leap forward," and the people on top were still "encouraging" the peasants to sell "surplus grain" to the state. My uncle, who was Deputy Director of the commune, could not understand how such a situation could come about under the leadership of the Communist Party.

"A lot of the leaders in the Central Committee come from peasant backgrounds. Could they really believe that one *mu* of land could produce ten thousand catties of grain? Why do they let the newspaper reporters print such outrageous exaggerations? If they keep on exaggerating, everyone will starve to death!" He wrote a letter to the Central Committee exposing the fact that the production reports for the commune and county were unfounded, describing the sufferings of the people, and asking the Central Committee to send someone to investigate the matter. His letter was intercepted on route.

One day the commune suddenly called a mass meeting to "struggle against active counterrevolutionary elements." The county Chief of Security was in charge of the proceedings. My father and I both went. The last thing we expected was that the target of the struggle would be my uncle, bound up hand and foot. . . .

After the struggle meeting, they were going to take him to the county seat to be held there in custody. But on the way my uncle by a sudden frenzied effort was able to throw off his escorts and hurl himself headlong into the river. He could not even move his hands, which were tied behind his back, and he had no strength left to struggle. . . .

The corpse of this "active counterrevolutionary" who had "committed suicide to avoid punishment" was pulled out of the river and made the object of criticism at a meeting held there at the scene. Death, you have cheated him! What if his "cohorts" want to find a place to give him a peaceful burial? It is not permitted! Just dig a trench on the spot, and furthermore you can't use a coffin!

That is the way it happened. My aunt was pregnant at the time, and with some difficulty she made her way over to the corpse and put a clean suit of clothing on him there in front of everyone. Then shovel after shovelful of yellow earth fell onto his clean clothing. He was buried. My uncle was not yet 40 years old . . .

"Even if I go to jail for it I am going to find a way to bring your uncle's corpse back home and nail together a few boards to make him a coffin." After my father came back from the river he spent all night smoking his pipe, one bowl after another. "Is it a crime to say something truthful to help out the peasants?" He kept muttering things like this to himself. The next evening he took some planks from the bed, and he and I secretly made a crate-like coffin. We groped our way down to the riverside in the dark, dug up my uncle's body, put it into the coffin and buried it in our private plot behind the house.

The people in the village may have known, or they may not have. In any case, no one ever told our secret.

"From now on our two families will live together as one. When we have plenty to eat, you will have plenty too; when we have less you will have less too, just like when my brother was alive."

My father's thoughts and feelings had never been influenced by the theory or practice of "class struggle." It had never occurred to him to turn himself into a "tool of class struggle." This was probably because he was too ordinary and insignificant. No one tried to use him, and he had nothing he was afraid of losing in the "class struggle." Every year, every month, every day, every hour, and every place, the wind blew and rain fell, and any work unit or any family could be hurled into a different class. Even a single individual could find himself in different classes yesterday, today, and tomorrow.

Lots of people learned the art of adjusting their emotional center of gravity and changing their banners and insignia from time to time according to the "requirements of class struggle." They learned how to test the wind, recognize the current party line, join the ranks, draw lines, form factions, create cliques . . . But my father never went in for that sort of thing. In fact, he *was* too ordinary, too insignificant, what effect could he have on any "class struggle"?

But "class struggle" had an enormous effect on him. It expropriated him. At the same time, it gave him an opportunity to reveal the simplicity, dignity, and beauty of his soul. This soul gave me precious nourishment. I drank my father's milk . . .

After this, the two families joined to form one. My aunt and her son came to live at our house. We had mouths to feed but no grain or livestock. We ate everything we had, and sold everything we could sell. The adults could endure this without crying or complaining, but what about the children? My little brother was only seven or eight, and my uncle's son even younger, only six years old. And didn't the child in my aunt's belly need nourishment even more?

My father and I, two big strong fellows, spent every day dredging in ditches and in the river, and digging around in uncultivated spots. Mother, who had bound feet, took my little sister with her to the fields to look for sweet potatoes that the harvesters had missed. In order not to "smear mud on the face of the people's commune," my mother and sister had sewn little pockets in their clothing, into which they could fit slices of potatoes. How much could they carry this way? They dug a hole in the ground to make a stove, cooked some of the potatoes, and stuffed them into their own bellies . . .

Mother gave one cooked sweet potato to my father, and he pressed it into his nephew's hand. My brother started to cry, and Mother wiped his eyes and led him away.

Days seemed like years! My brother could not endure such hardships, and was the first to "depart." My mother became ill and never recovered . . .

"Kowtow to your uncle!" My aunt pulled my cousin over to my father. "Uncle, I can't bear watching your family suffer and die because of us. I will take my child with me and try to get away from this famine-stricken area. After a few years we will come back."

For a long time my father kept puffing on his pipe. The tobacco pouch was filled with dried acacia leaves. Finally, holding back his tears, he waved his hand and said, "If you can get away, you might as well try it! I have let my brother down . . ."

Not long after this, my mother followed in my brother's footsteps and "departed" too. Only three of us were left in the family; my father, my sister, and me. By then neither my father nor sister could get out of bed. I was the only one who could move about and make the daily search for food. And my whole body was already bloated. Like my mother, I sewed pockets all over my clothing and went to the fields to look for sweet potatoes that had not been harvested. There weren't any more close by, so I had to go farther away. I would bring home fibrous tubers no bigger than my finger, as if they were precious jewels.

But my father did not improve. Day by day he wasted away. Every evening I sat by his bed and filled his pipe for him. As I watched the dried leaves burning in the pipe bowl, my heart was suffering even more than if it had been held over the fire! If my heart, my blood, my love, could be transformed into tobacco . . .

"Pa, please don't smoke this anymore," I pleaded as I filled the pipe. "No, son, all his life your pa has only had this one indulgence. Why not let me keep on smoking in my old age . . ."

Where did Sun Yue manage to get such good tobacco? She would not know that you can smoke acacia leaves, and that you can fill your stomach with the smoke.

One day my father called me over to his bed and I filled his pipe for him. He took the pipe, but was already too weak to smoke it. I couldn't keep from crying. The corner of my father's mouth moved slightly—was he trying to smile at me? The motion released a flood of tears. As I wiped away his tears, he clasped my hand. He kept looking at me, and the tears flowed down the deep gullies of his cheeks. "There are still a few sweet potatoes left in the hamper. I saved them up before. It is all right for me to die, but you cannot die. If you die, who would be able to know what kind of a man you are? And there's your uncle . . . You must find your aunt . . . your sister is growing up . . ."

He did not finish speaking. He did not smoke his "tobacco."

I knelt by my father's bed, and for a long time did not get up.

I picked up the pipe, which had fallen to the ground. My first puff of "tobacco" was the smoke of burning acacia leaves that my father had left for me . . .

My uncle and I have both been exonerated. My aunt brought home her son and the daughter who was born during the troubles. "If your father were still alive . . ." My aunt would bring him up every now and then. I always replied, "He is undoubtedly at peace." I believed that my father's soul in heaven would certainly feel gratified, because he never thought of himself. But, Father, how can I not keep you in my heart?

Whenever I pick up the pipe I think of you. Through the pipe I drink your milk, a father's milk. "Mothers' milk is blood transformed"; fathers' milk is also blood transformed. Mothers' milk is stored in the breast, but fathers' milk is stored in the heart.

My father did not leave me any mementos except for the pipe. And no one else thought of remembering him, or having a funeral service. He was too ordinary, too insignificant. What did his great sacrifice have to do with history? History only records the lives and activities of great figures. People like my father can only be lumped together under the term "the masses of the people." Lots of people admit that history was created by "the people," but when they leaf through history books, or write about history, how many individual living, feeling, ordinary people do they see?

I remember my father, and mourn him. My eulogy is the manuscript I wrote—*Marxism and Humanism*. To carry on class struggle in order to eliminate class oppression and exploitation is necessary, high-minded, and proper; to artificially create class distinctions and tear apart people and families in order to carry on "class struggle" is cruel and unconscionable. The former liberates the people, while the latter harms the people. The former truly treats people as human beings, while the latter treats people as tools that can talk.

Sun Yue has not read this manuscript. Several times I have thought of letting her see it, but her attitude held me back. The day before yesterday I ran into the editor of the press, and he told me it would soon be coming out . . .

I will send Sun Yue a copy, and write on it, "Offering my thoughts and aspirations of more than twenty years . . ."

No, that would not be appropriate. That would lead to

misunderstanding. I should write, "To Comrade Sun Yue, for comments and criticism."

"Comrade!" "Comrade!" We used to sing, "Our proudest name is Comrade, More glorious than any other name." But today, when we use this term to address someone, it often creates a feeling of coldness and distance. Why is that?

"Comrade Sun Yue!" Are the thoughts and aspirations of over twenty years summed up in this name? It makes me shiver. But this is the way it is, and the only way it can be. Those diaries will accompany me forever, along with a little yellow blossom made of paper.

The case which had lasted more than twenty years has thus closed. It started from "nothing" and has ended in "nothing." A young fellow has turned into a middle-aged man. When he lies down he is still the same length, and when he stands up he is still as tall as before. He comes and goes with no strings attached.

"There is only one road before me, to live my life alone." No, Sun Yue, I don't want that for you. Give this road to me!

I will always treasure this pipe. The pipe was my father's. The tobacco pouch was Sun Yue's . . . such fine stitches . . . ★

Chapter 20 of the novel *Ren a, ren!*. Guangzhou: Guangdong renmin chubanshe, 1980.

Translated by Jeannette L. Faurot

Downpour on a Leaky Roof

Photo by Saundra Sturdevant

by Zhu Lin

Daylight took on the chill of water as darkness set in. A jumble of houses straddled the main street like a line of great yellow-earth bricks, the paleness of their faded thatched roofs contrasting with the pitch darkness of the locust grove. Flickering yellow oil lamps no longer lit the windows. The sleepless lay on their pillows and listened to the leaves in the wind, rustling like the swish of flood waters.

But light still burned in Louwa's home. A small lamp homemade from an ink bottle hung at the bed head. It had no shade, and as the yellow flame flickered, wisps of sooty smoke fluttered up like long black scarves from the twisted paper wick.

There was nothing in the room that the smoke could harm; no mosquito net on the bed, no bench on the floor. A rough table nailed together from logs stood in the center, with bundles of straw on either side for stools. By the wall were three earthenware jars half a man high; they were meant for grain, but now contained only the shabby clothes and worn shoes of the children.

Three boys, Big Tiger, Second Tiger and Third Tiger, were sleeping soundly, curled up together on the cold bed under a cover of wheat straw. Shuhai, the daughter, was also asleep, tucked into a quilt stuffed with stubble. The household's sole cotton-padded quilt was laid over Louwa's wife.

In the last few days her elephantiasis had flared up again. Her leg was swollen from ankle to thigh, and her body burned like a glowing coal. In order to save fuel, she hadn't asked her husband to boil water for her during the day, but by nighttime her thirst was unbearable. She raised her head from the pillow and begged Louwa to get her a drink.

Louwa heard his wife's call. He hurriedly draped his jacket over his shoulders and got out of bed. He lit the lamp, gathered up a bundle of straw and went into the kitchen. The grate rattled as he pulled it out.

Shuhai's mother's face was flushed as she wheezed and gasped in the flickering lamplight. When Louwa brought in the boiled water, he saw she was helplessly weak, so he lifted her up and, supporting her in the crook of his arm, brought the bowl of water to her lips.

After she'd taken a few mouthfuls of the water, her spirits seemed to revive a little. She took the bowl and said, "I'll do it myself."

Shuhai woke up and poked her head out from under the quilt. Her eyes open wide, she said, "Pa, I just remembered, we still have some of the pills ma took when she was sick last time."

"Get up quick and fetch them for her," said Louwa.

"Okay," said Shuhai, and jumped barelegged onto the floor. Doubling her little body over, she buried her head in one of the earthenware jars. After a long search she pulled out a grubby little medicine bottle and gave it a shake; there were still a few pills in it.

"Are these the right ones? You don't want her taking the wrong thing," said Louwa dubiously as he took the bottle.

"They're the ones," Shuhai insisted. "Second Tiger wanted to take them to play with once before, but I wouldn't let him have them and hid them here."

"Ha, our little girl's a clever one." Louwa's thick lips creased in a grin. He helped his wife take the medicine, then blew out the lamp and settled back down to sleep.

But sleep would not come to the two people on the bed. Louwa rested his hand on his wife's feverish body and said remorsefully, "Wife, when we pick up the relief money tomorrow, the first thing I'll do is fetch a doctor to look at you."

"Don't worry about me," Shuhai's mother sighed, "you'd better buy something to eat first."

As they spoke, a gust of wind forced its way through the

crack in the window, raising dust in the darkness of the room. As Louwa tucked the quilt under his wife, she rolled over and said, "What upsets me most is those few dozen eggs. We saved them all winter for nothing. Otherwise you could have taken them to market, sold them and bought us a few pounds of grain."

"*Ai*, what could we do but hand them in? Didn't you see what happened to the old guy in the Western part of the village—he hid some eggs, and when the brigade found out, they hung a placard round his neck and paraded him around the village. What a shameful thing that was!" said Louwa dolefully.

His wife made no reply. She remembered the day the old fellow had been paraded round the village beating a gong, a placard hung round his neck announcing "Criminal Egg-hoarder." She couldn't face that, and the thought of it set her heart pounding. But she still disagreed with her husband. "What's so shameful about it? The eggs were laid by his own hens, but he's still expected to hand them in to the authorities, what justice is there in that?"

"For that matter, where's the justice in firing the Old Party Secretary after he's slaved his guts out for so many years?"

Louwa's forthrightness silenced his wife's questioning; it seemed there was some mysterious truth that neither of them could fathom. After a while, Louwa sighed and said, "Let's sleep now, I'll be up early in the morning to get the relief money."

"How much will our share be?" she asked anxiously.

"We'll get the same as everyone else. However much it is, the first thing is to get you a doctor." In the darkness, Louwa's voice was firm.

"What about food? We can't feed the children on air." Nervously she drew close to her husband.

Louwa pondered. "We'll buy some to start with, then we'll get Shuhai to go to the lowlands east of the reed beds to glean some of the wheat and sweet potatoes that got flooded. With luck that'll keep us going."

His wife murmured resigned acquiescence. Louwa closed his eyes and slipped into a fuddled sleep.

He woke again before dawn, and once awake he could not go back to sleep. First of all he was concerned about his wife's illness—she'd been groaning all night and didn't seem any better. Secondly he was afraid that other people would already have gleaned all the wheat and sweet potatoes, so he went to rouse the children; but when he remembered there'd been no food the evening before, he couldn't face the thought of sending his kids out hungry into the dead of night. Helpless and sleepless, he slumped against the bed and smoked.

By the time he'd smoked a couple of pipes, pale light was penetrating the window. Louwa felt it was time to move, so he slipped softly from the bed, and reached underneath for a basket. In the basket was the family's last morsel of coarse flour—the Old Party Secretary had sent his grandson Little Treasure round with it a few days before. He drew out a scoop of the flour, thought again, and shook half of it back into the basket before making his way out into the kitchen.

Louwa put water in the pot and was about to light the fire beneath it, when he clapped his hands and stood up, resolved that it would be better to wake Shuhai after all and send her straight off to glean as soon as they had eaten—he simply couldn't relax for thinking about the flooded wheat and sweet potatoes. His own priority was to line up for the relief money, and that was something he couldn't delay.

Shuhai was already gone when he went back into the room; the three little Tigers still slept sweetly, their bodies intertwined. As soon as Louwa woke one, the others would nod off again, so he gave up the idea of waking them, and went back to his cooking.

The vegetable basket was gone, but there were still a few sweet potatoes beside the cooking pot. Louwa washed and diced them painstakingly, then tipped them into the pot to boil. When they'd boiled, he took the scoop of flour and shook it in bit by bit, chopsticks stirring it as he did so with skill born of long practice.

At this moment Shuhai came dashing in, her feet slip-slopping against the floor. She was wearing only a thin print jacket. Her shoes were soaked and her lips blue with cold as she set the basket down by the door. Shivering, she said, "Look, Ma, I got up early and picked half a basket of wild vegetables."

Her mother looked up from the pillow with tears in her eyes and said, "Poor child, you're starving. Get your father to give you some gruel to warm you. Then when he's got the relief money he can go out and buy some grain."

Slurping the gruel, Shuhai said, "I wonder if we'll even get real steamed bread to eat?" and gazed at her father.

Louwa bowed his head, put his face in his hands and stared at the ground by his feet, thinking, "When we pick up the relief money . . ."

After breakfast, Louwa told Shuhai to take Big Tiger off to glean wheat in the flooded fields; he instructed Second Tiger to look after the youngest at home; then he rearranged the quilt on his wife's bed and helped her eat half a bowl of gruel before he too left the house and headed for brigade headquarters.

Louwa was thirty-eight, but he looked like a man in his forties or fifties. He'd been born the year of the insurrection against the Japanese, when his mother had given birth at the foot of a Japanese artillery bunker, which accounted for his name Louwa, "bunker baby." Louwa had grown up pulling grain stalks for food, fighting with local militiamen, eating wherever a meal could be found. Things had improved with Liberation; he married, had children. But in the last few years, with more mouths to feed and his wife sick, he just hadn't been able to make ends meet. When the Old Party Secretary had been in office, he would always help them out with food and necessities in the lean period before the harvest. Louwa was an honest man, and it hurt him to receive charity, but he had no way of repaying, and all he could do was work harder than ever. Times were tough, but somehow they always managed to get by. He could never have anticipated this year's floods. The waters had simply cleaned them out. Louwa's house was on low-lying land; the day of the rains and the flooding, his concern had been to save his wife and children, while his pig and chickens had all been drowned. When the floods subsided, all he had left was a basket of eggs, which he planned to sell, to buy grain. How could he have guessed that the Brigade Leader would take even these away from him? Exhaustion and anxiety had brought on a relapse in his wife's illness; it's all too true that the rains pour down hardest on a leaking roof! Now his only concern was to pick up his relief money as soon as he could, get his wife's illness treated, and buy food for his children—such were the fond wishes of the honest Louwa.

He arrived none too early. There was already a long line snaking its way from the door of the brigade office; at its head a crowd of women stood in the wind busily stitching shoe-soles, some twisting yarn round mutton bones in their hands. Thrill at the prospect of the relief money made them laugh and chatter excitedly. All had eaten gruel for breakfast so none of them felt cold.

Louwa dutifully joined the end of the line, his mind at work, resenting the way that the time was crawling by. One minute he worried about his wife's illness, the next he was concerned his share of the relief money wouldn't be enough, and oh dear, should he get the doctor first or buy food . . .

After a good deal of time had passed there was some restlessness in the line. People were getting impatient, and conversation turned to grumbling.

"It's almost noon, how come there's nothing moving in there?"

"No one's said a word about when they're going to hand it out."

"I had a couple of bowls of gruel early, but my stomach's rumbling now."

"I'm famished, we might as well go home and get a meal started."

"What is there to cook? We have to wait for our money to buy grain."

As they were speaking, they saw Juanjuan come running out of the accountant's office. The crowd swarmed around her, excitedly pestering her with questions; but Juanjuan's face was ashen, she barged through them wordlessly and dashed away without a backward glance.

They all looked at each other, but no one had a clue what was going on; so they just lined up and waited as before. Louwa felt his eyelids quiver, his heart pound. After another while, the word came down the line; "Everyone should go home, the relief money's been lost."

"What? The relief money lost?" Louwa was bewildered, his mind incapable for a moment of accepting the news. The line was already in chaos, people pressing forward and pounding on the door of the accountant's office. "How the hell can the money get lost? What do we pay the accountant for?"

They crowded around, screaming and cursing in despair, but to no avail. The office was empty and Juanjuan had long since fled.

Louwa couldn't join in the cursing. He stood dumbstruck, his head hanging dejectedly. Running through his mind again and again were the thoughts, "food . . . wife's sickness . . ."

A breeze blew up, rippling the pale grasses in the fields this way and that. Louwa couldn't make up his mind; should he wait around a bit longer or head home? Many people hadn't left yet. They seemed still to cling to some hope.

As Louwa hesitated, seven-year old Second Tiger ran stumbling towards his father, his little hands flailing wildly.

Louwa sensed his son's alarm, and quickly called out, "Second Tiger, what are you running for?"

Second Tiger was trembling all over, too shocked to speak.

Heart pounding, Louwa grabbed hold of his son. "Tell me quick, what's wrong with your Ma?"

"It's . . . not Ma, it's sister . . ."

"What's wrong with her?"

"Sister fell . . . fell in the water."

"What? Is she . . ."

"She's home, asleep . . . asleep on an ox."

His face grey as iron, Louwa dragged Second Tiger home.

Sure enough, there was a crowd of people at the door. When they saw Louwa coming, they parted to let him through.

Louwa sprang forward, and saw his daughter Shuhai draped over an ox's back, her body arched like a bow. Her hair hung lifelessly down; one hand still tightly clasped a few ears of wheat.

The mother dashed dishevelled out of the house and slumped at the ox's feet, crashing her head down and screaming, "Child, let me go with you!"

Some of the women, fearing an accident, called out, "Grab her, grab her!"

Something exploded in Louwa's brain. He seized Shuhai's body and clasped it to himself, madly crying, "Shuhai! Shuhai! Shuhai!"

The girl would never reply. Her lovely eyes had lost their gleam, her nose was clogged with mud, her lips were purple, and white saliva trickled from her mouth.

Big Tiger stood to one side and sobbed, "We went east of the reed beds but all the wheat had been gleaned, so sister said let's go to the west side where the water's deeper, no one's been there. I said it's too deep, I'm scared, I won't go. Sister said if we don't get any, there'll be nothing for lunch when we get home. I went along with her. When we got there, she said you're little stand here while I have a look. There was water everywhere, sister went in and bent over to feel underwater. Later I couldn't see her anymore, I called to her . . . she didn't answer . . ."

By this time, Big Tiger was incoherent with crying. The listeners were all grieved, and murmured to each other what a fine child Shuhai had been. Louwa hadn't taken in all that his son had told him, and didn't know what the others were saying, but those words that penetrated his ears pierced his heart like arrows. His ears buzzed, his mind was paralyzed. He put his hand on Shuhai's chest and rubbed it furiously, as if trying to make her heart start beating once more . . .

Some could not bear to watch any longer. "Louwa," they said, "the child's dead."

Louwa's tears trickled down over the little corpse, and he thought, Shuhai's dead. I told her to glean the wheat, to fall in the water and drown. I'm her father, and I . . .

"Louwa, the child's dead, you can't bring her back, you'd do better to prepare for the funeral."

"That's right, you have to look after your own health too, just look at Shuhai's mother . . ."

Only then did Louwa notice that his wife had collapsed on the ground, faint from weeping. Hastily he set his child down and went to lift up his wife; with many helping hands, he carried her into their house.

It was quite a while before Shuhai's mother revived. She opened her eyes, looked up at the crowd and said shamefacedly, "Don't mind me, it's getting late, you should be going home to prepare a meal."

Seeing there would be nothing more of interest happening, one by one the bystanders said their few words of condolence and slipped away.

Louwa sat on the bed and clasped his wife's hand. Head bowed, he asked her, "Well, wife, what can we do now?"

Just as Shuhai's mother was about to reply, tears came streaming down. Clasping Louwa's hand tightly, she said: "Husband, Shuhai was such a good girl, and she didn't even get to eat the bread roll she wanted so much before she died. We couldn't do much for her when she was alive, let's at least do something for her now. How . . . how much relief money did you get?"

Louwa's eye's darkened. He glared at her and rasped, "I

didn't . . . didn't get any at all."

"Why didn't you?" she asked in amazement.

"They said the relief money's been lost."

"Lost? Are they still going to give it out?"

"If it's lost, how can they still give it to us?"

"So there won't be any relief money?"

"No, there won't."

Shuhai's mother gave a cry of anguish. "How in heaven's name can our family survive?"

Her cry shocked Louwa, who rubbed her chest and pounded her back to quiet her down. She leaned against the pillow and gazed at Louwa through her tears. "My being sick these last two years has brought you so much suffering . . ."

Louwa shook his head. "Don't blame yourself, we're one family, we're in this together. We'd best work out what we're going to do now."

His wife looked at the ground. "If we can't think of anything, we could go and see the Old Party Secretary."

"The Old Party Secretary . . . ," head in his hands, Louwa spoke the name he had not mentioned for quite a while. Shuhai's mother thought for a while, then she said, "No, we shouldn't. Last time when Little Treasure brought that bit of flour over, the bricklayer spotted him and the boy was criticized. If that happened again . . . let's not make more trouble for him. Besides, his family's hard up enough as it is. I think we should go and see Secretary Cui first."

Louwa felt that with things as they were, that was about all they could do. He said, "all right," stood up, and headed out.

"Husband," she called out suddenly.

"What is it?" Louwa spun round to face her.

"It's nothing, go ahead." She swiftly turned her face away.

Louwa glanced at his wife again and hurried off.

It was noon, and the road was quiet. Smoke spiralled above the roofs of the yellow earth houses.

There was drinking at Cui Haiying's house. It sounded as if there was quite a party going on. Louwa peered in at the doorway, but as he was bracing himself to step forward, he shrank back. Even Louwa himself couldn't explain why he was so scared to open his mouth and ask this favor.

His wife's sickly look, his children's starving faces, and the ears of wheat clasped in Shuhai's hand flashed through his mind, giving him the extra impulse to pluck up his courage and step over the threshold.

"Yap! Yap!" With a burst of barking, a huge yellow dog sprang at him from behind the woodpile. Louwa dodged, but not before the dog had ripped away a piece of his ragged jacket. Timidly he called out, "Secretary Cui."

"Aha, it's you, Louwa, come on in, sit down!" Cui Haiying welcomed Louwa, and threw a bone to the dog. It seized the bone with a fawning glance at its master, and stayed away from Louwa.

Louwa didn't dare sit—he didn't even dare look, so dazed was he by the table laden with wine and food, and the people all around it. Looking to one side, he stammered, "Secretary Cui, I have to talk to you."

Frowning, Secretary Cui laid down his chopsticks and led Louwa outside. His breath stank of alcohol. "What is it?"

Louwa sensed he'd come at a bad time, but he licked his lips, set his face and said his piece.

When he'd heard Louwa out, Cui Haiying lit a cigarette and took a drag. "The brigade has no money."

"But I'm completely broke," said Louwa awkwardly. He looked up and pleaded with Cui Haiying. "I've nothing. If you could just lend me a couple of yuan to buy some food, I'll pay you back after the harvest, honestly."

"Louwa," said Cui Haiying, giving him a friendly pat on the shoulder, "it's not that I don't want to lend you money, it's just that I don't want to set a precedent. We all know the brigade is having its problems at the moment because of the flood; it's not only your family that's broke. If I lent to one family and not the others, that wouldn't do, would it?"

"But I'm . . ."

Cui Haiying interrupted Louwa as soon as he opened his mouth, "I'm aware you're an extreme case, you are in difficulties. But we mustn't just think of the 'me' under our noses, the ground beneath our feet, we must fill our hearts with the whole globe, bear the world situation in mind. We must deal correctly with the relationship between the state, the collective, and the individual, we must be revolutionaries, not supplicants."

"Then I'll . . . I'll just have to go out and pull up grain-stalks or beg, yes beg, for food," spat out the anguished Louwa. But when he thought of taking up the beggar's staff again after thirty years, his eyes suddenly reddened. He was silent for a moment, then blurted, "No, no, I can't. It's the new society now, and if I went out begging, everyone would call me a worthless idler!"

Cui Haiying smirked, "That's okay, just get the brigade office to give you a note."

"A note?" Louwa stared incredulously.

"Sure." Cui Haiying pulled a notepad out of his pocket. Resting it on his knee, he scrawled a couple of lines on the top sheet and gave it to Louwa. "Here you go, get Juanjuan to put the brigade stamp on it." With this, he pinched out his half-smoked cigarette and tossed it on the ground to indicate the interview was at an end.

Stunned, Louwa folded the scrap of paper and went to find Juanjuan to get it stamped; then he made his way home.

For some reason, the door of his house was shut. Louwa gave it a light push, but it still wouldn't open. So he forced it, breaking down the door. He saw he had knocked the little table aside. Looking up, he saw his wife balancing on their two bundles of straw, securing a noose to the rafters. Louwa slumped to his knees, grasped his wife's legs and groaned, "Wife, wife, you mustn't die!"

When she heard him call out, her will faltered; she let go the rope and fell into his arms sobbing convulsively.

As he clasped his trembling wife, his hand resting on her emaciated arm, the ten years of love they had shared flashed through Louwa's mind . . .

In that moment Louwa realized that his wife's love for him was the most important thing of all. Yet he, a man, couldn't even support . . . Louwa clenched his fist and savagely punched his own head. The blow shocked his wife, who grasped his arm, "Husband, what's wrong with you?"

"Me?" Louwa let his hand drop lifelessly, and great tears coursed down. "I'm a beggar. Come, I'll take you with me."

The sun was sinking in the West, but the family's cooking pot remained unlit. Louwa found a strip of matting and buried Shuhai in it, marking the little grave with a hexagonal clod of earth and sprinkling it with tears. Then, his arm around his wife and carrying his children in the baskets of a carrying-pole, he trudged out of the village.

Shafts of sunlight pierced the clouds, gleaming on the

peaks of the Tiger Mountain range, twinkling on the flooded fields of the Tiger Mountain brigade, sparkling in the puddles on the yellow-earth highway. Bathed in the last rays of the evening sunlight, Louwa plodded with his family down the muddy road away from the village. ★

Chapter 13 of the novel *The Path of Life* (*Shenghuo de lu*). Beijing: Renmin chubanshe, 1979.

Translated by Richard King

Fu Da Regains His Wife

Photo by Saundra Sturdevant

by Yang Zhenwen

It was getting dark when Fu Da came back home from work and hurriedly began to chop some vegetables and wild herbs to feed the pigs.

Suddenly, a man came in and asked him, "Where is your daughter?"

Struck dumb, Fu Da turned his head to the door. "Eh, eh, Qin, Ch. . . Chu. . . Chu. . . Chairman Quin, y. . . y. . . you. . ." Qin Guangxuan had held the position of Chairman of the Brigade Revolutionary Committee quite a few years ago. But now, though Qin is no longer a Chairman, Fu Da not only still calls him "Chairman," respects him, believes in him and follows his words as he did before, but also speaks to him with the same slight stutter he has when talking to any current leader. Seeing Qin come in, he immediately put aside what he was doing and rushed to the kitchen to brew some tea for his Chairman Qin. Only at the moment he reached the cooking stove did he remember that there was no boiled water left because his daughter Yaoxiang had gone to visit her grandmother that day and no one else was home to help him.

"Well, well, well. . ." He shook his head from side to side, his two open hands dropping disconsolately, as if he couldn't find any place to hide himself for shame. "Well, well . . . "

With a slight smile, Qin handed him a cigarette.

"No, thanks, no . . . "

"Oh, don't treat me like a stranger . . . What's the difference between yours and mine?" said Qin unhappily.

Fu Da, on hearing this, had to accept the cigarette. Qin struck his lighter and offered the flame to Fu Da. "Where is your daughter?" he asked again.

"She's g. . . g. . . gone to her g. . . g. . . grandmother."

"What for?"

"Her g. . . g. . . grandmother is s. . . s. . . sick and has sent a m. . . message to ask her to g. . . g. . . go to her . . ."

"You fool!" Qin spit on the ground, "You're still being kept in the dark."

Perplexed and alarmed, Fu Da looked at him with wide open eyes.

"Yuegui has come back," said Qin, dusting the cigarette ashes from his clothes.

"Ah, b. . . b. . . but she died m. . . m. . . many years ago." Fu Da sighed deeply. Then he begged Qin, "D. . . d. . . don't make fun of me."

"Who on earth wants to make fun of you? Someone went to the town to collect night soil the day before yesterday and saw her getting off the train with four other people."

"Five altogether?"

"Yuegui, her new husband and their three sons."

Fu Da shot Qin a glance, finding no amusement on his face. His heart began to leap fast, blood flooding his face and sweat soaking through his whole body. His cigarette had gone out for some time, but Fu Da's thick and stubby fingers were still clamping it and putting it to his lips from time to time. He drew and drew on it, not giving it up till the saliva soaked the cigarette paper completely and the tobacco dropped out.

Qin began to talk. "You and Yuegui had a legal marriage, didn't you? Don't you know that you can go to your mother-in-law's home to bring Yuegui back to your home? You're not a bachelor, but you're living like a bachelor. It's a life even more pitiable than a bachelor's life. Haven't you lived this way long enough?"

The news that Yuegui had now come back to visit her mother agitated him and made him as restless as a boiling river or the sea at floodtide blown by a force-nine wind. In bed, he could not close his eyes the whole night. He hurriedly got up before dawn. He went into the garden under the starlit sky and picked some fresh squash. For years after Yuegui left home, he had constantly paid visits to her mother. Whenever he went to her house, he never forgot to take her some fresh fruit or vegetables in season. After filling his big basket full, he washed his face and changed into the blue khaki jacket he usually wore only on New Years and festival days. Then he walked out in very high spirits.

The sun hadn't climbed up over the mountain, but half of the sky in the east had already brightened in many-colored splendor. Everywhere under the sun was green, green in the fields and green in the mountains. The morning birds were singing by the roadside and in the bamboo grove.

Fu Da was born and grew up here, but today, for the first time, he felt his home village was as beautiful as a picture. The air seemed extraordinarily fragrant and sweet to him, as if someone had sprayed honey into it.

Farther away, people from the co-op were working in the rice fields. When they saw Fu Da walking along the road, they began to whisper to one another, exchanging comments in low voices. In their facial expressions, one could see a mixture of sympathy, pity and also curiosity. Concentrating on walking fast, Fu Da didn't take any notice of those people. Sweetness filled his heart as if he had drunk several bowls of cassia wine.

Along with such sweetness, the happy memory of how his mother took him to Yuegui's home to settle the marriage for him came to his mind. He remembered that he wore the same blue jacket that day, and it was at the same early hour that, with his mother, he set out on the road to Yuegui's home, feeling happy and shy. His mother had constantly been teaching him how to behave in an easy and confident manner so as to strengthen Yuegui's respect for him. But once they arrived there, he could not raise his head, as if something were wrong with his neck. Thus his eyes could not see too much around him; yet his ears were very sharp. The whispering in the side-room was plainly audible; Yuegui's mother asked her daughter to offer some tea to Fu Da and his mother—in fact she wanted to have her daughter make her appearance known to them. Unable to withstand her mother's mixed urgings and threats, Yuegui had no alternative but to come out of the room with two cups of tea. Blood surged up to Fu Da's face when he heard the steps approaching him, and he buried his head deeper in his chest. His mother hurriedly urged, "Oh, you don't need to be so formal! Fu Da, have some tea, Yuegui is bringing you some tea." The moment he lifted his head, his eyes barely met hers, shyly. It seemed as if Fu Da was seeing two sparkling stars hanging in the night sky; they were bright and deep. The meeting of their eyes, though it was only for an instant, made Fu Da's brain dizzy, his body weak and numb like a drunkard's.

Now, walking on the same road after all those years, Fu Da seemed to see those two bashful eyes again. They were still like stars sparkling in the dark sky, deep and bright. Although that meeting with Yuegui settled the marriage, he didn't even notice whether Yuegui was plump or thin, whether her face was round or long. He could not remember even to this day whether he took the tea from Yuegui.

That year, even though it was seven or eight years after Liberation, older people in the village were still superstitious. The parents on both sides secretly had their children's fortunes told. The fortuneteller said, they're a good match. Fu Da's mother was fond of Yuegui for her virtue and Yuegui's mother liked Fu Da for his honesty. Before long the marriage was settled. After their marriage they became an affectionate couple, with never a single quarrel between them. In the village there were not many young daughters-in-law who were on good terms with their mother-in-law. Yet, Fu Da's mother loved Yuegui dearly and treated her like her own daughter; Yuegui, on the other hand, showed filial obedience to her mother-in-law. The next year, she bore a child they called Yaoxiang.

However, such a satisfactory and harmonious life lasted only until Yaoxiang was two years old, the year when public dining rooms were set up on a large scale in the countryside.*

Then one night, a winter night, when snowflakes swirled in the air, Fu Da arrived home after the night shift of digging in the fields. This endless hard battle day and night had long ago exhausted him, leaving him hungry and cold. He wanted to eat, but his daily ration of half a pound of rice had been eaten already; he wanted to wash his feet in warm water, but the cooking stove had been removed.

By edict, nobody was supposed to eat at home. Yuegui was then a cook in the communal dining room. When Fu Da came back, she was still busy working there, preparing breakfast for the next morning. Tired to death, Fu Da climbed onto the bed and threw himself down on it. The weak moans of his mother constantly floated in from the next room. He knew well that his mother was also suffering from hunger.

Suddenly after midnight, the beating of a gong and a shrill piercing whistle struck terror into the people of the village. Fu Da was awakened by the noise, unaware of what was happening. Immediately he heard someone knocking loudly on his door.

"Fu Da, get up, get up, in a hurry!" Qin Guangxuan was yelling outside.

Fu Da jumped to the floor—quickly for fear of being slow —and opened the door.

"What is the m. . . m. . . matter, B. . . B. . . Brigade Leader?" Qin was the Brigade Leader at the time.

"Go to the denunciation meeting! Someone has attempted to sabotage the public dining room," Qin said firmly.

"Who w. . . w. . . was it?"

"You'll know when you get there." Qin paused, and went on in a serious tone, "Fu Da, your family have been living as poor peasants for three generations, haven't they?"

"Y. . . y. . . yes, th. . . th. . . three generations all belong to the class of p. . . p. . . poor peasants."

"You must take a firm proletarian stand."

"Yes, a f. . . f. . . firm stand."

A gas lamp was hanging under the eaves of the public dining room, sending out a brilliant white light. In front of it had gathered hundreds of men and women. They scrunched their necks down into their collars, shivering in the piercing north wind and swirling snow, as silent as cicadas in the cold weather. The air was so full of tension that the people hardly dared breathe.

Fu Da walked towards the dining room. Suddenly his legs became stiff, as if nailed to the ground. His eyes stared, nearly bursting out of their sockets. Was it Yuegui, his wife, who was on the steps under the gas lamp? She stood there with her head bowed, a bowl in her hand, a pot lid hanging before her with this inscription; "A thief who sabotaged the public dining room." Fu Da saw clearly that Yuegui's shoulders were quivering. Tears as big as pearls were running down her cheeks.

Qin Guangxuan poked Fu Da's back with his flashlight from behind.

"Why are you so dumbstruck? A while ago you said quite

---

* In 1958, during the Great Leap Forward—ed.

correctly that a firm proletarian stand should be taken."

Fu Da took a sudden big stride over to the steps and, roaring like an enraged lion, slapped Yuegui's face; but his lips were quivering as he shouted, "You bitch, I'll b. . . b. . . beat you to death, I . . ."

Yuegui's body rocked from his slap. The bowl in her hand dropped and broke, the white rice inside spilling all over. Bright red blood ran from the corners of her mouth. But, she tried to control her body and keep her balance. She shot a glance at Fu Da and held back her tears. She bit her lips with her teeth, letting her husband slap her face, letting the blood run down . . .

The next morning, when Fu Da and his mother woke up, they found a small bowl full of washed rice at the side of each bed. From that day on, Yuegui never returned. Later on, he heard by chance that she had run away to Jiangxi province. But she could not make a living there and had drowned herself.

She ran away, she died. Fu Da could not tell whether his feelings about it were more of regret or of resentment. But he kept saying, "That bitch . . ." Soon, his mother died too. Fu Da worked as hard and as quietly as a bull in the fields during the day. When he came home from the fields, he had to feed and wash the two-year-old Yiaoxiang. Taking care of the baby seemed to require more effort than carrying a one-hundred-fifty-pound load. But, in spite of the hardship, he never complained and took it as his fated duty—almost completely forgetting Yuegui.

Who could have dreamed that Yuegui hadn't really died! After twenty years, she had unexpectedly come back to visit her mother! If the news had been reported by anyone else, Fu Da would not have believed it. But it was Chairman Qin who told him!

Chairman Qin, an authority in Fu Da's eyes, spoke authoritative words which can never be wrong! Qin said to him, "You and Yuegui had a legal marriage . . ."

"That's right, I still have the marriage certificate issued by the county government." Thinking of all this, Fu Da began to feel proud of himself. "Yuegui and I went through a formal wedding ceremony in which we also worshipped our ancestors . . ."

Even stagnant water has a moment when it is moved by the spring wind. Fu Da recalled the night when he and Yuegui got married. The boys and girls in the village came to have a jolly time in the bridal chamber till midnight. Fu Da at that time was anxious to dismiss them. But when he and Yuegui were finally left alone, he suddenly felt his heart pounding nervously. He wanted to look at Yuegui, but he dared not lift his head; he wanted to talk to her, but dared not open his mouth. In such a dilemma, sitting on a red-colored stool, he remained wordless, with his head bowed low. He remembered that it was Yuegui who went to bolt the door after the guests were gone. When she passed by him, he became aware of a kind of sweet scent. Infatuated by the fragrance, he finally found the courage to lift his head and look towards Yuegui. Though he had gone to her home to settle the marriage, and that day knelt down together with her to make reverence to the ancestors, he had never dared glance at her fully. Now he saw that she was wearing a black-and-red-checkered jacket. Her cheeks were rosy, her nose straight, her mouth well-proportioned. Fu Da had never dreamed that she could be so beautiful. Yuegui, sitting on the edge of the red-colored bed with her head down, felt that Fu Da was fixing his eyes on her; she purposely turned her face to the other side. As she turned, Fu Da caught sight of a scar on the left side of her forehead where she had once been injured on a work project opening up waste land. "Ah, why! How did you get that scar?" He blurted the words out without thinking. Yuegui, struck dumb by his bluntness, her two star-like eyes staring at him, pretended to be angry. Rough as he was, Fu Da this time noticed a change in her facial expression. "You saw the scar on my face? You don't like it, do you?" Fu Da immediately answered, "I like that scar," and a smile returned to her face again. Soon they blew out the light, undressed, and went to bed. They lay far away from each other, not uttering a single word, as if they had fallen asleep right away. Suddenly they heard a loud "bang" from under the bed. Shocked, Yuegui turned to Fu Da and held him. "Never mind," he said, "it's only fireworks. They left them here. Watch me get those guys." He was ready to get out of bed to catch those "jokers," but Yuegui held him tighter and tighter . . .

"Ha, ha, they didn't make things half bad for us!" Fu Da mused, recalling that night he had passed more than twenty years ago.

He walked and thought, walked and thought, as if in a half-drunken and half-foolish state. He felt that his legs were very light, as if they were being carried by the wind. When it was about ten o'clock, he had already covered more than forty *li*. However, when that familiar old mulberry tree came into view, his legs became stiff, as if they were suddenly rooted in the ground. For a moment, Qin Guangxuan's words lost their authority over him and he felt uneasy and even frightened. He asked himself, "Why should I come here? To meet Yuegui? Will she go back home with me? I slapped her face so bitterly . . ." He looked down at his hand. If Yuegui bore a grudge, he would be more than willing to hand her a knife and allow her to chop off his hand. But, he was quite certain that Yuegui would not forgive and she would not take the knife offered by him either. Moreover, Fu Da remembered that Qin told him Yuegui's new husband had also come to visit his mother-in-law. What shall I do when we meet each other? He began to regret his coming there and decided to turn back.

Right at that moment, Yuegui's mother saw him from the window. She came out and called, "Fu Da!"

"Mother, I have come to bring you some squash." Blushing he stepped into the room.

Yuegui's mother didn't reply. Fu Da glanced covertly at her, finding her eyes red and swollen. Obviously she had been crying.

"I've come to call Yaoxiang back, our pigs are waiting to be fed." He was too flustered to know why he said that.

Yuegui's mother understood his false excuse, shook her head, and said sadly, "I know you've come to meet Yuegui. But she's gone with her family. Yaoxiang has gone to the railway station to see them off."

After having lunch at his mother-in-law's home, Fu Da set off on his way back home alone. Though he was not then as happy, as drunken, or as foolish as he had been on his way to meet Yuegui that morning, he didn't feel much sorrow. On the contrary, he felt relieved of a heavy load. Outside the village, people were still working in the rice fields. Seeing Fu Da return from some distance, they began to whisper to one another, exchanging comments in low voices. In their facial expressions, one could again see sympathy, pity, and also curiosity. However, Fu Da, pondering what his mother-in-law told him during lunch, paid no attention. She had told him that it was true that Yuegui wanted to drown herself, but she was rescued by a young peasant who took her into his care. Later on, they got married and now had three sons. They had a hard time managing until last year, when people were allowed to raise their own pigs. Now the whole family could afford to come for a visit because they had sold a big pig . . .

The moment Fu Da stepped into the doorway, he was shocked. A woman was squatting in the middle of the central room, chopping pig's food on the floor. Wasn't it Yuegui? Rosy cheeks, straight nose, well-proportioned mouth, in a black-and-red-checkered jacket . . .

Yaoxiang was so frightened by the way Fu Da was staring at her that she stood up hurriedly and cried out, "Father! Father!"

The illusion disappeared. Yet, his eyes were still fixed on that black-and-red-checkered jacket—he would be able to recognize it right away even if it were burned into ashes, f Yuegui wore it on their wedding day!

Yaoxiang seemed to realize suddenly what was happening and explained, "My mother took it off and gave it to me when she left. She came here, too."

"What? You say?" Fu Da couldn't wait.

"Yes, she did. Before she went to the railway station, she purposely made a detour to come here. She also asked me to take her to my grandmother's grave so she could pay her respects." She went into the room as she spoke and brought back a pair of new shoes.

"She made them for you!"

Fu Da quickly took the shoes and held them in his hands. His face broadened into a smile.

All the details concerning Fu Da's attempt to bring Yuegui back home spread quickly throughout the village. Many people commented behind Fu Da's back; "Fu Da is too honest. If I were he, I, at least, would bring back one of my sons. They have three of them!" Among the villagers, Qin Guangxuan seemed most actively to take Fu Da's part. He came to Fu Da's home again.

"You should bring a suit against Yuegui and her new husband. Do you know?" he told Fu Da.

"To bring what . . . a suit? . . . of clothes?"

"No, go to court and bring a lawsuit. You don't know, but these days the government stresses the rule of law."

Fu Da got his drift. But this time, for a change, he shook his head and said "no" to this figure of authority. Moreover, he spoke back without a single stutter.

"They sold a big pig in order to visit her mother."

"What does it matter if they sold a pig or not? Yuegui is a bigamist. Her new husband illegally possesses the wife of another . . ."

"Yuegui made a pair of shoes for me!" Fu Da happily defended her, as if he wanted Qin to share in his happiness. He went into the room and took the pair of new shoes from the chest. "Look here, Chairman Qin!"

Qin Guangxuan disdained to look at them. He cursed Fu Da as "a dumb dodo," and left the room frustrated and angry. Fu Da didn't see him off this time. He held the shoes in his hands, not knowing how to express the sweetness he was feeling deep in his heart. ★

Originally published in *Renmin wenxue*, no. 12, 1980.

Translated by Ping Yen and Michael S. Duke

A World of Their Own

> *Poets should establish through their works a world of their own, a genuine and independent world, an upright world, a world of justice and humanity.*
> —*Bei Dao*

Bei Dao, Gu Cheng, and Shu Ting—in that order—are the three finest young poets in China. Although their supporters have hailed their poetry as the new style most expressive of the spirit of the post-Mao era, their conservative detractors have attacked it as "obscure poetry" (*menglong shi*), sparking a continuing debate that has run to hundreds of articles from 1979 to date.

Bei Dao ("Northern Island") is the best-known pen name of Zhao Zhenkai, a young man from Peking who began publishing poetry in 1972. He wrote his remarkable protest poem, "The Answer," while participating in the Tiananmen demonstrations of 5 April 1976. It was not included in the standard anthologies because it had already transcended the conventional political rhetoric of the poems inspired by that occasion. Bei Dao writes free verse forms, and his diction, whether colloquial or bookish, conforms to the standard language of educated Peking citizens. His powerful imagery chiefly takes that busy city as its background, but reaches out to nature, especially the sea, in search of the tranquility Chinese poets have always sought there. His striking symbolism sometimes involves private associations, but for the most part his verse is readily comprehensible to the educated urbanites who have always been the only real audience for modern Chinese poetry.*

Gu Cheng is the youngest of the three poets. Son of the poet Gu Gong, he began writing poetry in his teens while living in the atmosphere of a "cultural desert" (his father's phrase) on an army farm during the Cultural Revolution. Gu Cheng's poetry represents his sensitive reaction to the world around him as well as a world of his own imagination where he has sought refuge from the unreality of the "real" world of China in the 1970s. For example, when philistine moralists criticized him for a line in "All Is Finished" that compares the Jialing River near Chongqing to a wet shroud, a line that horrified even his father, his reply was what we in the English-speaking world would expect from a poet: "In the realm of art, the world of my perception is more real than the appearance of things." Gu Cheng is a master of color images: his preoccupation with darkness is often overshadowed by his intense search for light, but his is a light more illuminating than the stale references to the "dawn of a new era" so popular among older "revolutionary" poetasters.

Shu Ting is the daughter of an intellectual family that suffered greatly during the Cultural Revolution when her relatives were imprisoned and her mother died. Her poetry is decidedly more romantic, both personally and politically, than Bei Dao's or Gu Cheng's. She quite often expresses a melancholy sense of personal disappointment from unsuccessful quests for love and friendship which might well be interpreted allegorically. The other side of her melancholy is a romantic avowal of a mission, as in "Perhaps," and a heroic demand for truth, as in "Voice of a Generation."*

The last five poems in our anthology represent the most recent works of Xie Ye, Jiang Wenyan, and Zhang Zhen. These three are members of a younger generation of women poets now emerging into prominence in China. ★

---

* The poems "The Answer," "Rainy Night," "Habituation," "Declaration," "Night: Theme and Variations," "In a Decade," "The Artist's Life," "The Snowline," "Comet," and "All" first appeared in English translation in *Notes from the City of the Sun: Poems by Bei Dao,* edited and translated by Bonnie S. McDougall (Cornell East Asia Papers, No. 34, Ithaca, NY: Cornell China-Japan Program, 1983). They are reprinted here at Ms. McDougall's suggestion and with the kind permission of the China-Japan Program, Cornell University. The other poems by Bei Dao have been supplied to us from Ms. McDougall's private collection.

* My thanks to Bonnie S. McDougall and Shiao-ling Yu for their assistance on these introductory notes.

Poems by Bei Dao

Photo by Saundra Sturdevant

The Answer

Baseness is the password of the base,
Honor is the epitaph of the honorable.
Look how the gilded sky is covered
With the drifting, crooked shadows of the dead.

The Ice Age is over now,
Why is there still ice everywhere?
The Cape of Good Hope has been discovered,
Why do a thousand sails contest the Dead Sea?

I come into this world
Bringing only paper, rope, a shadow,
To proclaim before the judgment
The voices of the judged:

Let me tell you, world,
I—do—not—believe!
If a thousand challengers lie beneath your feet,
Count me as number one thousand and one.

I don't believe the sky is blue;
I don't believe in the sound of thunder;
I don't believe that dreams are false;
I don't believe that death has no revenge.

If the sea is destined to breach the dikes,
Let the brackish water pour into my heart;
If the land is destined to rise,
Let humanity choose anew a peak for our existence.

A new juncture and glimmering stars
Adorn the unobstructed sky,
They are five thousand year old pictographs,
The staring eyes of future generations.

Résumé

I once goosestepped across the square
my head shaved bare
the better to seek the sun
but in that season of madness
I changed direction, meeting
the expressionless goats on the other side of the fence
until I saw my ideals
on blank paper that seemed from a saline-alkaline soil
I curved my spine
believing I had found the only
way to express the truth, like
a baked fish dreaming of the sea
Long live. . . ! I shouted the blasted cry once only
and then sprouted a beard
tangled like countless centuries
I was obliged to do battle with history
and at knife-point formed a family
alliance with idols, not indeed to cope with
the world that is fragmented in a fly's eye
among piles of endlessly bickering books
we calmly divided into equal parts
the few coins we made from selling off the stars
in a single night I gambled away
my belt, and returned naked again to the world
lighting a noiseless cigarette
a gun bringing death to that midnight
when heaven and earth changed places
I hung upside down
in an old tree that looked like a mop
gazing into the distance

Accomplices

many years have passed, mica
gleams in the mud
with a bright and evil light
like the sun in a viper's eyes
in a jungle of hands, roads branch off and disappear
where is the young deer
perhaps only a graveyard can change
this wilderness and assemble a town
freedom is nothing but
the distance between the hunter and the hunted
when we turn and look back
the arc drawn by bats
against the vast background of our fathers' portraits
fades with the dusk

we are not guiltless
long ago we became accomplices
of the history in the mirror, waiting for the day
to be deposited in lava
and turn into a cold spring
to meet the darkness once again

Portrait of a Young Poet

the inspiration drawn from your sleeve
is never-ending; you
pass day and night through strung-out lines and
lanes; you
were old when you were born
even though ambition grows as ever
around the edges of your baldness
taking out your false teeth, you
look even more childish
as soon as one's back is turned you scribble your name
on a public lavatory wall
thanks to a poor constitution, you
have to swallow several hormone pills a day
making your voice as tender
as the cat next door in heat
nine sneezes in a row
drop on paper, you
don't mind repetition
saying again that money isn't clean
but everyone is pretty keen on it
a fire engine wails insanely
reminding you to praise
the moon which has paid its insurance premium
or the axe, which hasn't paid
ponderously heavy
it weighs more than thought
the weather is mortally cold; blood
darkens, numb
is the night
like a frost-bitten toe, you
limp
in and out of the brake beside the road
meeting louts wreathed with laurel
every tree
with its own owl

running into people you know is a pain
how they do like to bring up the past
the past, yes, you and me
skunks, all of us

The Echo

you can't get out of this valley
in the funeral procession
you can't let go of the coffin by yourself
make peace with death, or let the autumn
continue to stay at home
stay in the tin can beside the stove
and bear infertile buds
the avalanche has started—
the echo seeks the mental connections
between you and others: good fortune
lasts, good fortune lasts until tomorrow
but joins tomorrow's
sunbeam, coming from
a jewel hidden in your breast
an evil jewel
you can't get out of this valley, because
the funeral is yours

Strangers

on the museum's
marble floor, you
took a bad fall, a shoe
slid over the ice-locked river
into the distance, I sat on the table
feeling seasick
endlessly dialing
not knowing whom I was calling
the stop-work bell rang three times
following the silent crowd
you gazed hopelessly at the red light
sunset in a tropical rain forest
is enthralling, I turned inside out
the banana-skin like glove
shaking out sand and loose tobacco
then I shaved off my lonely beard
together with the soap foam
spattered the dull
mirror, you stepped across the puddle
seeing the unfamiliar figure
behind was the sky of a billboard
a glass dove
fell on the floor, I
crawled under the bed in search
my hand was scratched by the gleaming stars
sucking on a lollypop
in the dim cinema
you wept over the sad
tale, I switched on the light
and laughed, leaning against the door
with so many chances to get to know you
it would seem that we are not
strangers, the door knob
has turned a little

Without Title

a perpetual stranger
am I to the world
I don't understand its language
my silence it can't comprehend
all we have to exchange
is a touch of disdain
as if we meet in a mirror

a perpetual stranger
am I to myself
I fear the dark
but use my body to block
the only lamp
my shadow is my beloved
my heart the enemy

Orphans

we are two orphans
who have formed a family
we will leave behind another orphan
in the lengthy
file of orphans trailing pale shadows
all the strident flowers
will bear fruit
the world will know no peace
it is the true father
of all orphans

A Blank

poverty is a blank
freedom is a blank
in the sockets of a marble statue:
victory is a blank
black birds pouring from the horizon
reveal tomorrow's age spots:
despair is a blank
at the bottom of a friend's cup:
betrayal is a blank
on the lover's photograph:
disgust is a blank
in the long-awaited letter:
time is a blank
a swarm of ominous flies
settle on the hospital ceiling:
history is a blank
a running genealogy
where only the dead are recognized

Underground Station

the cement electricity poles
were once logs of wood
drifting downriver
do you believe that?
eagles never fly here
though rabbitskin hats of every size and shape
are on show in the street
do you believe that?
only at night when all is still
flocks of goats pour into town
and are dyed bright colors by neon lights
do you believe that?

Another Legend

dead heroes are forgotten
they are silent, they
pass through a sea of faces
their anger can only light
the cigarette in a man's hand
even with the help of a ladder
they can no longer predict anything:
each weather vane goes its own way
only when each huddles
at the foot of his hollow statue
does he realize the depth of despair
they always come and go at night
suddenly illuminated by the solitary lamp
but difficult to distinguish nonetheless
like faces
pressed against frosted glass

finally, they slip through the narrow gate
covered all over with dust
taking charge of the solitary key

Temptation

from time immemorial
it has been a temptation
luring sailors to surrender their lives
an embankment preventing
the tilted land from slipping to the bottom of the sea

a dolphin leaps over the stars
and falls back, the white beach
disappears in generous moonlight
water covers the embankment
and the empty, deserted square
jellyfish cling stranded to every lamppost
water mounts the steps
and pours booming through the doors and windows
chasing the man who is dreaming of the sea

Without Title

it has always been so
that fire is the center of winter
when the woods are ablaze
only stones that don't want to come closer
keep up their furious howl

the bell hanging on the deer's antler has stopped ringing
life is one opportunity
a single one only
whoever checks the time
will suddenly find himself old

One Step

the shadow of the pagoda moves across the grass, pointing at you
or at me, at different moments:
we are only one step away
parting or meeting again
is an ever-repeating
theme: hate only one step away
the sky sways, on its foundation of fear
the buildings open windows in every direction
we live inside them
or outside: death only one step away
the child has learned to talk to walls
the history of the city is sealed by old men
in their hearts: dotage only one step away

Boddhisattva

the flowing folds of your robe
are your faint respiration

on each palm of your thousand arms
stares an unblinking eye
they caress the static silence
making all things perpetually intermingle
as in a dream

you sit cross-legged on lotus
joy has its source in mud

enduring centuries of hunger and thirst
the pearl set in your forehead
stands for the sea's matchless power
that renders a pebble as transparent
as the water

you face the day soberly
though still sound asleep

your sexless
half-naked bosom swells
it is only an urge for motherhood
to feed the sufferings of this mortal world
making them grow

Rainy Night

As the shattered night in the flooded ditch
Was rocking a new leaf
As if rocking its child to sleep
As the lamplight threaded raindrops
Studded your shoulders
Gleaming and rolling down
You said no
In such a resolute tone
But a smile revealed your heart's secret

With moist palms the low black clouds
Kneaded your hair
Kneading in the fragrance of flowers and my burning breath
Our shadows lengthened in the street lights
Connected each crossing, each dream
Catching in their net the riddle of our happiness
Tears from earlier torments
Wetted your handkerchief
Forgotten in a pitch-black doorway

Even if tomorrow morning
The muzzle and the bleeding sun
Make me surrender freedom, youth and pen
I will never surrender this evening
I will never surrender you
Let walls stop up my mouth
Let iron bars divide my sky
As long as my heart keeps pounding, the blood will ebb and flow
And your smile will be imprinted on the crimson moon
Rising each night outside my tiny window
Recalling memories

Habituation

I'm used to how you light my cigarette in the dark
As the flame quivers you always ask softly
Guess what I've burned

I'm used to how you sit in the boat humming
The oars dripping water fragment the sun in the mist
How trailing weary, wilful footsteps
You refuse to rewarm our old dreams on the bench
How you race me, your hair swinging from side to side
Separating shoulders, and laugh with carefree abandon

I'm used to how you call out in the valley
Listening afterwards for the echo that chases our names
How you bring your books, always asking questions
Pursing your lips as you write down the answer over your hand
How your warm breath wraps around my neck like a scarf
Under the deep blue street lights in winter

Yes, I'm used to
How you strike the flint that burns
The dark I'm used to

Declaration

Perhaps the final hour is come
I haven't left a testament
only a pen, for my mother
I am no hero
In an age without heroes
I just want to be a man

The still horizon
divides the ranks of the living and the dead

I can only choose the sky
I will not kneel on the ground
allowing the executioners to look tall
the better to obstruct the wind of freedom

From star-like bullet holes shall flow
a blood-red dawn

Night: Theme and Variations

The roads converge here
parallel beams of light
are a longwinded but suddenly interrupted dialogue
suffused with the drivers' pungent smoke
and rough, indistinct curses
railings have replaced the queues
light seeping out from between the cracks in the doorboards
is cast with cigarette butts to the roadside
for nimble feet to tread on
an old man's forgotten walking-stick against a billboard
looks as if it were ready to go
the stone water lily has withered
in the fountain tall buildings slowly topple
the rising moon suddenly strikes
the hour again and again
arousing the ancient time inside the palace wall
the sundial calibrates errors as it turns
waiting for the grand rite of the dawn
brocade dress ribbons stand up rustling in the wind
brushing away the dust on the stone steps
the shadow of a tramp slinks past the wall
red and green neon lights blaze for him
and keep him from sleeping all night
a lost cat scurries up on a bench
gazing down at the smoke soft gleam of the waves
but the mercury vapor lamp rudely lifts open the curtain
peering at the secrets that others store
disturbs the dream, rousing the lonely
behind a small door
a hand draws the catch softly
as if pulling a rifle bolt

In a Decade

Over the forgotten land
the years entangled with the horse's yoke bells
rang out throughout the night, and the road's panting
under the swaying heavy load changed into a song
passed on by people everywhere
to the sound of an incantation a woman's necklace
rose into the night sky as if in confirmation
the fluorescent dial struck licentiously at will
time is as honest as a wrought-iron fence
except for the wind trimmed by withered branches
no one can pass over it or come and go
flowers that have only bloomed in books
eternally imprisoned, become the mistress of truth
but yesterday's broken lamp
is so resplendent in the hearts of the blind
right up until the time when they are shot
a final portrait of the assassin is left behind
in eyes that have suddenly opened

The Artist's Life

go and buy a radish
—mother said
hey, mind the safety line
—the policeman said
where are you, o ocean
—the drunkard said
why have all the street lights exploded
—I said
a blind man passing by
nimbly raised his cane
like pulling out an antenna
an ambulance arriving with a screech
took me to the hospital

then I became a model patient
sneezing loud and clear
closing my eyes to figure out the mealtimes
donating a series of blood transfusions to bedbugs
with no time to sigh
in the end I was taken on as a doctor too
holding a thick hypodermic
I pace up and down in the corridor
to while away the evenings

The Snowline

forget what I've said
forget the bird shot down from the sky
forget the reefs
let them sink once more into the deep
forget even the sun
only a lamp left full of dust and ashes
is shining
in that eternal position

after a series of avalanches
the cliffs above the snowline
seal everything in silence
from gentle grassy shores
below the snowline
trickles a stream

Comet

Come back, or leave forever
don't stand like that at the door
like a statue made of stone
discussing everything between us
with a look that expects no answer

In fact what is hard to imagine
is not darkness but the dawn
how long will the lamplight last
perhaps a comet may appear
trailing debris from the ruins
and a list of failures
letting them glitter, burn up and turn to ash

Come back, and we'll rebuild our home
or leave forever, like a comet
sparkling and cold like frost
discarding the dark and sinking back into darkness again
going through the white corridor connecting two evenings

in the valley where echoes arise on all sides
you sing alone

All

All is fate
All is cloud
All is a beginning without an end
All is a search that dies at birth
All joy lacks smiles
All sorrow lacks tears
All language is repetition

All contact a first encounter
All love is in the heart
All past is in a dream
All hope carries annotations
All faith carries groans
All explosions have a moment of quiet
All deaths have a lingering echo

Translations by Bonnie S. McDougall. See note on p. 39 for the sources of these poems.

Poems by Gu Cheng

Photo by Saundra Sturdevant

Nameless Little Flowers

As I was returning home from cutting grass, a light rain was falling. I saw flowers by the roadside glistening with dewdrops and wrote this poem.

Wild flowers
Hither and thither
Like lost buttons
Scattered by the roadside.

They do not have Chrysanthemums'
Gold curls
Nor peonies'
Dazzling looks
They have only small flowers
And thin weak leaves,
Yet their faint fragrance
Is dissolved into the beautiful spring day.

My poems
Are like these nameless little flowers,
Following the wind and rain of the season
Quietly blooming
In this lonely world.

1971, Shandong
From the collection Nameless Little Flowers

My Curriculum Vitae

I'm a child of sorrow;
I've never grown up.
From the grassy banks of the northland
I came, along a
White road,* and walked into
A city full of gears and wheels;
Walked into a narrow lane,
A wooden shed, and to every downcast heart,
In the midst of hazy smoke
I continue to tell my green-colored story.
I trust my audience—
The sky, and
The water droplets splashing from the sea;
They'll cover up all of me,
Cover up that never-to-be found
Grave. I know
At that time, all the grass and little flowers
Will crowd around me, at
An instant of dim lamplight
Gently kiss my sorrow.

Wenxue-bao, 10 March, 1983

---

* The road is white from the alkali that covers it.

Fantasia of Life
(excerpts)

Without any aim,
I float in the blue sky,
Letting the waterfall of sunlight
Wash my skin black.

The sun tows my boat,
Pulling me along with ropes of powerful light.
Step by step,
I thus traveled the distance of twelve-hours.
The wind pushes me
To the east and to the west.
The sun disappears in the twilight.

Night comes,
I sail into the harbor of the Milky Way.
Thousands of stars stare at me,
And I cast down
The crescent moon—my golden anchor.

The sun bakes the earth,
As if toasting a piece of bread.
I walk on
In my bare feet.
My footprints, like seal impressions
Cover the great earth.

And the world also melts into
My life.
I want to sing
A song about the human race:
Thousands of years later,
It still reverberates in the universe.

> 1971, returning from Weihe (in Shandong Province) in the heat of summer. From the collection *Nameless Little Flowers*

Night in the Countryside

The thick, dark night
Glues together heaven and earth.
Stars are mixed with candlelights,
The Milky Way joins the irrigation ditch.
Our little thatched hut
Becomes a neighbor to the moon palace.
Let's go in to drink a cup of cassia tea!*
We might also inquire about the problem of residence.

> 1970 Shandong

---

* According to Chinese legend, a cassia tree grows in the moon palace. The sweet-scented cassia flowers are often used to flavor tea.

The Origins of Stars and the Moon

Tree branches wanted to pierce through the sky,
But only managed to poke a few small holes.
Lights from outer space filtered in,
And people called them the moon and the stars.

> Quoted in *Qishi niandai* (*The Seventies*, Hong Kong), no. 12 (1982)

The Red Guards' Graves

In Chongqing (Chunking), in the Shapingpa Park there lies a stretch of Red Guards' graves amongst overgrown weeds and shrubs, facing the Tombs of Revolutionary Martyrs on Gele Mountain in the distance.

There is no trace of human presence.
I and my poetry happen to pass by, but what can we say...

A Dim Little Path Led Me Into Your Midst
(one of six poems)

A dim little path
Led me
Into your midst.
Like a strand of forgotten sunlight,
Standing together
With the tall grasses
And the short trees,
I do not represent history,
Do not represent the voice
Emitted from the highest place.
I've come
Only because of my age.

One by one, you
Fell to the ground
With happy tears in your eyes,
With imaginary guns in your hands.
Your fingers
Are still clean,
They've opened only school books
And heroes' stories.
Perhaps out of
A common habit
On the last page
You painted your own self-portraits.

On the page in my heart
There's no picture of any kind.
It's getting damp,
Moistened by the blue dewdrops
On the tips of leaves.
When I open it
I cannot use the fountain pen
Nor the writing brush;

I can only use the gentlest breath
Of my life
To trace some
Marks for people to speculate.

October, 1980. From the collection
The Hanging Green Apple

All Is Finished

In a twinkling—
The landslide ceased,
The riverside was piled high with skulls of giants.

The junk in mourning,
Slowly passes by,
And unfolds the dull-yellow shroud.

So many beautiful trees,
Their trunks gnarled from pain,
Weepingly comfort the fallen heroes.

The moon, hacked into a sliver,
Is hidden in the dense fog by God.
All is finished.

The heavy shadows of the mountain,
Representing blurred history,
Continue to record everything in silence.

Chang'an, July, 1980

To My Honored Teacher Andersen

Andersen and this writer had both worked as amateur carpenters.

You push your carpenter's plane
As if paddling a canoe,
Letting it drift slowly
On the smooth sea . . .

Wood shavings scatter like waves,
Disappearing at the end of the horizon;
Water ripples resemble undulating verses,
Bringing season's greetings.

You have no flag,
No gold or silver, or multi-colored silk,
Yet all the kings in the world
Cannot match your wealth.

You transport a heavenly kingdom,
Transport the balloons of flowers and dreams.
All the pure childlike hearts
Are your ports of call.

Shi kan, No. 4, 1980

Impressions

The sky is gray,
The road is gray,
The buildings are gray,
The rain is gray.

In this dead grayness
Two children walk by;
One is bright red,
The other light green.

Shi kan, No. 10, 1980.
English translation first published in
Renditions, No. 16 (Autumn, 1981)

Farewell

Today
you and I
will step over the ancient threshold
don't wish me well
don't say goodbye
they're like a performance
silence is best
in reserve there's no deception
leave thoughts of the past to the future
like leaving dreams to the night
tears to the sea
wind to the sails on the night sea

Wenhuibao yuekan, June 1981

The "Garland's" Soliloquy

According to tradition, "Garland" is a high quality Shaoxing wine which is buried in the ground on a wedding day and not opened until a sixty-year cycle has passed.

My skull vault is full and smooth
storing fire, spring water
and amber yearnings
juice of poetry, fragrance of dreams
obscure pleas and blessings

These memories come from paddies stuck
full with rice and gleaming like coarse china
from the breathing of milk-vetch, and earthen cellar
the skin color of unnamed herbs
reflections of sails, and history dispersed in the mud

At an hour when red candles flickered
I was buried, not
in mourning, but to be born
a custom brought by the monsoon
and a secret between lovers

I hear the leaves falling, the plough digging, the tamp pounding
the sloughing off of cicada and chrysalis
the soothing questions of earthworm and mole
(they imagine me formed of
a great round shell from an ancient shore)

But of my creator?
the opening of plank and paneled doors
the splintering of kindling, the children's guardian bells
memories and footsteps, gradually getting heavier
are all beyond my hearing

Yearning, I ripen in yearning
like an underground tuber
—forgotten by the sunlight, a dismal fruit
in an hermetic seal that allows no seepage
the choicest love completes its fermentation

I imagine the giddy hour
white hair and piping laughter
I shall pour out all my cries
and in a brief moment of silence
dissolve into starry night and blue void

April 1981, Shaoxing
Haixia, January 1981

The Boat from the Distant Past

Many thousands of years ago, a small boat sailed up the River Seine.

Exhausted, it moored at a small island in the middle of the river.

And so the small island gained life, a fishing village, and a figurative name—Roof Over the Waters.

The great city of Paris is the son of Roof Over the Waters. It has not forgotten its past. The sacred emblem of Paris, the city's symbol, is a boat from the distant past. The boat advances through the waves, sails hoisted high.

1

The waves deliver my destiny
and all
the sunlight that will not drown
the warm strength of my palms
takes me forward
dividing the sea and the sky
to make the acquaintance of kindly shoals and
eccentric reefs
passing through an archipelago—a mouth
where two great continents gradually meet
sending through the shortest night
a hoping heart
to expectant eyes

2

A curious sea lion
swims up from the polar region
behind it a splendid tiger shark
its obscure stripes expanding
an octopus hastily retreats
after a violent embrace
making the scattering fish flicker uncertainly
only the boat-boring shell firmly upholds its love
showing its teeth in a honeyed kiss
towards these creatures
I only have silence
awaiting hostile rejection
with pride or humility

3

I know the sea's mood
and the reason for its generosity
an inky warm current
wells up from a coral forest
inviting the transparent icy water
to the dance
a myriad secret thoughts
are born and vanish
fixed and mobile lives
merge into rock, generation upon generation
decorating time
with the pattern of their bones
making a symbol of the sea's memories

4

Throngs of noble clouds
move in from the horizon
trailing long silvery-grey skirts
under this arrogant cover
I open sail
and all-searching hands
not in supplication
they have nothing
to arouse my attention
I only make enquiries
of the poor and humble winds
coming from the forest
they have news of my companions

5

Yes
I cherish the memory of those companions
upright redwood and whitewood pines
we gathered by a volcanic pool
bending to watch the flying birds
singing together
even the oldest moon
became a child
and guessed at riddles with new mushrooms in a green dream
perhaps you spent your whole lives partying
until fire and thunder struck
your disaster is to rise to heaven's halls
but my misfortune is to sink to the ocean depths

6

Perhaps I may come in peace
to my declining years
farewell a wanderer's fate
and under a towrope's courteous guidance
sail into the fond embrace of inland waters
perhaps, also, a small shoal there
will offer me rest
and let the sun draw the ache from my rheumatic bones
perhaps, also, a pair of lovers, the world forgotten
will come softly up to me
moving colorful boulders
to prop me up
and rest in peace under my cover

7

Limp from the stormy wind and rain
I lie in a gravelly ditch
a wisp of cooking smoke tells the sky
and all the life that belongs in the sky
I am a roof
I am still on my voyage
though no longer do I carry flowers of hope
but fruit that has swelled in good fortune
I voyage in heaven's sea
moored at the bank of life
naked children pour from my windows and doors
leaping into the sunlight
to play with lively little crabs

Dangdai wenxue, February 1981, pp. 95-96

Translations by Shiao-ling Yu except for "Farewell," "The 'Garland's' Soliloquy," and "The Boat from the Distant Past," which are by Bonnie S. McDougall.

Poems by Shu Ting

Photo by Saundra Sturdevant

Oh Mother

Your pale fingers smoothing my hair,
I hold fast to the lapel of your clothes
As if I were still a child,
Oh Mother,
To cling to your vanishing shadow,
I dare not open my eyes,
Even though the morning rays have shattered my dream.

I still keep that red scarf,
Afraid washing will make it
Lose your lingering fragrance.
Oh Mother,
How unfeelingly time flows.
I dare not open my memory's manifold screen,
For fear it, too, will fade.

Because of a little splinter, I used to come crying to you,
Now I'm wearing a crown of thorns,
But I don't dare,
Don't dare to let out a single moan.
Oh Mother,
I often gaze at your photo with sorrow,
Even if my calls can penetrate the earth,
Dare I disturb you from your rest?

I still dare not display my love,
Although I've written many songs
To flowers, sea and the dawn.
Oh Mother,
My sweet remembrance of you
Is not a torrent, not a waterfall,
But a voiceless old well hidden amongst flowers and trees.

Xinge ji, pp. 238-39

Giving

I was full of regret for you
Beside the gunwales flooded by the moonlight.
On the roads dampened by light rain
You arched your shoulders, tucked your hands in your sleeves
As if afraid of the cold.
Lost in your own thoughts,
You did not notice
My footsteps beside you
And how slowly they followed.
If you were fire,
I would be the charcoal;
I want to comfort you thus
But I don't dare to.

I was overjoyed for you,
For the lights flickering on your window,
For your bending silhouette in front of your bookcase.
When you bared your awakening to me,
Saying that spring tide had once more overflowed
Your banks,
You did not ask
How I felt night after night
When I passed by your window.
If you were a tree,
I would be the soil;
I want to remind you of this
But I don't dare to.

Xinge ji, pp. 243-44

When You Pass By My Window

When you pass by my window,
Bless me, please,
For the light is still on.

The light is on—
In the gloomy night,
Like a floating fisherman's lamp.
You can imagine my little cabin,
Like a little boat tossing in a windstorm
But I did not sink,
For the light is still on.

The light is on—
My shadow on the curtain
Is that of a stooped old man,
No vigorous gestures,
My back bent even more than before.
But my heart has not grown old,
For the light is still on.

The light is on—
With a burning love,
It acknowledges greetings from all sides.
The light is on—
With dignity and pride,
It looks down at oppressions of all kinds.
Ah, when did it take on a distinct character?
Since you began to understand me.

For the light is still on—
Bless me, please,
When you pass by my window.

Xinge ji, pp. 245-46

Perhaps

—In response to a writer's loneliness

Perhaps our thoughts
Will never have readers
Perhaps our road was wrong in the beginning
And is still wrong in the end;
Perhaps we can light up one lantern after another
Only to have them blown out by a fierce wind one by one;
Perhaps we can burn out our lives to illuminate darkness,
But we have no fire to warm ourselves.

Perhaps after we shed all our tears
The soil will become more fertile;
Perhaps when we praise the sun
We'll be praised in return;
Perhaps the heavier our burdens become
The loftier our faith will grow;
Perhaps we can protest against all sufferings
But remain silent over our own misfortunes.

Perhaps
Because of some irresistible call
We do not have any choice.

Xinge ji, p. 271

Assembly Line

In the assembly line of time
Night closely follows night;
We come off the assembly line in the factory,
Again in assembly line formation we march home.
Above our heads
The assembly line of stars stretches across the sky,
Beside us
Little trees stand dazed in the assembly line.

The stars must be tired,
Thousands of years have passed,
Their journey never changed.
The little trees have all fallen sick,
Smoke and monotony caused them
To lose their contours and colors;
All these I've sensed
Through a feeling of common rhythm.

But how strange
The only thing that I cannot sense
Is my own existence;
As if like the trees and stars,
Perhaps out of habit,
Perhaps out of sorrow,
I'm powerless to show any concern
For my own inevitable fate.

Xinge ji, pp. 277-78

Voice of a Generation

I'll never complain
Of what I went through.
Wasted youth,
Distorted conscience,
Painful memories
From many a sleepless night.
I've overthrown one doctrine after another.
I've smashed one shackle after another;
What's left in my heart
Is a vast expanse of wasteland . . .
But I've stood up,
On the vast horizon I stand,
No one, by whatever means,
Can push me down again.

If it were I who lay inside a "martyr's" tomb,
Moss covering the inscriptions on my tombstone;
If it were I who was locked behind iron bars,
Arguing my case with fetters and chains;
If it were I, haggard and worn,
Toiling endlessly to redeem my sins;
If it were I, if it were only
My personal tragedy—
Perhaps I'd have already forgiven,
My tears and indignation
Can also calm down.

But, for the sake of the children's fathers
For the sake of the fathers' children;
So that we no longer tremble before the silent reproaches
Coming from under the monuments everywhere;
So that we no longer dodge
The sight of the homeless on the streets;
So that innocent children a hundred years from now
Won't have to guess the meaning of the history we left behind;
For this blot on our motherland,
For this tortuous experience of our nation,
For the purity of the sky
And the honesty of our road
I demand truth!

Xinge ji, pp. 273-74
Translation of the first stanza first published
in *Renditions*, No. 16 (Autumn, 1981) ★

Translations by Shiao-ling Yu

Poems by Xie Ye, Jiang Wenyan, and Zhang Zhen

Photo by Saundra Sturdevant

I Don't Believe, I Believe

by Xie Ye

When I leave
I don't believe you can smile
or go and look at doves with joyous eyes
or dance
along the path, planning the future
letting your fancy run wild

When I leave
I don't believe, I don't believe
the lamp is really extinguished, the stars and the letter
discarded, your soul a darkness
I don't believe you look on me like that
that you would really let me go

I don't believe, I really don't believe
I believe in
words and heart in deep silence
in the sun behind the dark clouds
in the rock quietly melting in the earth's deepest layers
I believe in dreams, in the waiting in dreams

I believe in waiting, I'm afraid it is
endless, dark, I'm afraid it is in the grave
as long as the path is alive
strewn with white and purple lilac
you might turn towards me
saying everything, then say: I love

I believe, I am fortunate
so fortunate I can't breathe

I can't answer your questions
I have waited too long, become
a valley, become
a spring and a skylark's song in a valley

Xinghuo, 1982

When I Grew Up

by Jiang Wenyan

When I was little I was terribly stupid
grown up, I'm still not very clever

I was a child, then
wiping my nose on my sleeve
a blind man asked me the way
I took his cane in my hand
and led him into a corner
and ran off, sniggering
his curses chasing me

Now I'm grown up, I've also gone blind
life's road to me is a blur
I let others take my cane and lead me
an inexpressible confusion in my mind
I think of the blind man I cheated
the cane stabs my heart
curses chase me

Hebei wenxue, January 1981

Dark Clouds

by Jiang Wenyan

My father picked me up from the leaves and grass
and gave me to a warm current of air
my mother picked me up from the breakers' foam
and gave me to the sun
the sun gave us to the wind
to the dust and the cold
we gave ourselves
to the mountains, their thirsty flowers
to the branches, their smiling leaves
to the furrows, their golden crops
put the paper boat with that
in the child's dream in the gutter

Guangzhou wenxue, October 1981

Your Heart Is a Field in Early Spring

to M

by Zhang Zhen

In the beginning I did not dare
walk along the railway line that held no hope
I was afraid that the parallel rails
might suddenly intertwine
       in the fiery kiss of the setting sun
I was afraid that the love
abandoned between the sleepers
might pour out a patch of grass
in the interweaving of blunt footsteps
       drowning static time

Afterwards I knew
from your translucent eyes
also in your awkward innocent gestures
the evening breeze raised joyful eyelashes
the clamor of frogs
dissolved into immaculate music
finally also in your total sincerity
the story of always evasive anguish
I began to believe
your heart
was a field in early spring

The two sides of the abandoned railway
still spread out
unextinguishable spring
on the dim horizon shines an unreachable light
so there's no need for us
to step out in despair
obediently like a child
I raise my neck
let the music of early spring drench the open desert
and plough pure lines of verse

Qingnian shitan, No. 2, September 1983, pp. 33-34

The Forest

by Zhang Zhen

Do you remember
we almost mistook each other
like two trees gazing at each other, in despair
from opposite ends of the forest
be glad at the two stars' chance encounter
you stretch out your hand to me
in the forest's still autumn night

Don't be like this, please,
rustling the fallen leaves
arousing the mast's droop
and the boat corpse's drift
on my unquiet sea
I want to moor at your bosom
never more to sail forth

Are you angry?
branch shadows spread over your forehead
like your fine black hair
covering solid thoughts
forgive me
if the forest is really boundless
I should like to lose the way with you

Don't you believe me
there's no need to make such an inspection
as if searching for another lover
I let this kiss burn
in the winter night in the forest
it will always navigate for us
from here down to the sea

Qingnian shitan, No. 2, 1983, p. 34

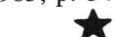

Translations by Bonnie S. McDougall.

Intellectual Youth in Quest of Light and Truth

Youth
Red waves
soak a solitary oar

—*Bei Dao*

The black night has given me black eyes,
But I use them to search for light.

—*Gu Cheng*

I'll never complain
. . .
But . . .
For the purity of the sky
And the honesty of our road
I demand truth!

—*Shu Ting*

Over half of China's one billion people are under thirty today. As in the May Fourth Era, the largest audience for modern Chinese literature is the millions of urbanized "intellectual youth" (zhishi qingnian), a term that includes not only college students and graduates but all those with the equivalent of a high school education. To say that this post-Mao youth generation is engaged *en masse* in a quest for light and truth may sound a bit romantic, but it is not too far off the mark if by light and truth is meant a deeper meaning and significance to life than economic production and consumption, however basic those two may be to physical survival. Disillusioned by the chaotic events of the Cultural Revolution and both stimulated and frustrated by the new freedoms and restrictions of the present era, the young people of China are seeking spiritual values everywhere they can.

The tremendous popularity of Li Ping's autobiographical 1981 novella "When Sunset Clouds Disappear" (*Wanxia xiaoshi de shihou*) is a prime example of the present questing state of mind of many young Chinese, some of whom—ex-Red Guards—may admittedly be over thirty. The concluding section, "Autumn" (*Qiu*), is presented here because the protagonist's Socratic dialogue with the wise old Chan Buddhist monk about the necessity of science, art, and religion (representing Truth, Beauty, and Goodness) for the creation of a truly human civilization seems to represent the authentic voice of Chinese youth much better than official pronouncements on the building of "socialist spiritual civilization."

The following plot summary is by the translator, Daniel Bryant.

* * *

The narrator, Li Huaiping, is the son of a veteran cadre and military commander during the Revolution. Once, while still a young student, he went looking for a place to study in a quiet wooded park. There he met a young girl named Nanshan with whom he had an intense discussion of many ethical and historical questions. At the end of their talk, she lent him a volume of Shakespeare, a present from her mother—we learn that she has never seen her mother because her parents left China soon after she was born. A few months later, as a Red Guard leader, Li Huaiping is in charge of a raid on the home of one Chu Xuanwu, a former Nationalist army officer. In the course of the raid, Chu is interrogated at length by Li, who eventually realizes that it was his own father who accepted Chu's surrender. Li also discovers to his horror that Chu's granddaughter is none other than Nanshan, who was present during the raid. A few years later, when many educated young people are being sent to work in the countryside, Li goes to deliver some farewell gifts to departing friends at the railway station. Unable to reach their coach because of the crowds, he resorts to boarding the train at one end and making his way down the length of it. On his way he suddenly realizes that the compartment in front of him contains Nanshan, who is leaving for the countryside, and her grandparents, who have come to say farewell. Li eavesdrops on their conversation, learning that Nanshan turned to religion to support her during her trials. A little later, as the train pulls out of the station and Li again stands on the platform, he and Nanshan catch sight of one another. But once again, just as on the night of the raid, they are unable to communicate.

Twenty-five-year-old Li Chao is one of seven regional editors of a literary journal aimed at Chinese youth. He is also the son of the well-known writer Fang Zhi (d. 1980), whose 1979 story "Hidden Traitor" won a literary prize and who also tried to prevent his son from taking up the dangerous profession of writing during the Cultural Revolution. "Spring Chill" (*Chun han*) is one of the three stories Li published in 1979. Inspired perhaps by the cold political winds of the spring of 1979, when Deng Xiaoping cracked down on many unofficial publications, this story stridently expresses Chinese youth's desire to know and write the truth in spite of the very real risks involved. Professor Li Senquan's pitiful attempt to prevent his daughter's marriage to the one student who most resembles himself in his own youth adds another poignantly ironic touch. ★

Autumn

Photo by Saundra Sturdevant

by Li Ping

And now, twelve years had passed, twelve long years.

Late in autumn, an express train sped across the golden plains of eastern China on the Shanghai-Peking line. It came rushing out of the east along the curving tracks, its steady whistle borne on the wind, past endless ranges of hills, rivers, and plains. On it rushed like a storm toward the Yellow River, toward the North, toward the historic city that had left me so many unforgettable memories, Peking.

I sat alone by a broad window in one of the sleeper coaches, staring out at the scenes of autumn flashing by one after another: fields in the midst of an abundant harvest, distant blue hills, dense thickets of low trees, and great white clouds floating in the sky; thinking and daydreaming . . .

Twelve years, twelve long years! And now I had spent my entire youth on the open sea on a guided-missile destroyer.

* * *

I remembered with perfect clarity that cold night twelve years before when I had boarded the iron-sheathed transport wagons along with several thousand other new recruits. Packed into the carriages, we spent two days and nights en route and arrived at a great naval base on the south-east coast in the midst of a snow storm. It was at this heavily guarded base that we joined naval crews. With this, I bade farewell to my student days and entered the strict life of the military.

At the time, the Cultural Revolution had, after three years, created a kind of abnormal spiritual condition throughout the country. The military too had become deeply wrapped up in the same sort of thing. Ships' crews were mired down every day in interminable political study. They rarely performed any proper drills or exerecises, much less any adequate inspections or maneuvers. But the hardest part to bear was all the loyalty rituals and their ever-changing patterns: requesting instructions in the morning, reporting in the evening, "loyalty" formations at parade, quotation drills, and the Mao badges getting bigger and bigger. The absurd and outlandish kinds of saluting and bowing and scraping poisoned the atmosphere more and more as time went on.

I understood this unit, for I was a child of it myself. Very few military units in modern Chinese history had been able to equal it in doing away with the evil practices traditional in the military or in creating for itself a new, at times even deeply moving image. But now its glory had been badly tarnished by all these stupid, vulgar, and shallow ceremonies of modern superstition and servility.

I was a bold and high-spirited young man then. Although some of my values had gotten badly mixed up in the social and political confusion of the times, my basic preference for the good and beautiful over the false and ugly had not been overturned. And so, when I couldn't restrain myself any longer, I often revealed my disgust and dissatisfaction. As a result, once my comments went beyond the officially permitted limits, one of my comrades immediately informed on me.

The investigation was very strict, but after half a year, the Vice Commander-in-Chief* I had offended against suddenly became a thug for everyone to curse and spit at, so the incriminating evidence in my dossier turned me into a political hero. By this time, I had been serving as a real sailor

---

* Vice Commander-in-Chief refers to Lin Biao (1907–71) who was a vice-chairman of the Communist Party of China and Mao Zedong's "closest comrade-in-arms" from 1966 to 1971. He was reported killed in an airplane crash while trying to escape to the Soviet Union after an abortive attempt to assassinate Chairman Mao in September 1971.

on board a ship for less than three years. Some who were more capable, more reliable, and better qualified to assume important duties than I were discharged, while I was made an operations officer. And what did I have in my record? There were no voyages on the open sea, no lightning raids carried out in foul weather, no artillery practice using live ammunition, still less any good marks in military college; indeed, there were none of the things required by a junior naval officer . . . Fortunately, all this eventually changed.

* * *

The train ran so smoothly that it was soon in the mountains.

I took a cigarette from the pocket of my uniform which I had hung up, lit it, and began to think about my elderly father. Because of the bitter memories left behind from childhood, I had become completely indifferent to that unfinished but important part of my life. Yet whenever I thought of my father, I was ashamed of myself and felt a deep sense of guilt because I had left him lonely in his old age. The emotions I had buried deep in my heart for so many years suddenly revived, after an unexpected tragedy at home.

* * *

. . . It was a night four months earlier; the sea was heavy under a black sky. A huge warship rolled with the waves, pitching against the wharf.

All of a sudden, a mind-piercing battle alert roused everyone from his dreams. My comrades and I tumbled from our bunks, dashed out of our quarters, and ran along the passageways and ladders to our battle stations.

From the loudspeaker the captain ordered in his deep and resonant voice, "Attention all units! Attention all units! The naval base is under air attack. All hands remain at battle stations; blackout regulations are to be strictly enforced . . ."

Our ship set up great waves as it left the wharf in the darkness and sped out onto the deep black sea. The maneuvers had begun.

For six straight hours I fought the rolling seas while bent over the chart table, intently plotting the vessel's exact position from moment to moment, with the symbols on the chart joined in a red line showing our course. It was not until dawn, when the colors of sunrise appeared and I walked out on deck, having relinquished my station with much relief, that I discovered that a whole task force was spread out across the vast Pacific Ocean in a magnificent formation. The ships were steaming toward the dawn. That day we embarked on deep-sea exercises in Micronesia scheduled to last for 105 days.

My elderly father and mother had not been informed ahead of time that I was to participate in these maneuvers. Four months later, when the exercise was concluded and our ship returned to harbor, I received seven letters from my father all at once.

In the first, he wrote as usual that he and my mother were both in good health, and that I should go on about my duties without worrying about them. But in the second letter, my grief-stricken father informed me that my mother had suddenly passed away early one morning. He asked me to come home. The third letter was addressed to my unit's headquarters and asked why I hadn't written back after receiving such terrible news. But in the fourth letter my father asked headquarters to inform me of what had happened immediately on my return. Obviously they had already informed him that I was on maneuvers at sea.

After this, he had written me three letters, one after another. Nearly seventy himself, my father had clearly endured a terrible loss, but in these three letters he set out in very restrained language all the events connected with my mother's death and funeral. And so I learned that the unhappy event had occurred on the nineteenth day after we left the harbor. At one o'clock in the morning of that day, while the fleet was quietly passing by a group of islands, my mother had died in her sleep. It happened so suddenly that she suffered no pain. Her calmly sleeping face had become my mourning father's only consolation.

At the memorial service for my mother, my father read aloud a eulogy he had written himself, and then joined her fellow workers and comrades in taking her remains to the Revolutionary Cemetery for cremation. My father sent me a copy of the eulogy. In it, filled with the deep emotion of age, he described the life that they had shared for forty years. He said that they had been married abroad. They were two foreign students about to graduate in military science and industry just before the outbreak of the Soviet War of Defense against Nazi Germany. Not long after returning to Yan'an, they had gone separately to the Shanxi-Suiyan and Southern Henan Base Areas to devote themselves to the War of Resistance against Japan. After the establishment of new China, my mother had taken on the responsibility for running the household, in addition to her many other duties, and had rendered the greatest assistance to my father's work. But during the Cultural Revolution, since my father was being investigated, she too was implicated on account of her background as a returned student from the Soviet Union. She contracted a heart ailment as the result of beatings suffered in prison, and this led in the end to her fatal illness. My father wrote in his letter, "She was a good comrade, a good Party member, a good soldier, a companion who struggled alongside me for forty years. Her passing suggests that the time is not far off when I too shall go to be reunited with my comrades who fell in sacrifice. To be born, grow old, fall ill, and die is the common lot of human beings, for which I see no reason for grief. But as I look back over the past and sum up my life, I feel ashamed that I have not completely fulfilled my responsibilities as a member of the Communist Party. Thirty years after Liberation, our accomplishments have failed to bear out the great expectations of our martyrs; in addition, our revolutionary cause has suffered grave injury during ten years of catastrophe. What is gratifying is that in the midst of this difficult time of contention, the Party and the people have once again given proof of their invincible strength. The cause for which we have struggled has prevailed and advanced."

After my father learned that I was on maneuvers on the high seas, he wrote, "As those of my generation pass away one by one, the young people of your generation are our only hope. I was deeply stirred to learn that you were participating in ocean maneuvers with the Fleet; I am overjoyed and proud on your behalf. Historically, we Chinese have never been a sea-going people. It has only been the pitiless world conditions of the past century that have forced us to develop naval power. But during these hundred years, our navy has traveled a tortuous and unfortunate road. Only now has it finally and truly faced the sea . . . however you look at it, the navy has finally become strong. I am thoroughly delighted that you are a part of this bold undertaking, and your mother too was able to die without regrets. I am confident that when the fatherland has need of you, you will stand up and do your part, fulfilling your duties to the utmost and with complete integrity. At present, since the Fleet needs you, you had better stay there rather than worry about your family. And yet, whenever I recall your rash behavior during the confused struggles of the past, I remain uneasy. You are no longer a child, but you are inexperienced and lack an understanding of society; you must further temper yourself. I am now quite old. Your mother's passing makes me often think of my own condition. You and I have spent very little time together these past few years, so my one hope is that you will be able to come home and see me this autumn . . . Come home, Huai-p'ing, my only son. We should have another good chat while I am still alive."

As I read these letters from my father, I couldn't help weeping silently. It had been twelve years since their only son had been with them, and my mother hadn't been able to see me even when she died. How was my elderly father going to pass the years that remained to him, now that he was alone? An old man facing his own end, how much in need of comfort he must be! I had a sudden strong feeling that I had failed my responsibilities as a son.

And so I set out for home on the third day after returning to the harbor, without waiting to get settled down . . .

* * *

"Next stop, Taian; next stop, Taian . . . " The calm voice of the train announcer calling out the station broke off my reverie, "All passengers transferring to long-distance buses bound for Laiwu or Boshan, and all travelers visiting Taishan, please prepare to alight . . . !"

Several passengers had already stood up and begun to get their luggage down from the luggage rack.

I raised the window, stuck my head out, and looked up ahead; and there I saw a band of hills rising, one range after another, setting off a towering lofty peak. This I knew was Taishan, "beside which all other mountains look small." It showed an unusually clear outline under the clear autumn sky. The dense forests colored it with multiple washes of green and gold. In a moment, this scene stirred up waves of emotion in my heart.

Taishan has enjoyed the greatest esteem in Chinese history since ancient times. Even many, many millenia ago, when our Chinese nation was taking shape in the Yellow River valley, our ancestors had discovered this mountain towering up to the clouds. In all the five thousand years recorded in Chinese historical documents, how many pilgrims have come here to worship the Buddha, and how many Emperors have come here to worship Heaven and Earth! For generation after generation, our ancestors have left footprints, one atop another, on that ancient trail that winds slowly up to the highest summit.

In the past few years, I had heard a number of people speak of the mountain, and had seen it mentioned in a number of books. Its powerful aura and majestic appearance, its long history and interesting legends, had all strongly attracted my attention, so that I had come to cherish a fond desire to go to Taishan, make my way up the ancient trail, climb to the highest summit, and behold my fatherland from this point where it touched the sky!

And now, in the presence of these great mountains and rivers, all the individual memories that had gathered in me were suddenly transformed into a powerful desire to give myself to my country. The soldier's patriotic feelings that my father's letters had aroused in me rose fiercely in my breast, and I thought, "as a naval officer, my life has already become a part of my ship. Whatever happens, I will protect my country with my life. If our vessel should be sunk in battle someday, then as I leave this world behind, my heart should be filled with this ancient land and the great people that it has nurtured!"

I stubbed out my cigarette and stood up resolutely.

The train continued its rush toward the North. As it went thundering across the great steel bridge over the Yellow River, I had already made my way alone into the lofty ranges of the Taishan range.

On the mountain, the forest was dense and the undergrowth lush and green. The distinct cries of the birds in the woods were invigorating and the murmur of streams and pools, set deep in green grass and moss, refreshing. Among these waves of hills a single path paved with stone slabs meandered through the deep forest, winding upward toward the highest point of Taishan, Yue Summit, almost five thousand feet above sea level.

This was the only road. It was very rough, but there were no side paths at all. Thus, no traveler walking along the ancient track could lose himself deep in the mountains, whether he knew the way or not.

I had bought a green bamboo walking staff from a peasant under the Yuezong Arch, the starting point of the trail. In fact, I had no real need of such a thing to lean on while hiking in the mountains; I bought it only because its fresh green color and graceful shape caught my fancy. And so this staff became just a plaything that I could wave about to my heart's content.

Along the way I met travelers coming down in twos and threes. Their happy conversations, scattered here and there along the miles of the trail, kept me from feeling lonesome. Even more often, the ancient inscriptions carved on the sheer, water-stained cliffs that came into view one after another made me pause to reflect on these ancient remains of our ancestors. Being the Elder among the Five Sacred Mountains, this beautiful and mystic peak so aroused my interest and stirred my respect that it dispelled the fatigue of travel and sent me climbing without any hesitation in healthy strides up that choiceless road.

I was now an adult in my early thirties. Tempered by life, I no longer enjoyed idle frivolity and was accustomed to serious thinking on my own. As I hiked through the woods under a clear autumn sky, I could do so with a peaceful mind, enjoying the beauty of the landscape and savoring the profundity of the ancient sites, and, at the same time, as I followed the tracks, I could quietly look back over my life. It was as rugged and twisting as this trail, but also as free and clear of obstructions to my view.

But at Dismount Ridge, my bamboo staff brought me the acquaintance of an unusual traveling companion.

Dismount Ridge is a tiny gate tower hidden in the deep woods. After passing through the gateway, the path turns right and the steps become steep. If you are ascending the mountain on horseback, you must dismount here.

Just as I caught sight of it in the distance, I saw an old man striding vigorously along not far in front of me. He was walking effortlessly, bareheaded and dressed in loose clothing. When he arrived at Dismount Ridge, without hesitation he strode up onto the steps in front of the gate tower. But the steps were obviously too steep, forcing the old man to slow his pace and exert himself. I hurried up and supported him from behind, and when we had climbed the steps, we halted together in the gateway.

He turned around and looked at me with a kindly smile.

The old man I had supported had lived deep in the mountains for a long time. His bronzed face was all creased with wrinkles, but his manner was unusually robust. His thick eyebrows flecked with grey, penetrating gaze, kindly look, and silvery whiskers that reached to his chest compelled my respect and admiration.

"Must be your first trip up, eh, young man?" At close range, his resonant voice expressed the affability of an older person toward one younger.

"That's right."

"Have you come from the coast?"

"Yes."

"It must be lonely, climbing the mountain by yourself."

"I was just thinking of joining you; would that be all right?" I handed over my bamboo staff respectfully. "The trail is steep; you'd better use this!"

The old man took it with a smile and rapped it sharply on the ground several times, showing it to be very tough. "Good!" And with that word of praise, he called out at once, "Let's go!" and we continued our ascent.

The old man's manner was very uncommon. He had expressed not the slightest gratitude or modesty in accepting my help and respect, but he had put my mind to rest with a kind of friendly openness rarely offered to younger people.

This is how we became acquainted.

"How old are you?" I started chatting with him as we climbed.

"Seventy-seven!" The old man strode along using the staff.

"From your accent, I'd say that you weren't from around here."

"My family's from Guangdong."

I was really rather surprised, "Guangdong! How do you come to be living in Shantung?"

He laughed and stroked his whiskers, without answering directly, "Guangdong is east (*dong*) and so is Shandong. Anyway, it hasn't come time for me to go West for good yet!"

I started to laugh, amused by his cheerfulness. "Well, Sir, you're really something! So, you must be living on top of the mountain!"

"That's right."

"Is your whole family up there?"

"No," he shook his head, "I'm on my own."

"Then who supports you?"

"Supports me?" He laughed heartily, "I have a job of my own. I look after the ancient sites on top of the mountain, and sometimes I do a little guide work, so I draw pay on my own. Well, young man, if you walk along with old Taishan here, you're not likely to get lonely."

"If you would be good enough to take me up the mountain with you, it would be, if not 'the greatest luck in three incarnations,' at least 'the very best in this one.' "

We both began to laugh again.

And in fact it was the greatest good fortune to fall in with an old man like him. What more could I have wished for, especially since I was climbing Taishan for the first time? As I had expected, the old man's knowledge of the local lore very soon made me feel that the trip was not in vain.

All along the way, he pointed out the ancient sites and told me the history or legends connected with them, sometimes supplementing them with the wisdom of an old man. There was great skill concealed in his way of speaking, too. He would be sauntering along, telling me all about some traditional story in his enthusiastic way, but just when he had me listening spellbound, he would halt and casually point. Suddenly the site would be there, right before our eyes, as though he had made it appear by magic. The superbly vivid introductions of this long-time professional guide were so breathtaking that several times I nearly shouted aloud in delight. As I listened, Taishan gradually became not just a mountain, but a history and a myth.

As I followed this old man walking up the mountain with the staff, he never tried to exaggerate or to mystify me with any superficial tales, although he had lived in this magnificent landscape for a long time and had a thorough knowledge of all those old legends. In the midst of a dazzling ancient site, he would strictly distinguish between fact and fiction like an old-fashioned country scholar, and explain the real value and meaning of the place in clear and incisive language like a profound philosopher. I began to realize that although there were some really quite superficial things on Taishan, this old man whom I had chanced to meet at Dismount Ridge was in some ways really too deep to measure.

At noon, we reached the middle Gate of Heaven. It was here that I got a clear understanding of who the old man actually was.

The middle Gate of Heaven is a stone arch covered with inscriptions. The arch bestrides the trail, exactly marking the midway point in the journey between Daizong Arch and the Southern Gate of Heaven. From here, we had an equivalent distance to cover before reaching the summit.

Not far from the middle Gate of Heaven was a modern building. It was pale green, with a row of very large glass windows set into its broad, white-striped walls. One could just make out some resting travelers sitting inside the brightly lit hall.

The old man and I climbed the gleaming, polished stone stairs, pushed open the glass swinging door, which had "Middle Gate of Heaven Tea House" written on it, and passed through the dining room to reach the terrace. A number of travelers were seated here and there at simple, marble-topped iron tables under awnings that flapped in the wind. The guests drank tea, chatted, and enjoyed the vast prospect of open country.

I ordered the old man a pot of green tea and some snacks, and a cup of very strong coffee for myself. When we had taken an empty table and sat down, a feeling of calm and comfort suddenly made me feel very tired.

The entire Tinan Plain was now spread out below our feet. Beyond the mountains from the terrace, the mixture of green and yellow colors turned the earth into a huge, richly decorated rug stretching from the foot of the mountains to the distant horizon. As we looked straight out across the sky, all the thousands of clouds at the same altitude seemed like white naval vessels at anchor near and far on the sea.

I took out a cigarette and politely offered one to the old man.

"I don't smoke," he waved it away with a smile, "you go ahead."

"Your life is too austere. Now that you have reached such

an advanced age, you ought to enjoy yourself a little, but you don't even smoke."

"Mind and body, pure and calm, in nature all suffering vanishes," the old man replied casually.

"That's right; to live in a certain purity and suffering is good for body and mind alike," I said in agreement.

"No, you misunderstand me. Purity is not suffering, nor is suffering purity; being pure and without suffering, how could you call that purity and suffering? What I said was, when mind and body are pure and calm, all suffering naturally vanishes."

I began to have some reservations. "Yes, but suffering comes to everyone, so it is purity of mind that is crucial . . ."

"Yes," the old man took a sip of tea, "as the ancients said,

> Wisdom is originally without the tree;
> Nor is the mirror the same as the stand.
> Since there has never been a single object,
> Where could any dust or grit collect?

Although abstrusely put, it penetrates to the truth; a pity that worldly people are unwilling to think it over carefully!"

This took me by surprise, for it was a very famous four-line Buddhist *gatha* of the T'ang period.* I puzzled over this for a moment, then suddenly it all began to add up. I couldn't help staring dumbfounded at the old man.

His profound gaze was just then directed at the distant mountains. With his silver whiskers waving in the wind, he looked every inch the Taoist transcendent.

He turned and gave me a kindly look, "Well, young man, I don't suppose you know that I was the resident monk on the mountain."

I was amazed; I had never seen a monk before. By the time I was old enough to begin noticing the world around me, all those Buddha-worshipping propagators of superstition had already vanished without a trace. It was only after I became an adult that I began to have a slight understanding of the ancient and mysterious doctrines of Buddhism from reading some philosophy and history. Hence, those pious Buddhist monks seemed to me to be just as ancient and mysterious as Buddhism itself. Now, as I suddenly realized that a genuine monk was actually sitting right in front of me, and that I had already traveled with him a long ways, a feeling of strangeness and wonder almost paralyzed me, leaving me stunned.

He had noticed my agitation. "Well, how about it, Comrade Navy Man, will you come with me?"

"Oh! Oh, of course, I'd be delighted!" I was hard put to recover my usual self, and almost spilled my coffee, I was so astonished and pleased.

But ours was truly a strange association. A moment before, we had been a Navy officer and an old man living deep in the mountains, traveling together after meeting in the forest. But now, we were a Communist Party member and a Buddhist believer having an open and sincere discussion. I felt extraordinarily stimulated and refreshed.

It was only after this that I really began to see that the old gentleman, in every word and gesture, was a monk.

"Are the consecrated images of the masters and patriarchs still there on the mountain?" I asked, interested in all of Taishan's antiquities.

"Just as before," the old gentleman replied.

"Are Buddhist rituals still performed?"

"The clouds are stilled and the incense has wafted away."

"Most of the monks must have been returned to lay life, I suppose."

"The fallen leaves have returned to their root." He gently put his teacup back down on the marble table.

"Then how is it you have stayed on?"

"If the Buddha doesn't reject me, I won't reject the Buddha." He stroked his beard with satisfaction. "It has been many years now that I have been taking care of the blue lamps, the ancient Buddhas, and the sutra banners and precious scrolls."

The old man was already well along in years and could no longer give up the faith he had held for so long. He was completely devoted to Buddhism and would no doubt nourish the rest of his natural span by clinging to these antiquated doctrines. What a contradiction there was between his obstinate hold on superstition and his wise and knowledgeable manner!

By the time we got back on our way again, we had already talked a good deal about some profound and difficult problems in ancient philosophy. The old man's knowledge had proven quite thorough. We went from the Neo-Confucianism of the Song and Ming dynasties to the Esoteric Learning of the Wei and Jin, from Indian Brahmanism to Japanese Zen, from modern European science and technology to the philological scholarship of the Qing dynasty. I found it difficult to accept or understand much of what he said, but his abstruse and profound thought gave me a lot to reflect upon.

"Then what is philosophy, after all?" As we pushed open the door and walked down the stairs of the teahouse, I began to ask for his guidance concerning a few problems that I had long thought about without being able to solve. I had already determined that this old monk who had lived in the mountains for so long had a great store of broad and profound wisdom.

The old gentleman stepped onto the trail, over which a mild southeast breeze was blowing. "You want a precise definition, don't you? But that's impossible, because the subject is too vast; it embraces Heaven and Earth, ancient and modern, the spiritual and the human, everything from the cosmos to primary particles, from the world to the human mind; there is practically nothing it does not include. Indeed, although philosophers throughout history have written voluminously, no one has ever been able to establish a definition for philosophy itself."

We had gone beyond the foothills, and were progressing farther up into the higher mountains.

"That's a pity! This problem has troubled me for a long time without my being able to resolve it, in spite of actually having read quite a few books on philosophy."

The old man chuckled unintentionally. "In fact, if you ask me, our modern Chinese word for 'philosophy' doesn't really have a definition. In ancient times, our words for 'sagehood,' 'knowledge,' and 'wisdom' all had the same root, so when Western learning was first introduced, there was no reason why we shouldn't have called philosophy 'knowledge-

---

* The quatrain quoted by the old monk here is perhaps the best known Chan (Japanese: Zen) Buddhist poem ever recorded. By means of it an illiterate fuel-wood peddler demonstrated superior knowledge of the Way and was made the Sixth Patriarch Hui-neng (638–713). See Wing-tsit Chan, translated, *The Platform Scripture, The Basic Classic of Zen Buddhism* (New York: St. John's University Press, 1963).

ology' or 'wisdom-ology' instead of 'sagehood-ology,' as we did. Especially since the philosophers of earlier times were precisely those who considered ability to be a matter of giving knowledge free rein and preached the idea of perfecting their wisdom. They thought what men could not think and said what men could not say . . . "

"Therefore, they must have been able to know what men could not know."

"Nothing of the sort!" The old gentleman waved contemptuously. "Those men were just fools misleading themselves. The knowledge they sought wasn't knowledge at all. The skill of those philosophers lay only in speculation. But speculation is completely unreliable; what is reliable is scientific observation. As a consequence, the atomic theory of Democritus had to await confirmation by Dalton, and the Ptolemaic theory of the universe was overturned by Copernicus; scientists know Thales's theory that all things were composed of water to be preposterous twaddle, and political scientists regard Plato's 'Republic' as a lunatic's daydream. Since the ancients were weak in science and technology, they lacked any basis for observation, and had no choice but to rely on speculation, with the result that a history of philosophy is simply a great compendium of the endless guesses and speculations of the ancients on the subject of the nature of the world. Once natural science appeared, it meant the decline of that classical philosophy."

"Then why has modern philosophy appeared?"

"Because natural science is limited in its scope and cannot answer people's questions about society. This is the fundamental point of interest in modern philosophy, although by the time this point was reached, the nature of philosophy itself had completely changed."

The old gentleman had showered me with ideas. They blazed up like sparks in my mind. "Then are you saying that philosophy is only an ancient method of thought, its special characteristics being speculation and groundless conclusions, and that science is a modern method of thought, its special characteristics being observation and genuine inquiry? Do you believe that truths arrived at by speculation are unreliable, and that only truths verified by observation are reliable? Is it your judgment that the only foothold of philosophy is in areas that the power of science has not yet reached, and that once they come under scientific study philosophy will strike its tents and go into hiding, and that as a consequence philosophy will eventually be completely replaced by science in the course of the latter's continuing development?"

"What you say is too confused. It isn't necessarily a matter of groundless conclusions or genuine inquiry. If you really want to make an analogy, you might say that philosophy is thinking and science is seeing. Therefore, philosophy can reason about areas where science cannot see. And what you say is not entirely correct; science is concrete, but it is also limited; philosophy is indefinite, but it has breadth. Since the power of science will always be limited, it will never be able to entirely replace philosophy. Although humanity has been greatly misled by it . . . "

The old gentleman's comments set me thinking deeply. Although his manner of speaking was archaic and abstruse, what he said represented an entirely new system of thought that I had never heard of before. He seemed to be very unworldly, but his reasoning was very precise and his method clear, certainly not inconsistent with the practice of a professional scholar. He was well versed in the principles of philosophy, he valued science, and yet what he devoutly believed in was religion. I was afraid that I'd never be able to understand how so many contradictions could actually be united in one person.

As the trail stretched on up toward the lofty summit piercing the clouds, we halted at a bend where it turned sharply to the right, clinging to the mountain side. In front of us stood the needle-sharp Marvelous Rock, jutting upward alongside the trail and overlooking the winding canyon below. Boldly carved on the Marvelous Rock were three words in crimson, "Cloud Cutting Sword." It was here that I came close to offending against what the old gentleman most respected.

I stood beside him, running my hand over the rust-colored crag. "The shape is not bad, but can it really cut clouds?"

"In fact, it does live up to its name." The old gentleman glanced quickly into the canyon, then turned and looked away from the mountain. He finally pointed southward into the distance, "Look!"

I turned around, and there were innumerable white puffs of cloud floating leisurely in the sky above the vast plain. Most were drifting to the north, passing beyond the mountain on either side, but a few were drifting straight toward the pass. After a moment, one of them drifted into the pass and floated steadily toward the deep canyon. As it passed the diagonal line formed by the strange crag and the peak opposite, it seemed to be suddenly lifted up by some force. As it began its steep rise, it was instantly torn to shreds and dispersed like so much smoke.

I was so startled I almost cried aloud. But the old gentleman pointed the next cloud out to me. It was demolished in a single stroke in the same way, as it passed the crag. Several other clouds followed, but none of them was able to enter the canyon.

"Amazing! Really amazing!" I couldn't help calling out.

"Quiet, watch closely!" The old gentleman silenced me with a shout.

A huge mass of cloud was rushing toward the pass. In bulk it seemed as large as a four-story building, so that the brightest sunlight could not penetrate it and its shady side was a dark black. Its approach was so ponderous that I couldn't imagine how the graceful force of a moment before could obstruct it.

I stared wide-eyed, prepared to see this huge mass of cloud rush into the pass and collide head-on with the sheer wall at the far end.

It was being pushed steadily into the pass by the southeast wind, right past the Cloud Cutting Sword. But as it continued to rush toward the end of the valley, that same force rose up violently and tumbled it right over. At the same time, the dense woods filling the canyon below began to make a strange sighing sound, and when I stared downward, I found that the white cloud was being transformed into a light rain!

I was dumbstruck by this stupendous natural performance. I shook the solid crag with all my strength, shouting, "Cloud Cutting Sword! Do you really have so much mysterious power?"

Cloud Cutting Sword remained silent. Its roots were firmly joined to the solid of the earth, and it didn't move a hair.

I was a firm believer in science, and did not believe for a moment that there could be any miracles in the natural world. But now I could not imagine what the secret strength might be that turned white clouds into rain so lightly and easily.

As we continued walking upward, the old gentleman asked me, "Do you know what a front is?"

I thought for a moment, "Yes."

"What you just saw was a front."

The sort of front the old gentleman was referring to is one of the most fundamental of meteorological phenomena. When large masses of warm and cold air meet, a slanting plane of contact may be formed between them, and this plane of contact is called a "front." Over the broad area covered by such a front it is cloudy and rainy, and indeed, all natural occurrences of rain clouds are based on fronts. But a front requires a scope of at least a few hundred miles, if not a few thousand!

"A front? You really mean that a front can form in a canyon like this?"

"The large and the small are not the same, but their principles are alike. Look!" I looked off away from the mountain in the direction the old gentleman was pointing and saw endless clouds drifting in the sky. "The southeast wind brings with it warm air from the sea, but the air in the canyon is cold."

I looked into the valley, still dark and shaded. I began to understand; it was just that there was an invisible mass of cold air contained down there playing a rain-making trick on those warm clouds.

"But how can cold air be formed in the canyon?"

The old gentleman walked slowly on, "Perhaps it isn't formed, but stored. When a large mass of cold air withdraws from the mountains, it leaves some behind there." He gave me a kindly look. "In any case, you're a lucky man! I've been here over forty years, and this is only the third time I've seen such a marvelous sight of clouds turning to rain."

I started mulling things over; his scientific knowledge was so rich and well-rounded that I could no longer keep to myself a question that I hadn't been able to solve no matter how I thought about it. I strode a couple of steps ahead and caught up with him.

"I would like to ask you to explain something to me, Sir. Of course, my asking like this may not be very polite."

"Go ahead." The old gentleman was ready for me.

"Well, Sir, I don't mean to flatter you, but I find your philosophical wisdom very impressive, and I have to deeply admire your knowledge of science. But, precisely because of this, I simply can't understand: How can you still believe in religion! Please forgive my venturing to ask, but I can't understand it. You know, our age is one in which science has developed so extensively that it has not only discovered countless truths, it has verified many hypotheses the ancients were unable to and corrected many errors they couldn't; indeed, as you said yourself a moment ago, modern science has already replaced all of classical philosophy. And so this made me think of your religion; I mean, if it is almost as ancient as classical philosophy, has it not already proven to be equally antiquated by now? Is it possible that mankind's scientific knowledge has not already discovered all sorts of errors in it?"

I trailed bravely along after the old gentleman's firm steps, boldly expressing my personal opinions. "I cannot deny that Buddhism has a glorious history and traditions, but if someone understands astronomy and meteorology, he can't suppose that there are heavenly palaces for the gods constructed in the middle of the universe, and if he understands mechanics and physics, then he can't believe it possible for anyone to mount the clouds and ride the mist. But you are obviously someone with a thorough knowledge of science, and your learning convinces me that you must also be someone with a warm love of it, too. So I simply find it impossible to understand how you can go on believing in religion."

"Well, after all, what is so unbelievable about religion?"

"That should be self-evident; it isn't real. Its explanations of the world and its various legends about the past and future are imaginary."

The old gentleman ruminated silently.

This sort of question comes as a provocation to anyone who believes in a religion. Although it may only be a kind of request for information on the part of the person who asks, it often comes as something akin to blasphemy to the person who is asked, since it openly expresses doubt about a deity that properly should only be worshipped with devotion. At one time, religious belief constituted humanity's most fundamental object of reverence. How many violent conflicts have occurred in history between believers in different religions or different sects, all for the sake of defending their religious beliefs! I was sorry to have asked such a rude question. But fortunately, the old gentleman possessed great forebearance in this area. He did not express the slightest reproach. He just kept on walking quietly along, without making any reply. When I saw that he had no intention of discussing the question with me, I quickly and tactfully changed the subject. At the time, I saw nothing at all strange in the way the old gentleman had so easily allowed my atheism to gain the advantage.

I hadn't noticed when, but we had emerged from the forest by now and were climbing up through jagged rocks. All along the way, we continued to feel exhilarated, for almost every ancient site we came to furnished us with innumerable topics for conversation.

Finally, at four in the afternoon, we reached the last steep stretch of trail leading to the summit.

I gazed upwards, panting. There was a stairway stretching straight as an arrow right up into the sky. Far away, at the end of the stairs, was a gate tower with red walls and gold tiles standing against the sky, and through its tiny doorway a thin strip of the sky was visible, clear as glass. Seen from far below, it looked so small that it was just like a little carved stone tower in a *bonsai* vase.

The old gentleman was also panting slightly. He grabbed the railing and said, "This is the Ladder to Heaven; at the top is the Summit of Dai. What do you say, young man, shall we go up?"

I took his arm, "OK, let's go!"

The old gentleman climbed with firm steps. I followed close behind, climbing for all I was worth, but I was no match for this old man who had spent years climbing on this mountain. I very soon began to feel that my strength was not up to his.

"There's no hurry; be careful not to lose your breath!" When the old gentleman halted and extended a hand to steady me, I suddenly discovered that his arms were very strong.

At last my two legs, already as heavy as rock, carried me up to the very last step. I came to a halt, my chest heaving violently, and the rapid breathing brought on by the thin air of such a high altitude led me to feel a joy that I had never known before!

Now we had put ourselves above the sky. I leaned against the steel railing and turned to look back down the way we had come. A scene of incomparable breadth spread out below me; the earth was now a vast hazy expanse, and the lush green plains spread out around us. Far below, countless clouds drifted like burst cotton bolls. Beneath our feet lay rugged mountains and dense forests, with a goshawk circling among the lofty peaks. After looking carefully for a while, I spied the "Middle Gate of Heaven Tea Room," where we had taken our rest four hours earlier, looking like a chess piece placed there far below us.

Strong gusts of wind were tugging at my jacket and blowing so hard that the old gentleman's wide-cut garments billowed out and flapped around him. In the canyons, the forests shrouding the slopes heaved as though part of a tidal wave.

"Say, that's the Yellow River!" The old gentleman pointed toward the distant horizon.

There in the hazy distance, just a trace of a thin yellowish-brown line faintly crossed the farthest part of the plain, glittering in the sunlight.

"The Yellow River!" I cried out joyously to myself. Was that the birthplace from which our nation came? I had looked down on its turbid waves from a train and scooped its muddy water up in my hands beneath the great steel bridge at Jinan. During inland waters exercises, I had even navigated on its broad currents. But I had never imagined that the Yellow River, savage as a wild beast when in flood, could trace such beautiful curves across the boundless plains of our land and sparkle with such a gentle light under the sun's glowing rays.

An irresistible surge of emotion swirled through my breast, and I longed to stretch out my arms toward the vast land there in the haze and cry out with joy at the top of my lungs!

"Yellllloooooowwww . . . Riiiiiiiverrrrrrrrrr!"

More than a dozen echos carried my shout away until it was lost in the circling, surging mountain wind.

The old gentleman looked at me with a smile. "You are already at the acme in the human world."

Excited, I looked behind me and discovered the great gate tower with its red walls and golden tiles towering above us. The ancient tower was damaged and revealed old mud and building bricks where the surface of the wall had been broken. A few tufts of weeds were tossing in the wind above the glazed yellow tiles.

On either side of the gateway under this ruined tower, an inscription written in gold letters on a green background caught my eye. I read it aloud: "This gate stands guard over the Nine Celestial Levels—walk up to the marvelous site of the Three Heavens; these stairs ascend in ten thousand steps—look down on a splendid view of a thousand peaks!"

On the horizontal placard over the gate, three words were magnificently inscribed, "Southern Gate of Heaven."

Looking at this inscription carved higher than the clouds, I recovered my breath and heaved a heartfelt sigh of admiration, "Wonderful, beautifully written!"

But the old gentleman only laughed coldly and said, "Where in a hazy universe could there be three heavens? As we walked here along the trail, were there exactly ten thousand steps? Pah! I see nothing so wonderful or beautiful about that!" And with this, he dusted off his jacket, walked through the gate, and set off along the Heavenly Way without even a backward glance.

Catching this bucket of cold water on my head rather dampened my spirits!

I hurried to catch up with him. "You're wrong. This is art, and in art one may exaggerate, even make things up. So far as this couplet is concerned, unless it said 'Three Heavens' it wouldn't entirely express the altitude, and unless it said 'ten thousand steps' it wouldn't fully express the distance. Why can't that be wonderful or beautiful?"

"Exaggerate? Make things up?" The old gentleman laughed out loud. "As you ought to know, what isn't beautiful isn't true, and what isn't true isn't beautiful. Since the words do not accord with reality, what is the point in speaking of art?"

"That isn't so," I was racking my brains in order to argue logically, "Truth is not the same as beauty, nor is beauty identical with truth. Mathematics is dry and medicine messy; both are true, but they aren't beautiful. Dance can delight the eye and ear, and music can move the heart; they are beautiful, but there is nothing in them that we can call truth. It is evident from this that truth and beauty are not interdependent. When something is true but not beautiful, this only makes it more austere; when something is beautiful but not true, this only makes it more romantic. If truth were identical with beauty, then mathematics and medicine would be the highest arts. If beauty were identical with truth, then singing and dancing could replace science. No, Sir, this is simply impossible. Surely you realize that in our lives it often happens that there is ugliness in truth rather than beauty, and that there is fiction in beauty rather than truth. How can you say that truth is identical with beauty and that beauty is identical with truth? In fact, things that are unreal cannot only be beautiful, often they are the most beautiful of all."

The old gentleman had suddenly become completely unreasonable. He retorted in an acidly ironic tone, "You are entirely incorrect. The criterion by which we measure all things is their scientific nature; anything not in accordance with scientific explanations must naturally be overturned, without exception . . . "

"You're wrong! Absolutely, one-hundred-percent wrong!" I exclaimed, in relentless pursuit. "Investigating the truths of science is simply not the entire content of human spiritual life. Beyond this we also require the enjoyment of beauty and satisfaction in our emotional lives. If there were only science in our lives and no art, only investigation and no appreciation, human history would become a dry old textbook, and human life would lose all its joy!"

I simply could not understand why the old monk suddenly launched into this endlessly exaggerated and unrestrained praise of science.

The old gentleman halted and stood in the middle of the Heavenly Way. He gave me an unusually penetrating look, and then said with a faint smile, "Young man, what you say is quite right; humanity requires satisfaction in emotional life and the enjoyment of beauty, and science cannot supply these; it can only allow us to gain an understanding of nature. But what you say is not complete. According to you, there is something beyond truth, and this is beauty. But you have forgotten that beyond beauty there is goodness. It is the search for truth, beauty, *and* goodness that constitutes the whole spiritual life of humanity. What seeks truth is science; what seeks beauty is art; and what seeks goodness is religion. While we were on our way here, you said to me that religion was not real. But now I can say to you: since art need not be real, why must religion be real? The significance of art does not lie in its truth but in its beauty. In the same way, the significance of religion does not lie in its truth but in its goodness. There are many religions in the world, from those of Jesus and Allah in the West to Buddhism and Daoism in the East, and their branches and sects are numberless. Do you mean to say that none of them really has anything of value? Even if their doctrines are contradictory and confused, their main point is simply to guide people, so that the powerful may be merciful and the fortunate benevolent, so that the sufferings of human life are comforted and the void of the spirit has some support. So long as goodness is spread throughout the world, whether my Buddha exists or not is secondary. As for the sutra banners and precious scrolls, they serve only to make the mind reverent; fasting and meditation are simply a way of nurturing life. Everything about religion is in essence created by the human mind. If you believe it, it exists; if you don't, it doesn't; it's entirely a matter of sincere faith. As the ancients said long ago, 'my mind is my Buddha.' It should be apparent from this that religion takes morality as its basis, and does not really conflict with science. But in recent times ignorant people have set about testing and overturning the existence of Heaven on the basis of their experience in this dusty world, and it is for this reason that we have had these endless contending theories and quarrels!"

The old gentleman's air had become very serious. He sighed deeply, but said nothing more, maintaining his reverent state of mind, and pondering those mystic sayings of his as he walked on ahead.

His stratagem was now apparent, and I had been talked into a position from which I could hardly reply. I watched the old gentleman walking silently on and knew in my heart that we had reached the end of our discussion, so I too could only ponder as I followed close behind him, hiking on into the withered grass touching the sky on the mountain peak.

No, this wasn't superstition; nor was it a prostration before absurd legends, but rather a faith filled with wisdom. This faith might appear to be unfounded when viewed from the outside, or to have been completely misled by ancient stories. But those doctrines, though certainly not real in themselves, might wield a marvelous effect on the spirit, so that this Buddhist disciple could obtain a kind of mental calm and composure in the midst of the complicated life that he must have led. Once again I felt that this old man was too complex to figure out. Considered superficially, he was a muddleheaded old monk. But deep in his spirit, so deep that perhaps even his own wisdom did not often penetrate it, there was a clear-headed vision of the world.

In this silent manner we continued walking, right to the gate of the Jade Sunset Shrine.

There appeared before us a hall quite antique in appearance. In the center of it was a large gate with its doors firmly closed. They were painted red and had gold spikes. In front of the gate, four red-painted pillars held aloft a roof of glazed golden tiles, and from the roof rose a beautiful pavilion. Two great mountain gods of painted clay stood guard on either side of the gate, one holding a golden snake and the other a sharp sword. They bared their teeth at us in fierce grimaces.

The old gentleman pushed an electric switch beside the gate. It opened and we went straight through the temple, then turned through a small gate. What unfolded before us now was a neat and peaceful garden. But the building in the garden was old and plain, with half the paint flaked off, in great contrast to the imposing temple gate.

I followed the old gentleman into his living quarters, and casually laid my naval jacket and cap on an armchair. But he picked them up and hung them on a coat hook.

"You can bed down here tonight."

I immediately declined. "How could I? You've taken such good care of me along the way, how could I trouble you any more?"

He stopped me with a loud laugh. "You've got it all wrong! If it's inappropriate for a military officer to stay in a temple, of course please do as you see fit. But there's no need to be afraid of troubling me. To tell the truth, travelers are not at all easily admitted here. But since we have walked up together, we need not part like this. Besides, a companion is a rare treat for me. You have a seat; I'll be back once I've changed my clothes." And with this, he leaned the bamboo staff against a bookcase, showed me to the hot water, and was gone without a further word.

Left to myself in the room, I washed my face, then lit a cigarette and began to consider the meditation chamber itself.

In fact, it was just a study, for there wasn't the slightest flavor of religion about the room. It had snowy, whitewashed walls, a gleaming parquetry floor, and a fluorescent light on the ceiling, with a pretty push-button switch by the door to go with it, all just like what one would find in an ordinary city house. There was a table next to the window, with a glass desk calendar showing a date two days previous. Beside the calendar were an alarm clock and a transistor radio. There was a large bookcase with glass-paneled sliding doors against the wall, but the folding desk lamp attached to the bookcase was exactly like the one that I used on board ship.

I walked over to the bookcase and saw that there was a Persian walking stick leaning there beside my bamboo staff. It looked very valuable. The sandalwood-colored body was sheathed at both ends in gold. Thin strands of gold had been used to make a lozenge pattern on the handle, and the head was ornamented with shatterproof glass in the form of a blue jewel. I couldn't resist picking it up and hefting it, and found that it wasn't at all heavy.

All of these things were quite unlike what I had imagined to be a monk's way of life.

I stood in front of the bookcase and began to glance over his extensive collection. The books were of every sort and subject, all jumbled together. He had three full shelves of collected sets, in addition to periodicals, catalogs, and other volumes of every sort. Among historical works, I found a complete *Comprehensive Mirror for Aid in Government* and a *Draft History of the Qing Dynasty*; in philosophy, the *Zhuang zi, Huai nan zi,* and *Lü Shi chun qiu*, critical works such as the collected writings of Zhang Xuecheng and Hu Shi, foreign writers such as Locke, Rousseau, Hegel, and Marx, as well as works by Russell, Dewey, and others, and also a volume of Plutarch's *Lives*. There were even a few books in foreign languages. Of course, the most numerous were Buddhist texts and sutras. In the four shelves of old-style string-bound books, I saw innumerable arcane and obscure titles, such as the *Frost Sutra*, the *Diamond Sutra*, the *Hundred Topics from the Sea of Interpretations of the Flower Garland,* and the *Taishō Tripitaka,* all of which were no doubt Buddhist sutras, as well as the *T'ang Dynasty Biographies of Illustrious Monks*, the *Record of Monasteries in the Western Capital*, the *Record of Transmission of the Lamp of the Jingde Period*, the *Recorded Sayings of the Venerable Monks of Antiquity*, the *Mirror of the Sects*, and so forth. These books crammed the shelves to overflowing, and stuffed in among them were countless strips of paper with classification labels or extracts on them. The books themselves were a sea so vast that I felt I should drown if I were to pull out any one volume.*

I went back to the desk and noticed that a thick manuscript was placed squarely in the middle of it. At the head of the top sheet was a boldly written title, *A Comprehensive Interpretation of the Greater Vehicle*. I opened the manuscript in the middle and found a page covered with neat and compact script, with corrections in red. In the middle of the page was a title heading, "Chapter 73: The Essence of Nirvana." This was obviously an unfinished religious work by the old gentleman.

The door opened, and he came in holding a box made of red wood; he had brought back a dinner bought at the dining hall on the summit. He was now dressed in a short grey jacket and cloth shoes with very thick soles. After washing up, the old man glowed with vitality.

While we ate, I made up my mind; this day and the next, I definitely wanted to have a good chat with him. Insofar as possible without violating any of the old man's taboos, I longed to get to understand him better.

The table clock made a faint buzz; it was exactly six o'clock. I turned on the transistor radio with a click. Shandong Provincial Radio was just transmitting the weather forecast from the Central Meteorological Agency. The voice of the woman announcer was calm and monotonous, but she was reporting a huge change in the atmospheric conditions over Asia, a change abrupt as a thunderclap.

I realized that Taishan would soon be in the midst of a violent rainstorm.

When we had finished our soup and put down the bowls, the old gentleman handed me a towel and, to the accompaniment of pleasant music, said, "Young man, my Buddha is showing you unusual kindness today. At noon, he let you see the sight of clouds being cut at the Middle Gate of Heaven; and now, this evening, he's going to let you see the sunset over a sea of clouds from Moon-viewing Peak."

I felt a flush of excitement. Now I understood the real import of the weather report we had just heard; the thunder and rain were going to appear below our feet! What the few of us who were staying high on the mountain were going to see was a completely different sight.

Once we had cleaned up the dishes, we walked out of the temple together. When we came out of the gate and stood on the high terrace, the scene around Taishan had already changed. An endless sea of clouds had drowned everything. The broad and boundless plains of Shandong could no longer be seen, nor could the long rugged lines of the Taiyi Range, for magnificent masses of clouds were rolling beneath us, spread out to the horizon itself. The curling cloud tops showed gold and red amid light and shade in the slanting rays of the sun. Taishan hung suspended like a solitary island in an endless sea of clouds.

A magnificent scene was now visible at the Southern Gate of Heaven. Thick waves of clouds were surging up Taishan from the north, almost submerging the Gate, and then draining down the south slope along the Heavenly Stairway. This vast stream of clouds was rolling over the saddle between Moon-viewing Peak and Sun-viewing Peak, so that from a distance it looked just like a surging river flowing irresistibly from north of the mountain to the south and flooding everything in its path. Only the peak of the Southern Gate of Heaven remained floating above these white waves.

I sighed in amazement at this magnificent sight, then walked down the flight of steps through the temple gate with the old gentleman and on toward the west along the Heavenly Way. We were going to climb Moon-viewing Peak from the Southern Gate of Heaven to say farewell to the sun from the outlook on the summit.

Just then, a group of foreigners, perhaps two dozen in all, both men and women, came walking down from the Summit Guest House located almost a hundred yards above the Heavenly Way, clearly headed for Moon-viewing Peak to watch the sunset too. Bursts of happy laughter came continuously from this group of people dressed in trim suits and colorful new fashions who chatted in the slanting light of the setting sun and pointed this way and that. As they came down the narrow path and stepped onto the Heavenly Way, the old gentleman and I reached the same place; we all met at the intersection.

The old gentleman and I halted, wishing to let them go first. But my naval uniform and the old gentleman's monkish air had obviously attracted the foreigners' attention. They came to a halt too. Their laughter and talk died away, and they began looking us over with a fascinated air, several of the women laughing quietly and exchanging a few words in their language.

I looked at the old gentleman.

"We'd better walk behind them," he said with a smile.

At this, I gestured for them to go ahead. But they looked at each other without moving, as though they were selecting a representative.

The only military officer in the group stepped forward quickly with a smile. When he had come up in front of me, we exchanged salutes in the custom of military men and then clasped hands.

His manner was quite natural and unaffected. He bent his arm from an almost perpendicular position and, holding his index and middle fingers together, tapped them once against the hard visor of his cap. I couldn't help but look him over carefully. He was a European with an olive complexion, gentle eyes, and a thin, smart-looking mustache, which gave him a friendly and humorous look. He was wearing a grey uniform with crimson insignia sewn on the lapels, an eagle on one side and crossed swords on the other. The marks and patterns embroidered on his epaulets meant nothing to me, so I couldn't determine his rank. He was giving me a friendly once-over at the same time.

The foreigners laughed heartily, and a flashbulb popped. I gripped his hand firmly and tried greeting him in English with a "Hello."

He smiled and nodded, showing that he understood. But he replied with a complete sentence in a language that was not English, which I knew, but some kind of language tinged with Spanish. This made it difficult to determine his nationality.

We both looked over to one side, for a very simply dressed woman interpreter was walking quickly up to us. She gave me a friendly look and introduced us with a smile, "This is Captain Borsini. He says that he is very happy to have made your

---

* The manner in which all of these Buddhist sutras are listed here (e.g., the multi-volumed *Taishō Tripitaka* appears in a list of single titles) represents either Li Ping or his character's understandably sketchy knowledge of Buddhism.

acquaintance."

I was indeed very pleased, and immediately replied, "I am Li Huaiping, Chief Navigator of the *Zhongtiaoshan*. I am equally delighted to make your acquaintance, Captain."

After these friendly self-introductions, our hands relaxed. But the interpreter had not translated for me.

Captain Borsini turned to her and asked something else. But nothing came from her but silence.

This seemed strange to me. The interpreter's inexplicable silence was already beginning to affect the atmosphere of happiness and interest. So I turned and looked at her inquiringly. But when I recognized that familiar face, I was paralyzed.

Nanshan! Nanshan, from whom I had been completely cut off for twelve years! After vanishing from my life without a trace for so long, now she was standing before me once again, and this time she was standing so close!

I stared at her dumbstruck, unable to utter a single word for the longest time. My mind was stunned by this sudden meeting. But across her face, once so delicately pretty, a spirit of panic, uncertainty, and shock now played. As I stared fixedly at her turned-up eyebrows, wide-open eyes, questioning brow, and frightened lips, my heart began pounding uncontrollably.

Yes, the woman interpreter standing before me was none other than the girl I had first met more than a dozen years before. Her features, all so familiar, no less than her stunned look on our meeting again after so long a separation, confirmed that she was Nanshan. But now she was dressed as an adult cadre. I looked blankly up and down at those eyes. Now they showed faint wrinkles at the corners. The face was no longer so smooth and plump, the hair already a little dry. I had never noticed the faint freckles on her nose before . . . I could see clearly that tears had begun welling up in her eyes. Those damp pupils were no longer so black or so bright as they once had been. All these things were gradually blurring the image of the young girl in my heart. I began to realize that that brave and innocent girl had long since ceased to exist. The Nanshan of the present could no longer gather every happy feeling or mischievous thought in her merry laughter and frank manner or reveal them with such utter clarity. She could not, nor would she ever again. There was already a contemplative spirit in her breast, one that had transformed her carefree appearance forever and at the same time brought to her face the kind of serious and tempered manner that all women of middle age sometimes reveal.

Whispers began to stir in the group around us.

Nanshan's expression was undergoing rapid changes, showing shock, uncertainty, sadness, and then the pain she felt deep in her heart. When she succeeded at last in composing her mind in spite of the waves of violent emotion sweeping through it, she managed to fight back a tear that was about to fall and lowered her head in pain, biting her lip.

I gave the captain, who had been left forgotten at our side, a look of sincere apology. A man of deep feelings himself, the foreign officer was looking at us in astonishment. Then I looked apologetically around the group of foreigners. Some of them were astonished, some were sympathetic, some were smiling in good-will, and others were observing dispassionately. At last my embarrassed gaze halted on the face of the old gentleman. He was looking at us with an expression of deep concern.

"You two haven't seen each other for a long time?" he asked.

All the foreigners turned to look at the old man.

"Twelve years," I replied in a choked voice.

"There must be something in your past that is hard to forget, I suppose?"

"Yes . . . "

The old man lowered his head and pressed his palms together, slightly lowering his kindly eyes before us.

I could hardly keep my own tears from falling, but I didn't know how I could go about expressing my feelings.

"Thank you . . . ," Something seemed to be stuck in my throat.

"Thank you . . . ," Nanshan said also, in a faint, almost inaudible voice, making a slight bow of respect in the old man's direction.

The group of foreigners, who had been watching in amazement this revelation of emotion by Chinese, so well known for their sober self-restraint, obviously realized that it was inappropriate for so many people to stand around and watch. Someone said a few quiet words, and they signaled one another to leave. First, two of the older men smiled politely to Nanshan and turned to go. After this, everyone said a word or two of best wishes to her and went off in small groups. They walked slowly to the end of the Heavenly Way, passed through the stream of clouds at the Southern Gate of Heaven and reappeared on the opposite slope, from which, at times, one person or another would still turn back to look curiously toward us.

The captain and the old gentlemen were the last to leave. The captain, full of friendly feeling and very much aware that he had played an important part in our meeting once again, stretched out both arms emotionally, embraced our shoulders heartily, and said something. Then he gave the old gentleman an inquiring look, and when the latter nodded his head gravely, he took a step back, saluted me, and, without waiting for me to return his salute, turned with a smile and went off arm in arm with the old gentleman.

Now only Nanshan and I were left at the intersection of the Heavenly Way, but we said nothing for a long time. Not until the captain and the old gentleman had also climbed up the slope of Moon-viewing Peak together did I ask quietly, "What did the captain say?"

Nanshan didn't look at me. Watching the receding figures of the captain and the old gentleman, she replied simply, "He wished for our friendship to be renewed . . . "

We fell silent for a while.

Now I could look at her closely. She knew I was watching her, but she went on gazing at the figures of the travelers scattered over Moon-viewing Peak, without saying a word. By this time Moon-viewing Peak, towering high above the sea of clouds, had been coated with a layer of gold by the slanting rays of the setting sun. Nanshan's silhouette appeared unusually calm and gentle in the golden light. The golden beams once again outlined her long brows and lashes and illuminated her shining eyes. To see her gazing so calmly and fixedly brought back my image of her as a young girl, and I felt my heart tremble slightly. I watched her like this, and after hesitating for a long time, finally said, "I never thought that I might find you here."

"Nor did I," she smiled unnaturally.

"Nor did I ever think that it would be after so many years."

"Yes," she nodded.

By this time, countless old memories were churning in my mind. But with so much to say, for a moment I didn't know where to begin.

"Nanshan, the last time I saw you was on the train taking you to the frontier. If I'm not mistaken, you definitely saw me as the train was pulling out."

She looked at me, "Yes, I saw you."

"But I don't think you knew that before the train left I heard you talking with your family."

She smiled slightly. "Yes, I did. My brother saw you that day, so afterwards I guessed what had probably happened."

"You were right. I listened to you and your family for a long time from the passageway, and your conversation left an impression on me that still hasn't been erased."

"Really?" She looked me sincerely in the eye. "I'm glad."

We looked at each other, and there was another brief silence.

"I know that train was going to the north. Have you been on the steppes all these years?"

"There were three groups of educated young people on the train. One group was going to Inner Mongolia, one to Jilin, and one to the northeast frontier. Ours went to a league in Inner Mongolia. But after a year, we were transferred to the Xin'gan Mountains."

"Have you been herding livestock all this time?"

"No, I was herding on the steppes—I learned to ride there. After I got to the Xing'an Mountains, I worked at a forestry center."

"Logging?"

"No, I drove a tractor."

"And after that?"

"After that, our whole family returned to Jiangsu to work in agriculture. In 1974, I spent some time translating foreign material at a hospital in Wuxi. Starting three years later, in 1977, I was assigned to Hangzhou, Suzhou, Shanghai, and finally Nanjing, one after another, until I became an interpreter for the provincial Foreign Affairs Office, where I am now."

"When did you start?"

"At the end of 1978. So I've been doing this work for more than two years now."

"Look at me! We've only just met, and I've asked so many questions."

"That's OK; it's usually this way when people meet again after a long time."

We were able to smile openly now, but we still didn't look at each other.

"I imagine that what with all those changes and moves you must have met with quite a few surprises and disappointments."

"Yes, . . . I guess you could say that. But life has also matured me a lot. What about you? Have things gone well for you in the military these past years?"

I thought back over the defeats and setbacks that I had experienced, but I gave an affirmative answer, "Yes, very well."

She nodded, "I'm sure they have."

She spoke sincerely. She was happy that things had gone well for me, and perhaps she was also gratified by my good fortune. But I felt none of these things. Without meaning to, I laughed sardonically.

"What's wrong?"

"Oh, nothing. I was just thinking, hasn't there been anything you've wanted to ask me?"

She shook her head uncomprehendingly.

"Well, even today, you still don't know my name. If you'd like to, I think I should introduce myself, even though it is already very late."

She blinked once, but did not reveal her real feelings. "You don't have to do that; I've known for a long time."

I was quite surprised. "How could you know? I never had a chance to tell you!"

"But someone else told me."

"Who?"

"That's something I'd rather you didn't know."

"Why?"

"Perhaps it would be hard on you."

"It couldn't be."

She gazed out across the vast sea of clouds, thinking silently, the corners of her mouth curling in a faint smile.

"Please believe me; nothing you could say would hurt me."

Looking into the distance, she smiled sadly, "You are Li Huaiping . . ."

My heart began to beat rapidly. "That's right."

She was staring into the distance, as though she didn't intend to say anything more.

"But please tell me who it was, anyway."

Her eyes, fixed on the distance, narrowed slightly as she recalled those events long past. "He was a Red Guard; I don't know his name. That day, while you were interrogating my grandfather in the living room, I saw you through the glass in the door and recognized you. Then the boy hit me with a leather belt and said just to wait a minute until Li Huaiping had finished teaching my daddy a lesson and he would teach me one too. And so I learned your name then. But I have never mentioned it to anyone. Today is the first time I have said it, Li Huaiping."

My heart felt as though it had been lashed by a whip. I wanted to smile as she did, but my voice was shaking. "Since that day, I have never known a single day of peace; really, not a single day! . . ."

"Since that day, my heart has been as peaceful as a burnt-out coal."

All the while Nanshan was speaking of these memories, her whole person was projected far away onto the horizon, just like her gaze. She did not look at me at all, but spoke as though I were not beside her and she were only talking to herself.

Emotions compounded of regret and shame tormented me bitterly. But at my age, I had to repress at all costs the emotions aroused by these memories of my youth. "I hope . . . no, I believe the search that night couldn't have become a turning point in your life. Please believe me, you should go on being yourself forever!"

"The entire nation underwent the same great transformation. None of us could, or should, go on being the same person." She lowered her gaze, her face showing an extraordinary calm and indifference.

Changed, everything had changed! What used to be one way was now another, and what had been lost would never ever return. The mature and resolute woman on the threshold of middle age who stood before me now had once been a girl of such innocence and energy, one who had called up such beautiful longings in my heart! But I had smashed them with my own hands on that night that knew no pity. For years I had dreamed of meeting her again and of reviving those lost hopes. But not until today had she reappeared before me, and now it was too late. And the fate that had brought her back seemed to have done so only to prove to me that the girl of fifteen years ago no longer existed, that no shadow of my youthful dreams could ever again appear. Changed, everything had changed! But what were the reasons and forces that had made life deteriorate so? And what purpose had my destructive heartlessness served?

Everything in human life was so hard to understand!

Nanshan sighed softly and slowly turned to look at me.

"Do you still remember it, what we discussed the first time we met?"

I looked at her in confusion, painfully aware that I was incapable of recalling it. Indeed, although the happy scene of our first conversation in the woods was still distinct in my thoughts, I could hardly remember anything of what we had talked.

"What? Did it make no impression on you at all?"

I shook my head regretfully. "I really don't remember it clearly any more."

Nanshan gazed at me reproachfully. "How could you dismiss such a subject so lightly? How could you so casually forget those wonderful things you said on the subject of civilization and barbarism?"

"That's right, we did discuss that subject then, civilization and barbarism. But I have to admit that I had never thought about it carefully. As for what I said, those . . . they were only . . . what can I say? I can't think of any proper way to explain how I could have said such meaningless things then."

She looked at me, shaking her head. "No, what you said wasn't meaningless. Fifteen years ago, when I criticized men for always destroying the civilization they had created with barbarism, you told me that civilization and barbarism were as indivisible as a person and his shadow. You said that in ancient Greece men had created a beautiful mythology in the course of barbarous wars of plunder. You also said that the things that led men to civilization also led them to war; the first thing to bring men civilization was iron, but in all of history the great majority of weapons have been made of iron. You asked me, are the Greek myths stories of civilization or of barbarism? Was iron the angel of civilization or the fomenter of war? You said all this. If it all came from careful consideration, how could you forget it?"

I really didn't know what I could say.

Nanshan's emotions had by now been stirred into great waves by the memories of her youth. Her voice began to tremble. "You know, those were all things that made me think deeply. For thousands of years, mankind has struggled bitterly to establish an ideal civilization, but the cause of barbarism has advanced alongside that of civilization at the same pace. Men have slaughtered one another in countless struggles and conflicts of every kind for the sake of nation, state, religion, class, tribe, or party, even village or individual love. They have destroyed ancient halls without the slightest regret, apparently just to clear some space to build a new house. Is all of this good or bad? Is it right or wrong? What force is behind these things happening over and over again? And what meaning is there in the process?"

I looked at her silently; my heart filled with tears. Her sincere way of speaking had taken me back to that unforgettable clearing in the woods. How I wished that she would go on talking this way, go on and never stop! She heaved a long sigh. "The things that you said inspired me so deeply that I have been thinking about them for fifteen years. After fifteen years, my memory of you has grown indistinct and been forgotten, but what you said has never been blurred or erased, for I have been thinking for so long in order to find an answer. But now that I have met you again, hoping that you would be able to tell it to me, you say that you have forgotten all about what you said, and that really you had never even thought carefully about it. Do you really think these things are not worth everyone's careful thought?"

My emotions had suffered a heavy blow, and a cold teardrop rolled down my cheek. But I had no wish whatever to disguise my feelings, and said in a choked voice, "I should, I should thank you for your . . . your attention, but I can't, can't ever say anything of value to you again because, because only someone who had thought sincerely could have the right to answer, and I . . . "

"No, since you have never given the matter any careful thought, of course you need not say anything."

I sighed deeply. "But please tell me, after . . . thinking for fifteen years, what have you finally understood; where were you finally able to find an answer?"

She shook her head. "Surely every problem doesn't have a final explanation. Perhaps we shall never find answers, especially when we try to explain history with concepts such as good and evil."

So far as the two of us were concerned, that was the end of this inexhaustible subject. But I believe that there could be no better answer than Nanshan's.

By this time, the setting sun was rapidly nearing the horizon. Nanshan's whole body was tinted with the same golden color as the crags and summits below our feet.

I began to think of her grandfather. I had been dreaming for a long time of being able to bring Chu Xuanwu and my father together again some day.

"Are your grandfather and grandmother both well? When I went to look for you at 73 Lingyin Alley in the winter of 1976, you had already left Peking. I have been hoping to see Mr. Chu again for more than ten years, since I have a few things to tell him, things he would no doubt want very much to know."

"It's too late now," Nanshan said with a quiet sigh, "in January of 1976, the year you came looking for us, my grandfather and grandmother passed away one after another in their old home in Yixing. I was at the hospital in Wuxi when I suddenly got news of my grandmother's death from illness. But when I took leave and rushed back to Yixing, I was just barely in time to see my grandfather once before he died. Winter was unusually cold that year, and both of them contracted influenza . . . That was four years ago."

"Did your grandfather have anything to say on his deathbed?"

"No, nothing. Only just at the end he asked me to have his ashes buried together with my grandmother's."

I heaved a deep sigh, for now I no longer had any hope of seeing Chu Xuanwu again.

"Was his funeral well taken care of?"

"Very well. Chenchen wasn't home then, but fortunately local relatives helped out . . . "

"That's really rare . . . " I couldn't say anything more. The news of Chu Xuanwu's passing had plunged me deep in thought.

"Oh yes, I forgot to tell you; my father has returned to

China."

"Oh, what was his life like during the thirty-odd years he spent abroad?" I was deeply pleased to learn that Su Ziming had escaped from oppression and was still alive.

"Not long after he fled to Burma with Li Mi, he got out of the army and took up his former career in telecommunications, having been cut off from it by the sudden outbreak of the War of Resistance. Soon after, he moved to France with my mother, by way of Hong Kong, and got a job with a telecommunications company in Brest. He wasn't able to get in contact with my grandparents until 1957, when he ran into an old fellow student in Geneva. Later, in 1959, he visited Warsaw to send Chenchen home so that he could be educated in China. Since 1971, he began making one application after another to return home to visit his family, but he was never able to succeed because we lacked political influence. Finally, because of the change in policy concerning Overseas Chinese made in 1977, he was able to return to the embrace of the fatherland the year before last."

"And your mother? Hasn't she come back to China?"

"She wasn't able to come back. After my grandparents died, she grieved deeply. In the spring of the same year, she was killed in an automobile accident while driving in the outskirts of Paris. She was 55. From the time she bore me until her passing, I never saw her except in a few photographs and frames from a home movie camera."

Nanshan was calm and her voice remained steady as she told me this, but I could clearly detect an aching heart in her quiet words.

"And what about Nanchen? He must be doing fine now."

Now a faint friendly smile did appear in Nanshan's pensive face. She glanced toward me quickly and said, "He's a worker in an electricity plant in Peking and has a very satisfying life. He was married last year, just at harvest moon time, to a girl he had been in love with for four years."

"That's great . . ."

We both looked out over the sea of clouds, without saying anything more.

And now we heard a burst of happy shouting coming from far away on the slopes of Moon-viewing Peak. As Nanshan and I turned to look in that direction, we saw the fiery red evening sun hanging just above the boundless sea of clouds, beginning to send its incomparably splendid radiance out over the sky. Long rays of light—green, red, gold, and lavender—spread out over the western sky like an incomparably huge veil of gauze that covered half the heavens. Under this beautiful heavenly light, the boundless sea of clouds took on tints of every shade of rose, evoking sighs of admiration and cries of wonder. The splendid vision had begun.

We stared at the fiery disk in utter silence as it sank lower and lower down toward the turbulent sea of clouds. I had never seen the setting sun so huge, round, and distinct as today. It revolved steadily and slowly, but with irresistible force, toward the jade-blue western horizon, ponderously lowering its great bulk down toward another side of the world. Before the glowing disk entered the sea of clouds, it proudly discharged all its radiance, lighting the entire sky with breath-taking colors and tinting the sea of clouds and the Summit of Dai in a layer of gold.

By this time all of Moon-viewing Peak had become a jet black silhouette against the breath-taking radiance. The observation platform on the peak and all the travelers on the mountainside had become silhouettes set into a golden border. Against that backdrop glowing with gold and jade, the people stood facing the setting sun in a variety of poses and actions.

Some were standing still in amazement at this beautiful sight, without moving at all; some were raising both arms toward the setting sun, uttering their heartfelt praise and exclamations of joy. A few foreigners and photography buffs were anxiously recording the splendid scene with movie and still cameras. Far to one side of the crowd, the full sleeves of the gentleman billowed in the evening breeze and the Captain made gestures of various sorts as they talked congenially together.

Nanshan and I stood side by side at the center of the Heavenly Way, quietly watching Moon-viewing Peak and the setting sun. From that direction came continual praise and admiration, expressed in various languages.

"It's on fire . . . the earth is burning . . ."

"Apollo! The great god of fire . . ."

"Is that where the great Prometheus stole fire from Heaven? . . ."

"It isn't fire, but awesome nuclear energy . . ."

Everywhere the sighs of admiration were continual, the words of praise unending. The Captain had taken the old gentleman by the arm, his own arm forming a great arc against the golden heavens as he spoke. The old gentleman was shaking his head in contradiction. From far away the chuckling sound of the Captain's laughter could be heard.

At this point, the frozen waves suddenly split open on the horizon like the mouth of a beast of prey and began to swallow the blood-red sun. The westward-drifting sun seemed to know that it could not possibly turn back. It did not linger at the end of its road or look back toward the world of men. Without paying the slightest attention to the tiny people praising it and shouting for joy, it lay heavily down on the golden waves and sank calmly and fearlessly into the savage animal's maw. At the same time, it raised up the upper half of its red face, and proudly sent its last rays of light out across the sky. The sea of clouds began very swiftly to grow dark.

One foreign woman in a tight leather jacket with a wide belt seemed to be in unbearable pain as she watched the facing sunset. She clutched her arms in front of her chest and stared at the sun's descent. When the last last rays were cut off and it became only a few traces of blood-red color in the sky, she suddenly seized her long waved hair in her hands, covered her face, and burst into loud sobbing.

The others paid no attention to her sentimental outburst, but went on expressing their delight in the sun.

At last, the sea of clouds closed its dark mouth, and the sun was entirely gone.

As the last thread of sunset color faded on the horizon, I heard Nanshan sigh softly beside me!

"It will rise again," I said.

"No, it is rising now."

"Do you mean in their countries?"

She looked at the foreigners scattered around Moon-viewing Peak. "Yes."

"But it may set again there very soon."

"When it does, it will be rising here where we are."

"I believe so." I looked at her in agreement.

"So do I." Nanshan raised her eyes and we gazed at one another, exchanging understanding looks.

By this time, my emotions were so calm that I seemed to have dissolved into the tranquil dusk.

"But not everything can return in cycles in the same way. On the morning fifteen years ago, neither of us could have foreseen that an evening like this one might come. And what sort of dawn does this evening portend for us?"

"From what you say, you believe that human life can't be cyclic." She smiled slightly at me.

"I am positive about that. What about you?"

"I cannot affirm it, because I have no way of knowing what comes after life. But there is someone who can point out another world to you."

"Him?"

"Yes."

We both turned and looked toward Moon-viewing Peak. In the gradually darkening twilight, that old gentleman of the Southern Peak with his vaguely transcendent air was standing on the slope, listening to something that the Captain beside him was saying. By now the travelers had begun to drift back.

"Do you believe it?" I remembered what she had said on the train twelve years before.

She smiled, without saying anything.

"Twelve years ago, on the train, I heard you refer to God. Perhaps you share a common belief with the Captain and the others."

"No, that's not it at all." She turned to face me. "So far as faith is concerned, we Chinese have a better tradition of our own. For over a millenium, various Western religions have scoured our Chinese land like waves; from India, Greece, Judea, Rome, even from Arabia and Byzantium, but they have never won the hearts of our people. Among the finest traditions of Chinese Confucianism are the Chinese people's self-confidence, born of a knowledge of Heaven and an understanding of fate, and their magnanimity in the face of life and death, of success and failure. You may think that I have found some spiritual support from foreign countries, but my feelings have always been directed toward our own ancestors."

"In that case, perhaps our beliefs are the same."

"Perhaps so." She looked at me with a faint smile of uncertainty on her lips.

A faint light remained in the sky. Once deprived of the sun's rays, the vast, boundless sea of clouds began to surge and spout, rising slowly up toward the mountain peak. One patch after another of chilly, wind-borne fog assailed us.

Mixed in among the travelers, the foreigners passed by us in twos and threes, walking through the thin fog. Most of them smiled at us and then went politely past.

At this point, a middle-aged foreign woman dressed in a short overcoat of dark red leather came by with the young girl whom the sunset had moved to tears, and the two of them stopped in front of us.

"Can you tell us how he is related to you?" the woman in dark red asked Nanshan.

"He is a friend whom I haven't seen in a long time," Nanshan told her simply in English, nodding toward me in a friendly way. I shook the hand that the middle-aged woman extended to me.

"You are really fortunate. You know how charming Nan is," she said.

"Yes, I have always thought so, madam," I replied, also in English.

"All the best, officer."

"Thank you."

The young girl, whose eyes still glistened with tears, stepped forward. "I also wish you both the best."

"Thank you!"

"They both gave Nanshan a friendly good-bye kiss and left.

When almost all the travelers were gone, the old gentleman from Southern Peak and Captain Borsini came strolling slowly toward us from the Southern Gate of Heaven. This old gentleman who seemed to know everything obviously had thoroughly captivated the young foreign officer with his lofty manner. The Captain was walking along and at the same time using vigorous gestures of all sorts to assist his none-too-accomplished English as he explained something to the raptly listening old gentleman. Nanshan and I watched them silently as they sauntered up to us.

" . . . In ancient Egypt, he was called Aton. In ancient Greece, he was called Apollo. In ancient Arabia, he was called Allah. No matter where you look, his name always begins with the first letter, 'A.' So, in ancient times, did people everywhere revere him as the head of creation?"

"No, in ancient China, there was no sun god."

"I understood that China's sun god was named Kuafu."

"He wasn't a sun god; he was only a spirit who pursued the sun."

"Do you mean that there were never any myths about the sun in China?"

"Of course there were. According to Chinese legend, in ancient times there were ten suns, but later the husband of the moon goddess shot nine of them down . . . "

"Oh, didn't the earth catch fire? Just like," and here the Captain made a gesture imitating an explosion, "a napalm bomb?"

The old gentleman laughed. "No, all that fell down were nine dead crows."

"Crows?" the Captain was surprised. "Were they avatars of the sun? What ugly birds! A kind of, of omnivorous scavenger."

"But in ancient times they were worshipped as sacred birds. Just like frogs; a very ugly kind of frog was worshipped as an avatar of the moon."

"Why?"

"It's not clear; probably because of their loud voices."

They stopped in front of us, laughing loudly. Nanshan and I nodded to them.

The old gentleman looked at Nanshan kindly. "From the looks of it, I'd say that this is the first time either of you has climbed Taishan."

"No, I came once before with my grandparents when I was very young."

"What year was that?"

"In 1954, when I was six. I remember that everything on the mountain was very old and run-down then."

"And now?"

"Now everything is brand-new, but it appears much more superficial."

"Yes. But it was not without its superficialities then either!"

Nanshan nodded respectfully. "I understand what you mean, Sir . . . "

In fact, Nanshan and the old gentleman were in agreement about what had happened to the nation's cultural artifacts and about the changes that had taken place in popular culture.

"What were you just talking about?" I asked the Captain.

"Sun gods."

"It seems that you disagreed, am I right?"

He shrugged his shoulders. "I couldn't understand everything that he said."

Nanshan laughed, "On the way up, you were very interested in the suns of the whole world. Perhaps it was because I was acting as intermediary for all those suns!"

"Yes. I have been to Java, Bombay, Mecca, and Jerusalem, and everywhere I saw people bowing down on mountain tops and sandy beaches to pray aloud to the rising or setting sun."

"It must be a magnificent sight," I said.

"And very mystical."

"But what about you? Do you worship the sun yourself?" Nanshan asked.

"From the standpoint of scientific understanding, I worship the benefits that it confers on the earth, but not in religion."

"Then what do you worship in religion?"

The Captain pointed up toward the darkening heavens, "God, of course."

I raised my head and looked up toward the vast canopy of the heavens. I knew that up there were countless galaxies, each formed by billions of stars and planets. But there were still many people in the world like these, including the Captain, the old gentleman, perhaps also Nanshan (although she definitely wouldn't admit it), and the great majority of humanity, who believed that at the center of that field of gravity extending over countless, infinite light years, there was a supreme being. This supreme being existed in cold and dark space, utterly without air, water, light, or heat, and governed all things. I had never felt that such a universe could exist, but so far as they were concerned, it did.

Nanshan looked at him calmly, and then suddenly exclaimed, "You military men probably all believe in God. But you have smashed so many priceless skulls with your rifles all the same."

I was amazed to see her attitude turn so serious.

"Excuse me, Nan, but I am still young, and haven't been in combat."

"You may be yet, and it is quite possible that you will encounter your friend of today on the battlefield." She was clearly referring to me.

"Nanshan, I hope that we will meet as allies, and not as enemies."

"Yes," the Captain took my arm, "you can't foresee war between our two countries."

Nanshan looked right at us. "That isn't logical. Soldiers are enemies by nature. Their reason for existence is to prepare to kill other men just like yourselves on the battlefield."

The Captain twirled his moustache helplessly. "In that case, we must simply accept our fates, whether I kill him or he kills me, because both of us will be doing our utmost to fulfill our duties and commands. But . . . ," he gave my arm a friendly squeeze, "if Li fires at me, I shall be happy."

"And if it were you firing?" Nanshan persisted.

"So long as he were in uniform, I would be happy to fire on him. But not in your case. Attacking civilians is shameful. Can't you understand, Nan?"

Nanshan shook her head without changing her expression. "It's terrible."

"Yes, terrible." I could hear that my voice was shaking. This wasn't my fear of dying, but of killing. I had not been picturing what it would be like if Captain Borsini aimed his smiling rifle at me. What I was picturing was myself, a terrible vision of me in the living room at number 73, Lingyin Alley, smiling and pointing my rifle at that silent girl. This vision suddenly appeared before my mind's eye, but fantastic as it might seem, it wasn't a thing that couldn't happen.

The old gentleman obviously didn't approve of the three of us carrying on such an ignorant discussion, young as we were. He turned to the Captain and asked, "And what about your sun god? You persist in defending the sun's majesty, but you don't worship it. You are full of interest in legends about the sun, but then you talk grandly about war." He shook his head in disapproval. "Since you believe that Eastern and Western civilizations share a common origin, you should demonstrate that you are correct. So far as war is concerned, better wait until you have been in battle and then discuss it."

The Captain placed his right hand apologetically on his breast. "Excuse me, let us end this battle now."

"What, are you also a diffusionist?" asked Nanshan, looking at him in surprise.

"Yes, you could call it an absolute conviction of mine. I believe that everything human originated from the sun. Not only is all life on earth derived from solar power, but all of humanity's spiritual civilization also began with the sun as its object."

"So, you believe that sun worship is the common form of all primeval human religion?"

"Yes, but His Reverence says that ancient China definitely had no cult of the sun. Perhaps China's sun cult has not yet been discovered."

Nanshan said very positively, "I must say, Captain, that this historical view of yours, based not upon an examination of the evidence, but only upon an absolute conviction, is mistaken. Sun worship is not the form found in the earliest religions of any people; even in the totemistic cults of the most primitive tribes it is highly unusual to find the sun as an object. What you have seen at various places in the world is only a fire cult, one that takes shape quite late. Nor does the sun occupy an important place in the oldest religions. Take Apollo, now; he wasn't a supreme god, but only one of many. Besides that, Greek mythology is only a system of myths, and far from being a mature religion." She looked at the Captain genially. "It seems to me that you have entirely failed to understand the importance of monotheism in the history of religion. This is a criterion for distinguishing between religion and myth."

The old gentleman looked at Nanshan with satisfaction. "Moreover, the actual ruler in ancient Egypt wasn't Aton, but a different god, Amon. And Amon definitely wasn't the sun. Aton's position as ruler lasted less than thirty years during the history of Amon."

"And what was Amon?"

"He may have been a star at first, but in his essential nature he was an extraordinarily abstract and unchanging principle."

Their discussion had aroused my interest. But it was difficult for me to participate in their abstruse conversation. Of course, I was fully able to carry out a rebuttal of religion on the basis of my knowledge of physical science, and I could debate it from the standpoint of materialism, but I could not discuss religion itself, nor could I discuss with the same feelings that they had its origins, history, manifestations, or even the unusually complex role it had played in all of human cultural history. This was because I knew too little about religion. So far as this topic was concerned (and it was one that I would always find it hard to understand), I could only stand to one side and keep a regretful but admiring silence.

"But, is it still possible that Eastern and Western civilizations have a common origin?" the Captain asked.

"To decide this would require investigation of the migrations and relationships of primeval men."

"Evidence in this area must be limited, I should think."

"Yes. Forty years ago I followed the discussion of this problem. But since then there has been almost no progress with discoveries in this area."

Nanshan obviously sympathized deeply with the fact that the old gentleman's learning had gone hidden and unused. "If you had been teaching for the past forty years, who knows how many students' attention you might have drawn to this question."

The old gentleman stroked his beard and laughed. "I have been cut off from scholarship for many years. If I could lecture on the sutras, that would be fine indeed, but I couldn't do it on scholarly topics."

"What did His Reverence say?" asked the Captain.

Nanshan told him.

"But please tell me," the Captain asked, "if it wasn't the sun, what was the most decisive influence on the creation of human civilization?"

The old gentleman smiled, but didn't reply, turning instead to Nanshan. "What do you think?"

Nanshan thought for a moment and replied, "Rivers."

The old gentleman nodded his head again in satisfaction. And I too understood at once.

Nanshan said to the Captain, "Rivers have nurtured virtually all of the world's ancient civilizations. If it had not been for the Ganges, there would have been no ancient India; had it not been for the Nile, no ancient Egypt; were there no Euphrates and Tigris, ancient Babylon could not have existed, nor could have ancient China without the Yellow River. There can be no agriculture without rivers, and hence no formation of national civilizations. Therefore, as numerous archeological excavations show, even though remains of the anthropoid apes are spread throughout the Old World, once primitive man entered the Neolithic Age people settled down along the shores of the great rivers. The origins of human civilization present an extremely complex problem, Captain, but one thing is certain, and this is that rivers played a much more direct role than the sun in the appearance and development of human civilization."

Like anyone who has raised an honest question, the Captain instinctively looked for any possible holes in the answer he had received. "But what about ancient Greece? As you know, the only large river in Europe is the Danube, and it is far from the southern edge of the Balkans. What river nurtured the civilization of ancient Greece?"

Nanshan replied without hesitation, "The Mediterranean Sea. The Mediterranean Sea nurtured the Minoan civilization of Crete. But this civilization came much later, was commercial rather than agricultural, and was formed by combining strands from several great civilizations of high antiquity. The success of the Greeks was splendid and many-faceted, but it was not they who began human civilization, but rather the long vanished Babylonians, Egyptians, and Indians, as well as the Chinese, who still exist today."

The old gentleman looked at her very kindly. "But you don't believe in the common origin of Eastern and Western civilization too, do you?"

But Nanshan began to laugh, "Indeed we do; we ourselves were all converted to diffusionism long ago. But what we believe in is not the fire in the heavens, but rather the water on earth."

By now, the Captain's manner had become very modest and serious. He murmured to himself, "You amazing Chinese! I have been admiring the fine character of your people ever since I stepped onto your territory. And now, I have finally been converted by the natural endowment left to you by your great ancestors!"

"What sort of natural endowment do you believe our people has?"

"Seriousness, courtesy, civility, learning; everyone seems like a scholar. Nan, I admire your intelligence, and I esteem His Reverence's erudition!"

Nanshan smiled and passed the Captain's meaning on to the old gentleman, who laughed happily.

I listened to their conversation in silence. It harmonized like water mixing with milk. How different these three people were from one another! They belonged to different nationalities and differed in language, traditions, age, character, status, and experiences. And how different their religious beliefs were as well! And yet an intangible force had brought them cordially together, meeting one another with tolerance and conversing so agreeably. What kind of force was it? I understood intuitively that it was one both simple and powerful. It was this; deep in their hearts they felt that they were people of the same kind because they shared a common pursuit of truth, a common love of justice, a common respect for human civilization, and a common sense of responsibility for the future of the world. As I watched Nanshan joining in the discussion with such deep conviction, I felt an unusually poignant emotion rise up in my heart. I seemed to discover suddenly that Nanshan, whom I had always thought of as a person who held herself aloof out of self-respect, was in fact not alone in this world at all. No, she was not alone. In this world, in addition to the serene goodwill and honest feelings by which she got along so well with everyone around her, there was another link deep in her heart, one that joined her with people like these. People like these were numerous and widespread. Although they were dispersed all over the wide world, their common traits, honesty, wisdom, goodness, and fortitude, lofty ones inherent in humanity itself, formed in their persons a force that could never be defeated. It was only because of their existence that this world could seem so full of hope. how much of the essence of human excellence was gathered among them!

No, Nanshan was not alone at all. She lived as one of them.

By now, the sun and all its light had revolved to another side of the world. Without our noticing, the four of us, and all of Taishan, had been submerged in an obscuring night fog.

"Li," the Captain patted my shoulder cordially, "why aren't you joining in our discussion?"

"I can't. As you know, any kind of religion is alien to me."

"Oh! . . . Are you a member of the Communist Party?"

"All military officers are Communist Party members in our country."

He gave me a friendly look. "I'm very glad. I admire Communists. I believe that you are another segment of humanity imbued with the spirit of ideals and devotion. Of course, you believe in the theory of class struggle, while we believe in the power of ethics and morality. But different forms of consciousness should not keep us from mutual understanding and cooperation. So, for the sake of protecting human civilization, let us join hands in the cause of peace. God and Marx alike would probably approve of our generation avoiding conflict.''

I laughed heartily. "I'm afraid you underestimate our contentiousness. But even though the theory of class struggle is firmly and deeply rooted in our program, I want to say now that I join you gladly in this all the same."

Except for the old gentleman, who maintained absolute silence with respect to war, the Captain, Nanshan, and I all began laughing together. I don't know whether Nanshan thought of something in the midst of her laughter or not, but I definitely did not feel as I laughed that the real world could be at all so relaxed as our conversation together.''

At last, the Captain looked at his watch and said, "I'm very sorry, but I must leave you now."

I also took a look at my watch, and found it was already nine o'clock.

The Captain looked at me genially. "It has been a great pleasure for me to meet you; let's be friends forever, even at opposite ends of the earth."

"I wholeheartedly agree." We extended our hands and shook firmly.

The Captain then turned to the old gentleman with an air of great respect, and said, "Venerable Master, it has been the greatest good fortune for me to have met you here on this mythic mountaintop. You are an elder I won't forget as long as I live. If I may say that Nan is as clear as the flowing waters of the Heilongjiang, then you are as lofty as this Chinese Olympus. Perhaps some day I shall take up my pen to write of my impressions of China. I hope that when the time comes you will allow me to express my best wishes and respect toward you in my work."

The old gentleman did not show any modesty or gratitude, but just looked seriously at the Captain, joined his hands at the palms, and replied to the Captain's moving speech with words that no foreigner would find it easy to explain, "A-mi-tuo-fo . . ."

Nanshan looked at the old gentleman with deep feeling and explained to the Captain, "This is a god of good fortune in Buddhism. The recitation of the Amida Buddha's name is an ancient Chinese way of wishing happiness and good fortune."

The Captain was deeply moved. He placed one hand on his breast, bowed his head reverently, and uttered a similarly brief and difficult to explain European expression.

Nanshan said, "The Captain prays that God will bless and protect us all."

We said no more, but watched silently as the Captain turned and walked away. His broad strides took him onto the path to the guest house and he vanished into the twilight.

The old gentleman turned to look at us, and said, "I don't know what has happened in your lives. If I am not mistaken, the two of you might at one time have found a happy life at one time, but you didn't. Now you are suffering because you have lost it. Is that it?"

Nanshan and I looked at him sadly, unable to say a thing.

"I can tell that both of you are good people. Anyone can meet with frustrations and disappointments in life, but so long as a person is honest and firm, good and intelligent, that is all to the good. Let me tell you, a person who is unusual and unworldly, without emotional attachments, does not feel sorrow, but isn't happy either. And someone who has everything to his satisfaction can be depressed in the midst of constant happiness. A rich emotional life only comes with the alternation of sorrow and happiness through cause and effect. Li Huaiping, life has been kind to you. It seems to me that certain cruel events of your past will eventually turn out to your advantage. I hope that your spirit will find some consolation when you consider this."

These words were precious to me, especially at a time when my emotions were so unsettled. I nodded, deeply moved.

Lastly, the old gentleman turned to face Nanshan with deep affection, looking at her for a long time with head bowed, and then said, "You are a good child. I believe that the road you have taken may be the best one of all."

Nanshan looked at the old gentleman, her eyes revealing how deeply she was moved, but she did not reply.

The old gentleman said no more, but pressed his palms together in a gesture of benediction and farewell, then walked off along the Heavenly Way toward the Jade Sunrise Shrine. His gliding figure gradually vanished in the evening fog.

Once again Nanshan and I were left alone at the crossroad.

A full moon had silently appeared over the obscuring fog and was casting its silvery radiance on the mountaintop.

As I watched Nanshan standing silently there, waves of emotion began to assail my breast. From her reserved attitude, I already felt that she was perhaps just waiting to say goodbye, that after our farewell she would disappear from this world forever. Then I would never again be able to see the Nanshan who had left me so many unforgettable memories. But I couldn't think of anything appropriate to say to her.

Nanshan slowly turned to look at me, with the moonlight glistening in her eyes. She waited for me to speak. This aroused my courage.

"Nanshan . . ."

"Yes?"

"After we say goodbye this time, will we meet again?"

She shook her head calmly, and said gently but positively, "I doubt that we will."

"Why?" My heart had received a slight but powerful shock.

"We have already met four times by coincidence. Another such coincidence doesn't seem likely, does it?"

"But if we made a date?" You know, we ought to have met four hundred times, but we missed out on them all."

"We aren't young any more. At our age, do you think it is right for us to make dates?" There was an almost indiscernible laugh in her voice, but I could tell that it was forced.

"No, you should see me again, because I have some things I want to say to you, things I want to tell you."

"I don't think that is so important."

"But you don't know what it is I want to tell you about. It has to do with . . ."

"But I know that it isn't anything that we *have* to talk about."

"So, you really don't intend to listen to anything more I have to say?"

She looked at me. "No."

A painful feeling assailed my heart, and I was no longer able to control my excitement; my voice became urgent. "No, this is impossible! You aren't saying what you really feel! This refusal is as cruel to you as it is to me! Nanshan, after the way I treated you before, do you really not want to see any sign of repentance from me? It's impossible. I clearly saw you weeping that day. What was that? Proof of your indifferent feelings? No, quite the contrary! Why do you want to repress yourself? Don't go on like this, set your heart free! Mr. Chu was worried about this side of you. Especially when what I want to tell you is that your family . . ."

Her head sank in pain from waves of aroused emotions. She interrupted me, "Don't say any more, I don't need to hear anything."

"Do you hate us?"

"No!"

"Do you despise us?"

"Not that either."

"Then it isn't disgust?"

She went on shaking her head. "Still less."

"Then what is it?"

She raised her head again firmly, and looked bravely straight into my eyes. "Thirty-two years ago, in the winter of 1948, when you and I were born, my grandfather was captured by your father on the battlefield at Huaihai. This is what you were originally planning to tell my grandfather, and wanted to tell me now, right?"

Her words took me completely by surprise. In one burst she had said everything that I had waited more than a dozen years to tell her.

"My grandfather told you everything about my uncle's execution, my father's escape, and his own surrender, and you planned to tell me about it today. Did it really never occur to you that all these people were part of my family, and that all this is our family history? Did you really think it was reasonable to suppose that you could know these unforgettable things about our family and I would not?"

I had nothing to reply.

"As you ought to realize, those events are terrible memories for our family. We can't forget them, but we don't want to keep bringing them up, especially not in front of outsiders. My grandfather's life led him to bitter reflections; he spent the last half of his existence deep in remorse and melancholy. That evening, when you were interrogating him about that life, you could have no way of experiencing for yourself what torment such a thing could be for a human spirit. I know too much about all those things. You have no way of knowing how I sympathized with that old man. It wasn't just because I was his granddaughter. No, I was looking at people of the past from the viewpoint of a member of the younger generation. My elders marched toward the revolution one after another, expelling the Manchus, defeating Yuan Shikai, protecting the Constitution, the Northern Expedition, right down to the Civil War. They advanced without thought for their own lives, never wavering even in death, only to be attacked and killed one after another, or abandoned to beg by the roadside. This history is too bitter. It isn't anything like your father's glorious record. When you put these two kinds of history together, you are rubbing a wound that has not yet healed. So, I beg you, history is past; let us remember it in our hearts, forever, but don't bring it up again, so as not to stab at innocent hearts."

I couldn't raise the matter again. But I still couldn't resolve my own doubts. "But how could you know that the Chief-of-Staff Li who received your grandfather's surrender was my own father?"

Nanshan looked at me. "It was you. Don't you think you gave ample evidence that evening that you were Chief-of-Staff Li's son? You interrogated him about the battle so closely and showed yourself so excited at hearing anything about your father. On top of that, the two of you are strikingly similar in appearance. My grandfather gradually realized the truth. But this caused him even greater pain, because he felt that the Communists would never forgive him. After you left that evening, everyone in the house was very upset. But Grandfather told us the story of him and Chief-of-Staff Li anyway, and added that you might be Li's son. I was listening silently then, but I remembered everything. As you know, there was an additional layer of coincidence for me. But I never did tell my grandfather that I had met you already. That kind of coincidence might be something quite interesting for you, but it was nothing of the sort for us."

I sighed deeply. "I never would have guessed that the things I waited more than a dozen years to tell you, you learned only a few hours later than I did myself. Did the old man say anything about me?"

"He actually thought highly of you; he praised your bravery in action and your forthright decisiveness, and believed that you were a young man worthy of respect. But he said that he could not detect in you the stable seriousness and open-mindedness that your father had. He said that you were too inexperienced and not shrewd enough, and he even worried that once you entered life in earnest you would become depressed, because your way of revealing the sharp point of your blade would too readily subject you to attack. Was it really like that later?"

"Yes, it was. Mr Chu's prophecy was entirely correct . . ."

"That's really interesting." Nanshan's eyes began to glisten in the moonlight with that special smile of hers. Her smile showed almost the same innocence and satisfaction it had in the forest fifteen years before. "But what made him most concerned about you was how you passionately and recklessly threw yourselves into a cause you didn't understand in the slightest. He lamented that ever since the Revolution of 1911, so many hot-blooded young people had committed themselves to political movements of various kinds, with the result that the nation was immersed in unending turmoil for a full half-century. He said that it would be extremely difficult for this country of ours to progress to stability, and he only hoped that your carelessness would not become a grave national error. From our vantage point now, it seems that his concern was excessive, but that his hopes were not disappointed."

Hearing this, I was deeply moved by old Mr. Chu's feelings.

"But Nanshan, even if you already know all the things that I wanted to tell you, you can't have experienced my feelings. My heart is not made of iron. You ought to understand that that event, I mean our raid on your house, has been a great torment to me ever since. You ought to give me a chance to free myself from it."

She looked at me sincerely and signed gently, "I really

wouldn't have thought that you would take so seriously a thing unworthy even of mention. In fact, looking impartially at what you did, I should be grateful to you. At that time, when all of society had been militarized by hostility and suspicion, you treated our family with rarely matched kindness. Really, the impression you made on me at the time was rather a good one. After all, you had abandoned everything of your own to struggle for an ideal, even if it was mistaken."

"No, that's not true. I can believe that you do not feel hate and resentment; you probably have never learned those feelings. But I cannot believe that you do not feel pain. Think what an assault it was! Your home invaded, your way of life destroyed, your feelings ravaged, all that you respected trampled on . . . and besides, I saw you crying! Nanshan, I beg you, give up your forebearance, show the resentment and anger that you should feel! You have a right to do so, whether in law or in natural justice, and if you do I might feel better."

"What has been broken can be restored; what has been torn can be mended. Do you think that a single attack like that can make people go on grieving forever?"

"Yes! Many people were left with wounds that can never be healed. A house search—is it only a search of your house? All your possessions, imbued with personal feelings and family associations, gone for good . . . we destroyed the peace and harmony of your home . . ."

She smiled again. "Don't go on saying stupid things."

Now there was nothing left for me but to keep silent. It was evident to me that although my own emotions had sunk under waves of suffering since that house search, Nanshan had regained control of herself after the initial shock. No, she did not need any expression of apology or regret, because her mind had never lingered on that event.

Cold droplets of water borne along with the fog struck our faces in one wave after another, and the moon was sometimes veiled by the fog.

We remained silent. The sound of laughter came from the guest house far away. It was probably the foreigners, enjoying a happy outdoor get together with some Chinese travelers.

Nanshan glanced in that direction, and then said softly, "Huaiping, we had better say goodbye."

I felt a shock of disappointment. "Now?"

"Yes, now." She gave me a warm and friendly look in the moonlight, and extended her hand.

I reached out in confusion and grasped her hand firmly, firmly, for the first time in fifteen years, for the first time in our lives. As I grasped that warm hand, my heart was deeply stirred. This was she whom I had never won and was about to lose forever—the first sign of friendship that Nanshan had given me either as a young girl or as a grown woman. My heart began to pound furiously. I could not loosen my grip for a very long time.

She was affected by my emotions; shaking, she yielded her hand to mine, lowering her head sadly.

"Nanshan!" I was trying hard to keep my voice down, "For twelve years, under every sort of circumstances, I have been thinking of you. Sometimes you made me strong, and sometimes, weak . . . if you knew how much I wanted to be your friend, without being able to . . ."

"I accepted you as my friend, just now." She kept her eyes on the ground nearby.

"But you refuse to see me again."

"What good could come of it?"

"Because I hope that someday," I spoke resolutely and decisively, "I will be able to become your companion for life!"

Nanshan withdrew her hand slowly, raised her head, and said, with a look both gentle and reproachful, "You're mistaken, Huaiping. You ought to realize that everything between us is past now. Between our meetings as children and our reunion as adults lies all of our youth. Many things that could only have happened during that period have passed by along with it, forever. This is a fact whose consequences you and I should both face. It is true that we have had three unforgettable meetings, but even if what is past did not become the foundation for a beautiful future together, why must we become entangled in it? You know what a heavy burden on our spirits these painful old debts are! Huaiping, forget everything. If I had not suddenly met you here, I would have ceased to remember you. So, please accept my advice and forget me. For the sake of forgetting everything that has happened, really, we won't see each other again . . ."

"No, I can't! Nanshan, the influence that meeting you has had on me cannot be erased. That makes forgetting you something I cannot do, and should not. Surely you must understand this! When I met you, it changed my entire life. I cannot forget such a person. I cannot! Meeting her, and the way I treated her, have made me lose the most precious thing in life forever."

"What do you mean?"

"Love."

Love! This was the first time in all the fifteen years since we first met that I had actually thought or spoken of it between us. But when I suddenly said it aloud, that sweet and pitiless word deeply stirred two hearts no longer young.

Nanshan looked at me stunned, her eyes glistening with teardrops in the moonlight.

I could say no more, but I looked into those eyes sparkling with tears, my feelings a mixture of sorrow and regret, waiting for whatever reply she would make.

Those tears would never fall; they were gone.

"I'm waiting for your answer."

"No, it isn't an answer. I want to deny your belief about human life. It is too vulgar a belief for you."

I was pleased from the bottom of my heart to hear this criticism from her. Perhaps no other words could have made me feel more intimate and calm than this answer did.

"Go ahead, Nanshan."

"It seems to me that you think perfectly matched love is the greatest happiness in human life, and that a sentimental marriage is the greatest good fortune, just as ordinary people do. But you are all mistaken. Human life, just like the progressive course of all human history, is a prolonged process in which all sorts of very different things appear in their turn. At different stages, the main theme is different. If I put it this way, will you understand? At different stages in history, humanity has created entirely different cultures; primitive legends, ancient myths, medieval religion, literature in more recent times, and now modern science and technology. These products are all equally brilliant, illuminating mankind's babyhood, childhood, adolescence, youth, and maturity. They fulfill and adorn each different age and still impress and captivate us even after a thousand years. But if we were to revert to them, it would obviously be ridiculous, as though we were to go about creating ancient myths or medieval hymns today. Human life is just the same. Each successive stage of a person's life consists of different things. They can lead to entirely different kinds of happiness, but they are equally precious and great in value. In babyhood, the love of our parents; in childhood, the satisfaction of our curiosity; in adolescence, the establishment of a sense of honor; in youth, the fervor of love; in maturity, the exhilaration of struggle; in middle age, the joy of success; in old age, the respect of one's juniors; and in one's last years, the calm and satisfying feeling of looking back over a completed life without any shame or regret. These form the whole range of happiness of which human life is capable; they can all bring us great joy and leave us with precious memories. How can you say that love alone is the greatest happiness in human life? To be sure, pure love is warm and sweet, even lofty and sacred, to young hearts, but it is not in fact the whole content of human happiness. For many people, greater and more lasting happiness comes from industrious creation and from struggles filled with exhilaration. Isn't there a great deal written describing them in that vast sea of books? Any person with an ambition or, so far as you are concerned, any real man with some aspirations, should pay attention to this. It may be that you have lost the love that properly pertains to youth because the twists and turns in your life have gone by in such a rush, but you certainly haven't lost the whole of human happiness, nor even the greatest part of it. This depends on what sort of person you are and what you think is most important to human life. What the old gentleman said was quite true, a rich human life is only formed by the alternation of happiness and sorrow according to cause and effect. Can anyone attain the whole of human happiness? No, no one can. In the tortuous course of our lives we often attain one part and lose another. Now, you have lost the happiness of youth—in fact, too many people have—but, what about your middle years. Huaiping, you must give up this idea that makes you vulgar and weak! Springtime is the most beautiful season, but not the most precious. For someone who has something worth doing, maturity and middle age are the real golden years, because it is only then that you really mature. Our ancestors used to say, 'blossoms in spring and fruit in autumn.' Now you have just come to the autumn of human life, a season of abundant fruit. Perhaps there are no more blossoms, but there is a rich harvest all the same. Huaiping, the blossoms are lost, but the fruit is better. Love has withered away, but cherishing a memory is more inspiring. What do you think?"

My eyes had filled with tears.

I could no longer reply to that firm will of hers with any touching language, nor could I respond to her ardent spirit with any appearance of weakness! Nanshan was no longer a name or a person in my mind, but a kind of belief, a brand new belief that was beginning to exert an incomparable influence on my life!

I allowed a cold teardrop to hang on my cheek, but my heart was sober and resolved.

"Nanshan, I shall keep your words, and you, always in my heart, forever, forever, in my heart!"

She said nothing more, but silently extended her hand, and we firmly shook hands once again . . .

The fog had grown thicker. The moon shone with only a pale yellow light in the foggy sky.

"Nanshan," I looked directly at her.

"Yes?" She raised her head.

"There was a book; do you still remember it?"

She blinked her eyes. "Yes."

"Now that book has become a bequest from your mother. For fifteen years, I have always kept it with me as a treasure. If you would like me to return it, I . . ."

"No, keep it as a remembrance."

Another wave of warmth surged through my heart. "Thank you, Nanshan."

Our hands clasped once and then relaxed. I could feel the cool of the fog in the palm of my hand. She took a slow step back. I gravely raised my hand to the visor of my cap.

"Goodbye." She nodded her head slightly.

"Goodbye." I looked directly at her.

She didn't look at me again, but slowly turned and walked away along the path to the guest house. She walked away into the darkness with graceful and confident steps, treading the autumn grass, and soon vanished in the obscurity of the night. When she had reached the top of the guest house steps, beyond the reach of my vision, the calm sound of Nanshan's voice began to appear amid the talk and laughter that reached me from far away.

I stood by myself at the intersection on the Heavenly Way, looking intently through layer after layer of fog toward the place where Nanshan had disappeared, turning over in my memory the words she had left me, and which I had not entirely understood. By this time, my heart felt calm, composed, and full of strength.

From this time on, Nanshan was gone from my life for good. All the memories that she had left with me for fifteen years and all the longings of my youthful dreams were gone far away with her. Yes, what is past is gone; henceforth our field of vision should turn towards the broader future. ★

Originally published in *Shiuye (October)*, no. 1, 1981 as Part 4 of the novella "When Sunset Clouds Disappear" *(Wanxia xiaoshi de shihou)*.

Translated by Daniel Bryant

Spring Chill

Photo by Saundra Sturdevant

by Li Chao

It was a late spring day in 1979. Unrestrained laughter suddenly erupted in a long, silent corridor of the Central Municipal Hospital. Several youths wearing the badges of N University emerged from room No. 43 of the cardiac ward. A girl with her hands crossed in front of her chest bowed elegantly and said to someone inside the room, "So long Sir!" But her voice was drowned out by the young lads' roar, "Master, take care! Your disciples must take leave now!" Before they could finish talking, they were overcome by laughter.

Their teacher, old and drawn, was lying in a sick bed in the ward. He forced a smile and said, "Angels, excuse me for not being able to see you to the door . . . oh, right, tell Xiao Nan to stay for a while."

" 'Author'! Teacher wants to have a chat with you again. We'll leave first."

"I really don't understand. Xiao Nan is the laziest one in our Classical Chinese Language class. Why is Professor Li so fond of him?"

"So what! That's life. What's so strange about it?"

The laughing and chatting of the youths gradually died away at the end of the corridor. Xiao Nan, a slim and refined young man, gently shut the door and turned towards his teacher. "Professor Li, they're too ill-mannered. When you're recovered and teaching again you should punish them by having them recite from memory 'The Regulations For Students' one hundred times!"

Professor Li cast a warm glance at him. "You're the worst offender, talking about recitation from memory. How about you reciting it first, come on!"

Xiao Nan was shocked for a moment. Then he quickly grabbed a broom and said, *"Aiya,* Professor Li, don't embarrass me! How about punishing me by making me sweep the floor?" Seeing a faint smile on Professor Li's face, he couldn't help but feel proud of himself. On their way to the hospital, it was he who thought of this idea: instead of comforting a serious cardiac patient like Professor Li with sighs and condolences that would only make him feel worse, they should cheer him up by appearing to be happy, amusing, and childlike. How about that? It really worked!

As he swept at the front of the bed, suddenly he saw a piece of fine grid paper on the floor. He picked it up and took a look at it. It was a curve chart with "Electrocardiograph, room no. 43, Li" and the date on it. The curve was very uneven; the high points were like zigzags of varying sizes randomly drawn by the trembling hand of an epileptic. Xiao Nan kept silent but his heart immediately sank. He quietly finished sweeping the room, served his teacher a cup of hot tea, and said, "Professor, your disease is serious, you really should take care of yourself."

Professor Li sighed, "What good is it to take care of myself? Even if I'm well enough to teach, who is willing to listen to me seriously anyway?" Having said that, he looked at Xiao Nan with a smile.

Xiao Nan immediately blushed. He wanted to protest, but he held back stubbornly turning his head to one side, speechless.

Professor Li shook his head and gave a bitter smile. The past five months had made it clear to him how difficult it was to lead this young man back to a normal life and the proper academic path!

Five months ago, the Chinese Department had convened an academic report conference to celebrate the second anniversary of the fall of the Gang of Four. Li Senquan, the newly appointed Classical Chinese Language professor, gave a report entitled "My Views on Difficult Lines From 'Question of Heaven.' " Based on substantial materials from archaeology, folklore and ancient documents, he analyzed, among others, the two incomprehensible lines "Youhu was a tyrant; therefore Qi killed him so as to wipe out his vicious opponent. The reason Qi could attain the throne was because his father Yu harnessed the River so that the people could plant their grains." On the term "deed-exhaust" alone he cited over a hundred items and continued to lecture for over an hour. His new interpretations, substantial references, and profundity astonished the teachers and the students.

That night, the moon was hidden by the clouds and the barometric pressure was very low. Usually in this kind of weather he felt quite suffocated and restless. He tossed and turned and finally decided to take a walk in the campus garden. It was already past one o'clock, but the light was still on in one of the classrooms. He entered the room and found a student still studying. Li Senquan remembered his name was Xiao Nan and that he never paid much attention to Li's lectures. Taking this opportunity to get at the reasons behind it, he asked Xiao Nan to show him that day's lecture notes. But Xiao Nan was reluctant. So Li Senquan explained to him that reading the students' notes was a way to understand a teacher's standard of teaching and now he would like Xiao Nan to help him. Only then did Xiao Nan hand him his note book.

Strange notes! The main content of the report was very sketchy; it was only an outline. But there were many question marks among the notes and also a description which read,

> A wide forehead plus a bald head make Professor Li's brain occupy one half of his face. His facial skin is old and wrinkled. His clever but tired eyes only radiate coldness. Even when he hears applause, his eyes show no trace of a smile. Pale face, covered in cold sweat, age over forty, appearance sixty, physical condition seventy, a stillness of eighty . . .

Astonished, Li Senquan raised his eyes, examining Xiao Nan. The lad seemed to be aware of an approaching unpleasant remark; his eyes radiated excitement.

"It seems that your attention has been focused on the . . . portrait?" He said and then paused a moment. "That's a real shame. It means my lecture was terrible."

"No, it's my lack of interest in Classical Chinese Language that's to blame."

"Why?"

Silence. Li Senquan lit a cigarette as he eyed the youth, waiting for an answer.

As if having made a great resolution, Xiao Nan suddenly raised his eyes, and said challengingly, "Because our ancestors have been drowned in the ancient writings for too long! 'Ancestral records of Yao and Shun, the writings of Wen and Wu,' a burden of two thousand years has bent our backs and prevented us from moving even one step forward. The more we dig into the old writings the farther we are from the Four Modernizations . . . what do you think, teacher?"

Li Senquan avoided giving an answer, but asked instead, "Is it because of this that you fell in love with . . .," he lifted up the note book which contained his portrait, "literature?"

"Yes, only there is too much classical literature and too little contemporary literature for me."

Li Senquan forced a faint smile; he had an urge to stretch out his hand and to touch Xiao Nan's head like touching a lovable baby. But his faint smile hurt Xiao Nan, who was expecting a debate! Xiao Nan said gloomily, "Teacher, are you jeering at me?"

Li Senquan's eyes dropped coldly, "There's no need for me to jeer at you. Life itself will jeer at you. A few years from now, you'll jeer at yourself . . . Man is weak and powerless; he can't decide on his own path; he can only obey fate and society." He paused and then smiled gently, "It's already late. Let's talk again sometime. We know each other now."

He walked toward his dormitory, shaking his head, mumbling, "Naive, anxious, impatient. Oh, yes, young . . ." As he said this his heart suddenly felt a spasm of pain . . . "Ai, old, I'm already old."

This first exchange increased Xiao Nan's interest in Li Senquan's unfathomable personality. From then on he showed Professor Li his assignments often and asked him for suggestions. He had made up his mind to understand this person! He gradually discovered that Professor Li was not only well-versed in the classics, but learned in philosophy and ethics, too. He had mastered many schools of thought and yet showed no special preference for any one, neither likes nor dislikes. In knowledge, he had the mind of a computer, way beyond all kinds of challenges. In human relations, he was easygoing, almost without any temper. He could discuss academic problems with meticulous, old fashioned professors; nor did he refuse to play chess with mischievous students and rough workers. He coud get along quite well with certain vicious and perverse colleagues, although he never had a deep conversation with any one of them. He didn't boast of himself; he had no passion, no enemies, and no intentions of making any friends. He was a cold person.

"Was he vulgar or lofty?" Xiao Nan could never tell. Before long, Li Senquan had to be hospitalized because his rheumatic heart disease had flared up again. It was during this time that Xiao Nan heard people say Li Senquan was a distinguished philosophy graduate of a famous university and had been kept back to teach there after graduation. In 1957, for voicing some opinions of his to the administration he was branded a Rightist. Taking with him the daughter his divorced wife left behind, he returned to his village to be reformed through labor. He was called back only after being cleared of all false accusations at the time when intellectuals were being rehabilitated. He was chosen to teach in this university, but he decided not to work on philosophy any more. His heart condition had worsened while he was in the countryside. That was how Xiao Nan came to know about Li Senquan. Afterwards he often went to visit his teacher in the hospital. When Li Senquan was checking drafts of Xiao Nan's assignments, he often found the young man gazing at him with a sympathetic look. Accordingly Li Senquan began to treat Xiao Nan better than a teacher should, and anxiously watched his student's progress in creative work. Very often Li would put down a draft and look at Xiao Nan worriedly, "You really don't want to listen to me and devote your energy to the classics?" To this Xiao Nan always shook his head, remaining silent. Their differing views, however, did not affect their feelings toward each other at all; on the contrary, they seemed to become more intimate because of their differences. Strange!

Li Senquan's wandering thoughts were interrupted by Xiao Nan who obviously wanted to break the long silence in the ward and cheer up his teacher. "Professor Li, don't think I'm so good-for-nothing. I got 90 percent in my Classical Language test this time."

Li Senquan smiled, "Return of the prodigal, congratulations!"

"Huh, not at all. It should be deeply lamented!" He told Li Senquan that he only casually memorized words like *"zhi, hu, zhe,* and *ye"* to get a "shamefully" high mark. But in essay writing, he could only make a passing mark, even with original ideas. That was ridiculous!

As Xiao Nan talked excitedly, he suddenly noticed that Li Senquan's eyes were lit up, like fire and heat erupting from a newly opened oilfield. "Is it Xiaoyun outside the door?"

Xiao Nan went to open the door, laughing. "There's no sound outside. How could there be anyone?" But he was astonished when he opened the door. Professor Li was right. A girl was standing at the door! "Incredible! Is there such a thing as special communication between relatives?" he murmured to himself.

"How did you have time to come here today?" Li Senquan rose, with delighted surprise.

"The coach is sick. Our athletic team has half a day off. So here I am."

"Come in then, why are you standing at the door?"

"Because there was someone inside; it wasn't right for me to come in." So saying, the girl walked in, her face flushed. This slim and well-built athlete was unexpectedly soft and gentle in speech. She hesitated for a moment; too embarrassed to greet Xiao Nan, she walked straight to her father's sickbed. "Papa, didn't the doctor tell you to talk less and rest a lot? Why are you . . ."

"I know, I know. A lengthy disease will make a patient smarter than a cardiologist."

"Papa!" his daughter implored with her eyes.

"Oh, oh, oh, fine, I won't say any more. But you have to let me cure my disease!"

"Cure your disease?"

"That's right. Listening to this young man will make my heart stronger. It's better than medicine. Go on, young man, go on."

"His daughter makes him feel younger," Xiao Nan thought. He smiled slightly and told Li Senquan that the theme of his essay was to criticize the story "The Wounded."* Some classmates thought it was a piece of critical realism and therefore should be rejected; some thought it was not critical realism and thus should be accepted. His own view was "The Wounded" *was* critical realism and this was, in fact, its strong point. "Treating society is like treating a person, if there's no active criticism, there won't be any progress. Just singing praises will turn society conservative and decadent. The masses need actively critical works. History condones this type of literary work and so, from now on, I'll write it . . ."

"If you write that way, people will say you're criticizing Socialist Realism," Li Senquan interrupted him with concern.

"Socialism?" Xiao Nan gave a cold smile. "In recent years under the Gang of Four, our socialism has existed only in name. If the situation had continued in practice as well as in name, it would have led to state capitalism and feudal bureaucratism in no time at all . . . As for scientific socialism, many students of the future of modern capitalist countries will have to admit it is a definite trend. I believe that true socialist revolution and scientific-technical revolution are the two wheels of historical progress." Xiao Nan paused for a moment, staring at his teacher.

"You see, just because of this I got only a lousy passing mark. After I thought about this I came to realize how the teacher grades us, the worst memorization is far better than the best thinking."

Li Senquan fixed his sight on Xiao Nan, "To let you pass is doing you a great favor. If I were to correct your paper, I would give you a zero."

"You too? You want to give me a bad time?"

"No, on the contrary, I just don't want you to get into trouble. Don't get involved with anything like critical literature."

"Why?"

"Based on my twenty years of experience, literary creation and philosophy are quite similar; either you can't make anything out of it or you're in trouble once you are famous. I hope you won't get into trouble," Li Senquan said solemnly.

"In that case, I'd rather be famous. I hope our country will be strong and prosperous and soon achieve the Four Modernizations. I feel that the literature of this new era should face reality and life, reflect people's emotions and wishes, discuss society, politics, and human beings. I'm not afraid of suffering for these things. In a certain sense, if there is no suffering there's no genuine literary work. If a youth doesn't experience any suffering he won't mature. Then there won't be any historical advancement."

Li Senquan smiled. "Sure. That's poetic to a young man who doesn't know what suffering is." He recalled his past and sighed deeply.

"Do you think this is empty talk?" Xiao Nan stood up. His face turned pale. He felt his personality, enthusiasm and faith had been badly insulted, and in front of a girl. He did not look at her directly, but he sensed that she was staring at him intently. He clenched his fist, panting; he wanted to engage in a fierce debate, but he suddenly felt that piece of fine grid paper being crushed into a ball. Oh, the electrocardiograph! The zigzag lines, the irregular heart beat . . . Thinking about all these things he pursed his lips and said in a deep voice, "Well, someday I'll prove to you that suffering can't stop me . . . So long!"

He left. Xiaoyun asked softly, "Is he the Xiao Nan you always talk about, Papa?"

Her father nodded, "My best student. He's a bit stubborn, a bit arrogant, but he's upright; he's the bitter enemy of all vulgar phenomena." As if suddenly aware of something he waved his hand, "You girls don't understand this. Tell Papa, how is your training lately? Any improvement in your swimming speed?"

No answer. Xiaoyun stood in front of the window lost in thought. A long line appeared on her smooth, bright forehead.

---

* "The Wounded" *(Shanghen)* by Lu Xinhua was published in *Wenhuibao* on 11 August 1978. The sad story of a young girl's rejection of her mother during the Cultural Revolution era ends with the mother's death just before the girl returns home after an eight-year absence and the girl's rededication to the ideals of the Communist Party of China and its attack on the Gang of Four. It caused a great controversy in China and lent its title to the so-called Wounded Generation. It is actually very far from the kind of critical realism practiced in China before 1949. For an analysis, see Michael S. Duke, *Blooming and Contending: Chinese Literature in the Post-Mao Era* (Bloomington: Indiana University Press, forthcoming).

The Path

A few days later, after Xiaoyun left the Athletic Training Team, she saw Xiao Nan at the hundred-ten-meter spot. With his eyes fixed on her, Xiao Nan ran quickly and vigorously towards her. For some reason, Xiaoyun suddenly felt a bit scared. Trying to gather her feminine dignity, she waited for him to greet her. But, when he ran to the twenty-meter spot, he suddenly turned back. This puzzled her. After running for some distance, he stopped, turned around again, and walked toward her with a gloomy look on his face. Seeing that he was about to pass by, she couldn't help but ask "Hey! what are you looking for?"

"Oh!" He raised his head, astonished, and he looked at Xiaoyun in her blue athletic suit and white running shoes as if he were just waking up from a dream. (Just a moment before, he had seen but not recognized her.) After a long pause, it finally dawned on him, "Oh, you're Professor Li's . . ."

Li Yun nodded and asked, "What have you lost? Do you want me to help you look for it?"

"Look for what?" He quickly searched himself. "It seems I haven't lost anything."

"No? Then why are you walking back and forth so anxiously?"

Xiao Nan suddenly understood what had happened and gave a sneaky smile. "Oh yes, I'm looking for a person. Oh right, I'm going to tell you about a person's problem. I hope you can help me look for this person." He told her that this person was a naive girl whose father had been tortured to death in solitary confinement a few years ago. She had waited and waited, hoping some day her father would be cleared of the false accusations. The day had come. But, during the rehabilitation meeting, she suddenly fainted—because the secretary who chaired the meeting was exactly the same Special Case Division head who once broke her father's ribs with a bat. When people saw her collapse, they crowded around. The secretary came up and said, "Never mind, she's too excited."

Xiao Nan stopped talking and fixed his eyes on Xiaoyun with a question mark on his face. Xiaoyun was absorbed in the story.

"Finished?" she asked.

"Yes."

"Huh!" Xiaoyun stamped her feet. "This girl should have gone up to the platform and exposed the bad guy!"

"That's why I'm going to write this down and make it public for her."

"Is she your girlfriend?" Xiaoyun asked, her heart suddenly pounding.

Xiao Nan burst out laughing. "I don't have a girlfriend! This story came from my creative imagination. Just a while ago, I was walking back and forth, trying to picture this girl . . . Give me some suggestions, you know girls well."

"Me?" Xiaoyun blushed. "What can I say?"

"In that case, I've told you the story for nothing." Xiao Nan sighed.

"No, no." Xiaoyun was anxious. She thought seriously for a moment. "This is a good story. It makes people relate to many things in real life, makes them alert. It embarrasses the bad people . . ." She paused and then added, "Write it down, I . . . I mean, we hope to see it soon."

Xiao Nan's eyes began to light up like the bright clouds in the western sky.

The white poplar trees murmured as the couple slowly disappeared in the distance.

In the gardens lining the newly-widened country road, tablets, pavilions, and murmuring streams were to be found among the tall bamboo trees. When one walked along this road in a spring breeze, one must surely feel a clear and happy life force quietly filling up one's heart . . .

Perhaps it was because of this quiet environment that many colleges were built on both sides of this road. Here was Xiao Nan's N University, and not too far away, Xiaoyun's Provincial Athletic Training Institute. Students often strolled and meditated along this road. Perhaps by coincidence, or for some other reason, they met again on this road two days later.

Then again, on another day and another . . .

To talk with Xiao Nan and just to get to know him excited Xiaoyun. What is it in a person that attracts people most? Probably temperament. Xiao Nan's temperament was like a fire that burned inside his slim and lithe body. Whether because of his ardent love for life, his frankness, abundant sympathy, or because of his quick temper, impulsiveness, pride, and aggressiveness, Xiaoyun felt that being with him kindled her heart and opened her mind. The questions her father would not allow her to raise were answered and even the stars appeared nearer and brighter as she strolled along at night. Above all, she admired his abhorrence of viciousness and his passion for truth. She said jokingly, "It's lucky you weren't in Beijing during the Qingming Festival of 1976, otherwise I wouldn't be able to meet you." She flushed as she said this.

To befriend this girl also made Xiao Nan feel warm and happy. She was not strikingly beautiful, but her appearance and her pert swimmer's figure made her look serene and elegant. Her eyes were not like those "glittering big eyes" described in popular fiction; they were gentle and full of spirit. Her runner-up position in the 800-meter free-style swimming contest drew Xiao Nan's admiration. "Plain and elegant, though unconcerned about politics, she knows how to handle situations and she values morality. It's hard to find a girl like her these days," he thought. Only after they had known each other for a long time did he discover the strength and pride beneath her gentle appearance.

As they strolled that day, he found her deeply upset. She had been to the hospital to see her father. Li Senquan's liver had swollen and his heartbeat was very uneven. "It's been four months already. Papa's condition is getting worse every day; he's become a vegetable!"

Xiao Nan replied with a sigh, "But turning into a vegetable mentally is more terrible . . . He doesn't love good things; he doesn't hate bad things; he has no principles, no warm blood. His brain is over-developed and his heart is shrunken . . ."

He suddenly stopped talking—he discovered that she was not beside him. She had stopped walking. Her eyes were fixed in one direction and she looked extremely upset. He stepped forward quickly and asked anxiously, "Xiaoyun! What's wrong?"

After a long time Xiaoyun replied softly and firmly, "I won't allow anybody to say bad things about my Papa. Please don't ever say that sort of thing to me again!"

Xiao Nan said stubbornly and straightforwardly, "What else can I say? Isn't it a fact? Do you mean one's close relatives can't be criticized?"

Tears immediately filled Xiaoyun's eyes. "You really have no conscience." She turned her head and walked away.

This was the first time Xiaoyun became angry at Xiao Nan. He became scared and called her, but she wouldn't listen. When he caught up with her, he found her face covered with tears.

"Xiaoyun, Xiaoyun, what's wrong? Tell me clearly!" he said, perplexed.

Xiaoyun stood still, pressing her lips. After a while, she said, "It's easy for you to say, but do you know how much he has suffered? When he was only twenty-seven years old, he left his study and his wife. He was sent to labor reform in the countryside with a 'Rightist' label on him. He had a one-year-old daughter with him . . . The cadres there were quite good to him, saying 'Scholars are useless in the fields, let him make dog houses.' So he made dog houses for more than ten years!"

"Dog houses?"

"Dog houses. They were about this high and this wide, like a Chinese style pavillion, very nice looking, with a window and a door. They're not cold in winter or hot in summer. They're specially made for foreigners to get foreign exchange. They're made of cattail leaves. We were sent down near the Hongze Lake where there were lots of cattails. There was a weaving team in the brigade and that's where Papa was 'sent down.' But the place where Papa and I lived couldn't even compare with a dog house. The hole in the ceiling was so big that sparrows could fly in and out. On rainy days, the house was like a swamp; in winter it was a big layer of ice. Papa's income was based on how many dog houses he could make. He had to work very hard, and he wasn't good at his trade. He had to work so hard to support me that he couldn't straighten his back. For seventeen years he hasn't been able to move around. On top of this he had rheumatism and heart disease. Later, all this resulted in rheumatic heart disease. Even when he was suffering from illness, he still had to work. Do you know that?" She couldn't hold it in any more; she began to choke with tears. Xiao Nan was shocked and motionless.

Xiaoyun tried to calm down for a moment. She continued, "For more than ten years, whenever he couldn't sleep at night, he would get up, light a lamp, and read the classics he had brought along. When I woke up in the middle of the night I would ask why he was up. He would reply, 'Man must work, otherwise he will go crazy.' What had caused all this? It was all because he made a few remarks about the bureaucracy in 1957. Later, when people spat in his face, he would let it dry by itself. Whenever I saw ignorant people bullying him, giving him a hard time, I would get very angry and cry. But he would say, as if nothing serious had happened, 'They are so ignorant. If I fought with them I'd be even more ignorant!' He never flattered anyone, yet he got along with everybody. It is true he has no principles; I am his highest principle. He has no life of his own; I am his life . . . Do you know he was active and indignant in his youth? Do you know why he likes you? He says it's because he can see his own youth in you."

The road was quiet and the night was enshrouding them from all directions. Xiaoyun heard a pounding sound. It was Xiao Nan beating his own chest. "What happened afterwards?" he asked after a while, in a deep voice.

"Never mind. If you don't talk about it I won't feel bad. Don't mention it any more."

"No," Xiao Nan insisted, "You must tell me . . . letting it out is not the same as seeing it happen again."

"Afterwards . . . afterwards, I grew up. Papa grew old. I caught fish, cut cattails, and collected water caltrops to increase the family income. Papa's health deteriorated every year. It was so cold the winter I was sixteen that the Hongze Lake froze completely over. The ice spread out for several hundred miles and there was no way of catching any fish or cutting any cattails. Papa's heart condition got very serious. Since Papa couldn't get any work points, we simply didn't have a cent at home. We couldn't keep borrowing money from people all the time. I was so worried that I cried. But Papa said smilingly, 'Silly child, what are you crying for? This is the end of Papa's punishment, it's a good thing.' My heart was broken. I took some grain from home and went to exchange it for three catties of white wine. I ran to the edge of the Hongze Lake. At a spot where no one could see me I dug a hole in the ice and started drinking." At this moment, Xiao Nan cried out in shock, "You . . .!" But Xiaoyun didn't pay attention to him and continued, "Before, I used to think that there was no difference between wine and water. This time when I drank it I really felt its strength. The first mouthful of wine really burnt my stomach; it was like swallowing melted iron. I was afraid that I would relent, so I drank all the wine in one gulp. At that moment I felt I could burst my guts and let the wine flow out. Taking my chance while the wine was still doing its work, I took off my clothes, tied myself with a piece of rope to the trunk of a willow tree by the shore, and jumped into the ice hole." At this moment she suddenly felt that Xiao Nan was grabbing her hands. "Never mind, don't be afraid, the water only went up to my chest. 'When the weather is cold, the fish cling to the grass; there are abundant fish under the ice.' As soon as the fish sensed the heat of my body, they rushed towards me. I clenched my teeth and threw the fish out one by one. It took only a short time before I'd caught quite a few catties. When I came out of the hole the fish were all frozen on the ice. I had to use a spade to dig them out . . . Don't worry, I didn't feel cold at all. I felt much better than later when I had to put on a face to sell fish in the market." Before she had finished talking Xiao Nan embraced her tightly. She could feel his wet face and his trembling body. "Don't feel sad, this was a good thing. Otherwise, how could I win first prize in the District Amateur Swimming Competition and become an athlete? . . . Don't cry. You're a man!"

He did not answer nor could he speak. Instead he embraced her with all his youthful passion and strength, calling her in his heart, "Gentle, strong, compassionate, proud . . ."

And she? She smiled happily through her tears. A heart, a lofty soul, and a passionate embrace were all hers; God only knows how often she had longed for them in her painful loneliness.

One month later Li Senquan's disease got worse. Xiaoyun's eyes became dark circles after many sleepless nights taking care of her father. She said to Xiao Nan one day, "Nan, we should cheer Papa up. The reason why his disease has worsened is that he has too little happiness."

"What do you want to do?"

"Tell him about us. This will be a special medicine for him."

"How do you know?"

"Why, I'm his life. My happiness is his happiness. You're his favorite student. I don't know if he ever has liked anyone more than he does you. If you tell him about us, he'll be the happiest father in the world. He will surely say, 'At last, I haven't wasted my effort, children, now I can die in peace.'"

"Haven't you told him before?"

"I'm too embarrassed. Let's go together tomorrow. With you there, I'll have the courage to say it, and this will give him a happy surprise . . . All right? Bookworm!"

"Naughty girl!"

On this serene and beautiful road, they kissed for a long time in the passionate night breeze under the bright starlight.

The Ward Again

At night, the light was on again in room no. 43 of the cardiac ward. Xiaoyun glanced at Xiao Nan and then went first into the room, by herself. The door was closed again. Xiao Nan stole a glance at the patient before the door was shut, and his heart sank. In the past few months, Li Senquan's face had turned from pale to grey, it had wrinkled and shrunk. Like an overworked horse dying of fatigue at the finish line, this marathon runner in a whole life of suffering was about to collapse at the beginning of a peaceful life. His last living power for survival had now disappeared. Oh, pitiful old man! I hope our happiness will bring you laughter.

However, after Xiaoyun's soft and shy remarks, he could not hear a sound except the pounding of his heart . . . Oh, door no. 43! The door of happiness! Open, quick . . .

It was as if centuries had passed. "Crash!" Suddenly there was a sound of something breaking on the floor. "Papa, Papa, what's wrong?" Xiaoyun called sharply. Xiao Nan's heart tightened. He pushed the door but it was locked. What had happened? A layer of sweat beaded on his forehead.

Inside, after a bout of coughing there suddenly erupted a grievous cry, "You ignorant child! How could you have done such a thing?" Xiao Nan was shocked and numbed. He simply could not believe such a sharp broken cry came from that normally calm person! It seemed that Xiaoyun was explaining something, but her voice was lost in a series of groans. "No, don't say any more. I won't agree . . . Do you want to push me to my death?" His words were stopped by choking. Xiaoyun called to her father in a shocked voice, "Papa, Papa . . ."

Xiao Nan dashed to the door, pounding and kicking, causing the number plate No. 43 to swing back and forth. "Is he crazy? Or are we crazy? He? Or us?"

Suddenly he heard Li Senquan say, "That's him, I suppose. Go, open the door, I'm all right! Go!"

The door opened. Xiao Nan rushed into the room. In the lamp light he could see Li Senquan groaning in bed, with his hands pressing his chest. His face was pale, but his eyes were full of spirit. He ordered Xiaoyun, "Go out. Let me talk to him alone." When he saw that Xiaoyun left only after Xiao Nan consented, he couldn't help but sway back and forth, painfully. Xiao Nan hurriedly rushed forward to lift his teacher up, but was shocked to see his disgusted and even hostile look.

"Let go! I don't need your help! Don't you ever think of taking Xiaoyun away from me!"

He, surely, was not the familiar easygoing old man he used to know! He was just an emaciated old animal ready to protect its threatened offspring. Xiao Nan's heart froze deep inside.

"Why don't you agree?" he stammered.

"I'm her father, I love her. I want her to be happy."

Xiao Nan immediately said, "In that case, you should consent. I love her too. I, too, want her to be happy! We are in aggreement!"

"Not the same, a father can sacrifice everything for his daughter, but a husband can't sacrifice everything for his wife."

"I can even sacrifice my life for Xiaoyun!" Xiao Nan yelled.

"Very well. You don't need to sacrifice your life, so long as you give up your creative writing. Then, I will consent."

Their eyes were fixed upon each other. Xiao Nan's face turned pale. After a long while he said softly, "That is the only thing I can't give up."

"I knew you would say that. In that case, we're finished talking. Please go."

"You . . . why do you torture people this way?" Xiao Nan yelled.

"Go! I really have no energy to talk." Li Senquan waved his hand weakly.

"In that case I'll stay here until you have energy to talk and then I'll leave."

Li Senquan had no choice but to gather his spirit. "Is it necessary to say any more? Do you mean you don't realize that the writer's path is filled with corpses and wounded?"

"I know. I'm not afraid."

"You're not afraid. Then go ahead. But why are you dragging an innocent girl along with you?" As Li Senquan talked, he suddenly grew impulsive. "You said you want her to be happy, but how can you give her happiness? . . . Why don't you have pity on her? She has a rotten father who has made her motherless. She hasn't had a good life since she was born. When she was still a little girl she jumped into an ice hole in winter; she didn't even tell me when she came home . . . " Li Senquan suddenly turned his face away from Xiao Nan. Xiao Nan could hear tears in his words. "What a good girl! She hasn't committed any crime, she deserves a different life, a human being's life! Do you understand?" When he turned around, Xiao Nan could see purple traces on his lips. "You understand? If you do, how can you bear to drag her back into the ice hole? Do you mean that after she has suffered half her life because of her father, she still has to suffer for the rest of it because of her husband?" He pressed his chest and panted painfully, "You're selfish! You don't love her! I won't consent! I've ruined the first half of her life, I can't ruin the second!"

Xiao Nan lowered his head heavily, like an ox quietly receiving a beating. Li Senquan could see Xiao Nan's jaw tremble . . . After a long time Xiao Nan raised his head. "What you said is correct. I don't love her as much as you do. You can sacrifice everything to love her; I love her, but I can't sacrifice truth."

"Truth? Truth has no end, but life has. If you search for truth you'll end up in disillusionment and suffering . . . Before I was twenty or so I, too, thought of changing society and searching for truth, but now, now I only believe in the ancient oriental philosophy: transform your passion and cultivate your nature, don't fight against the world . . . .Child," Li Senquan's tone suddenly turned very earnest, "please listen to my experience. Society is too difficult to change. Until human beings change their hearts, obey society, and transcend their material surroundings, they will not have spiritual tranquility. Let's work on textual research; that way, you, Xiaoyun, and

I will be happy." At this moment, he had turned back into the person that Xiao Nan was familiar with. After all, he was deeply fond of Xiao Nan!

"But, do you mean Premier Zhou Enlai, General Peng Dehuai and the others died for nothing? Has the blood of hundreds of thousands of people flowed in vain these ten years and more? Can we stop after paying such a high price, without learning anything?" Xiao stood up. "Unfortunately, I don't feel right about forgetting all this, neither do I forget Marx's words. The reason why history needs to bring the masses to life is because it has to awaken them from historical ignorance. In those ten years, I have pulled the old cadres' hair; I have wounded people of the opposite faction; I have been a cynical 'escapee.' Conscience won't allow me to remain silent. I must write! . . . Don't worry, I won't drag your daughter along." He paused for a moment; two heavy tear drops rolled down his face. "Xiaoyun is free; I want her to be happy!" After saying this, he turned around and opened the door.

"No, don't go! You don't belong just to yourself. You're mine. I won't let you go!" Xiaoyun threw herself at him and forced him back into the room. She was weeping. "Papa, I loved him before, and I love him even more now. I don't know politics, but I know he is a real person and he won't betray me! I want to follow him even if I'm burned by the fire of heaven. Don't you want me to live like a human being? This is the life of a human being!" The two young people were overcome by great waves of emotion and tightly embraced each other.

After continuous coughing, her father vomited some pinkish phlegm, but no one noticed since everyone was overcome by emotion. Li Senquan, playing the roles of Jia Zheng and Jia's mother that he had always disliked so much, felt extreme physical and mental pain. However, he still managed to say, "What if you have children? It's easy for you two to sacrifice yourselves, but children are innocent! Do you still want to be like me, ruining your children's lives?"

Xiaoyun suddenly cried, "Papa, why are you looking for trouble? After the Gang of Four fell, disasters disappeared; they won't come back!"

Li Senquan gave an ironic smile. "Oh, yes, now everything has changed for the better and every policy has been implemented and my problem has been corrected, do you think I'm not happy? But I am 'Hoping everything will last forever, a thousand *li* of moonlight'! But, who can guarantee that another Jiang Qing won't arise from the Party; or another Lin Biao to engage in a power struggle? If they do, do you think we, the powerless common people, can stop them? After liberation we suffered twice. Will there be a third time?" He groaned and groaned. "I've suffered enough, enough! For over ten years I've hoped and hoped, but I've been disappointed again and again . . . Perhaps there will be a long period of peace from now on, but how can I bet my daughter's whole life on it! No, I won't consent." As he said this, purple marks spread over his face.

Her father's words made Xiaoyun tremble. She couldn't help but throw herself on the sick bed. "Papa, I beg you, agree. Didn't you say he was a distinguished youth?"

"Yes, it's just because of this that I won't agree."

"Then whom do you want me to marry?"

"Find the simplest person, someone who has no desire to accomplish anything, someone who only demands of himself that he not make mistakes. Even," Li Senquan clenched his teeth, "even a common citizen would be much better!" After he finished talking, he let himself fall back in the bed, as if he had used up all his energy in saying his last words.

Xiaoyun rose and drew back slowly, step by step, staring at her father as if she had just come to know him. "I never thought you were so selfish, so cruel, so mean . . ."

"Xiaoyun!" Xiao Nan forcibly drew her back. "Don't say any more, your father has suffered a great deal." Xiao Nan knew that even if there was danger before him, he would have a good future sooner or later. But, there is nothing more lamentable than the death of the heart. Li Senquan's heart was dead and he didn't believe in anything except his past. What good was it to argue with him?

However, Xiaoyun, who had always been gentle, now became unexpectedly stubborn. She said indignantly, "No, leave me alone! I can jump into the ice hole a thousand times for Papa, but I can't let him destroy our happiness!" She turned to her father. "Papa, we're not begging for mercy from you. If you don't accept us, I don't accept you as my father! You can't control us. Xiao Nan, let's go!"

But her father could hear no more of her reproach after the first two sentences. As if hit by a bullet he dropped his sweating head. He could only hear his own heart pounding unevenly, shaking and loudly breaking to pieces. His daughter's angry and despairing face gradually disappeared . . .

Xiaoyun and Xiao Nan's terrified cry covered his weak whisper, "Oh, heaven! Let me die in peace!"

At dawn, the nurse on duty led Xiao Nan and Xiaoyun to the emergency room. They had stayed up all night. Outside the door were the leaders from the university and the department, as well as Li's colleagues who came after hearing the news. A doctor approached and said, "The patient has a few last words to say to you. Time is short. He has suffered from a relapse of his rheumatic heart disease and sudden heart failure. Although we've tried our best to save him, there's not much time left."

"We've caused his death, we're guilty," Xiaoyun and Xiao Nan thought. They were confused as they blundered into the emergency room.

The patient opened his eyes, looking at Xiao Nan (What a sight!). He said brokenly, "Child, I . . . I only ask you to do one thing; don't marry Xiaoyun, I beg you!"

Xiao Nan stared numbly at Xiaoyun, speechless.

A painter could have painted Xiao Nan's expression as the face of a person run over by a car and certainly could have produced an immortal piece of art. He would challenge an emperor, fight with lions and tigers for the girl he loved, but how could he tear this little bed apart! How! Life has taken everything away from this patient, how can I deny his last pitiful request? How can I? How can I thrust another knife into this pain-stricken heart when it is about to stop beating?

"I agree," he said.

"Swear, child."

"OK, I swear, I'll never get married."

Xiaoyun groaned softly and fainted.

Xiao Nan looked at the patient and Xiaoyun. His face was half bathed in the lamp light from the room; the other half painted bronze by the incoming morning glow. He continued, "I also swear for the happiness of all girls and for the health of all old men, for my love, I will never put down my pen."

The old man mumbled to his unconscious daughter, "I've ruined you two, children. I'm guilty; curse me . . ."

His eyes slowly fixed on her face and stayed there forever.

Originally published in *Zhong shan*, no. 3, 1979, and reprinted in *Xinhua yuebao, wenzhai*, no. 12, 1979, from which this translation was made.

Translated by Laifong Leung

WOMEN THEN AND NOW

Of course it is necessary to give them legal equality to begin with. But from there on everything still remains to be done.

—Mao Zedong

Like most post-Mao critical realism, Zhang Xian's "The Widow" (*Weiwangren*) raises a problem that it does not attempt to solve: What is a widow supposed to do with the rest of her life? In the People's Republic of the 1980s, especially among the "revolutionary" Party hierarchy, the answer to this question seems to be the age old one of traditional "feudal" China; be a good mother by helping your children make suitable upwardly mobile marriages, be a faithful widow by venerating your husband's memory and continuing to live in his shadow, and give up any claims to love and individual happiness or even status in your own right. In the course of her long letter to her dead husband, Zhou Lianghui also introduces us to the rigid class distinctions that exist in the PRC as in the USSR. She shows us another segment of Chinese youth—cadre kids whose desire for social success makes them callous and unsympathetic toward workers like "that guy" the postman. The saddest case of all is the postman's mother who, after a life of suffering as a widow herself, does not want her son to marry a widow. In this story, Zhang Xian demonstrates that not all men are insensitive to the problems women face in China.

Zhang Kangkang, who comes from Harbin, is one of China's finest young writers. In "The Tolling of a Distant Bell" (*Youyuan de zhongsheng*), she and her co-auther Mei Jin construct a *déjà vu* story that reveals the social class distinctions in Chinese society through an ironic meeting between a former Ya'nan cadre who is now a high ranking member of "the party in power" (Hu Yaobang's phrase) and the woman he once loved. As is typical of Zhang Kangkang's narrative style, the authors cleverly highlight their message concerning the insidious persistence of "feudal" values in the new society by means of tangible symbols of time and personal connections between then and now. Among the latter are the tolling of the "distant" bell that abolishes the distance between memories of the past and experiences of the present and the gold watch that leads to the female protagonist's icy meeting with her former lover now turned bureaucrat. This meeting in turn leads to her decision to help her son marry the woman he loves in spite of parental refusal of consent due to upper-class (high-cadre) snobbery. This affirmation of the individual's right to happiness is also characteristic of Zhang Kangkang's fiction. ★

The Widow

by Zhang Xian

Photo by Saundra Sturdevant

Dear Weiming:

It's been twelve whole years since we parted. Twelve years today. During those twelve years I've written a steady stream of letters, and even though I've known that you'll never read any of them, I still can't help myself. For a lonely person who is thinking of someone else, writing letters is a comfort, a sort of sustenance, a way to ease the heart. As I sat before a sheet of clean white paper, trying to make some sense out of my confused thoughts and moods with my pen, you would appear before me and be by my side. I would embrace you and whisper into your ear intimate expressions that can be revealed only to a husband. Ah, dear Weiming! Only you know what a vulnerable woman I am!

Tonight the moonlight is hazier than usual, the subtle fragrance of orchids floats in the air. It's just as it was twelve years ago. I remember it as clearly as if it was yesterday: how you unhurriedly straightened your collar, slowly picked up your traveling bag, and walked over to the doorway, where you stopped for a moment, as though you had forgotten something. Yes, you had forgotten to kiss Lanlan and Wangwang goodbye. Maybe you had wanted to avoid waking them, or to keep them from realizing that Daddy was leaving, going away in humiliation with two shady characters. I remained completely composed and silent as I walked with you downstairs and across the courtyard, then watched the Peking Jeep disappear into the hazy moonlight. But as I turned back and saw those two little faces distorted by looks of sheer panic, plastered up against the window, I could no longer hold back my tears . . .

Lanlan is now a skilled auto mechanic. Last year she fell deeply in love with someone, although she kept it a secret from me. Her boyfriend, the second son of your old comrade-in-arms, Lao Shi, is a promising young actor with the Municipal Drama Troupe. The two of them are now busily making plans to start their own family. Wangwang left two days ago. He was admitted into Qinghua University—his entrance-exam score was the third highest in the city. I'm sure you can still remember the look of self-satisfaction that sometimes appeared on his upturned face. He spent the last few days busily running back and forth on errands: spreading the good news to relatives, hurriedly finishing a self portrait to leave with his elder sister as a memento, consoling a girl who had failed the exams—a classmate of his with large, shining eyes—and giving her every single book he had used to prepare for the exams. Yes, our children are no longer fledglings, and now they want to leave their confining little nest to soar into the bright blue sky that awaits them. They cannot be bothered with the aging and lonely mother bird that has stayed behind to watch over the old nest, or maybe the thought never even occurred to them. When Lanlan heartily announced that her "personal matter" had been "resolved," and Wangwang, playing the part of an experienced traveler, placed his canvas bag onto the luggage rack of the train, neither of them could figure out why Mommy was crying. How could they ever understand what was in their mother's heart!

Only you ever understood that, dear Weiming, only you. But now there is someone else who understands me, and that is he.

Oh, I should tell you who *he* is, since he's the reason I'm writing you this letter!

Your photograph is in front of me at this very moment. You are smiling from behind the glass, gazing warmly at me. I always thought that there was a trace of mockery in that smile of yours, which made me feel indescribably guilty. Dear Weiming, am I wrong? Shouldn't I have felt that way? Please tell me, and not as a Municipal Party Secretary would tell his subordinate or a husband would tell his wife. Weiming, tell me as you would a friend or a comrade, tell me how you feel, tell me what your thoughts are, give me your opinions . . .

You never met him. He played no role in our lives together. You were always busy in the service of the 250,000—later on 400,000—residents of the city: industry, agriculture, commerce; meetings, decision-making, grass-roots work . . . you never seemed to have any time for your own family, for your young wife. A common citizen like him had no place in your thoughts. And if he had, it would only have been as one out of 250,000 or one out of 400,000, which is next to nothing!

Weiming, do you still remember how we met? Do you still recall that day in 1954 when we were seeing in the new year, and Hospital Director Li dragged me, a nineteen-year-old girl fresh out of nursing school, over to meet you? Do you remember the shy look on my face? Do you remember how my hand trembled in yours as you clumsily danced across the floor?

My first meeting with him, however, was under totally different circumstances. In fact, I was barely aware of his arrival.

"Comrade Zhou Lianghui, a letter for you." He must have knocked at the door and I must have responded, but I have no recollection of it, since at the time I was so worried about you. He spoke very softly, only once, not wanting to disturb me, then placed the letter on the table beside the door and walked away noiselessly. I turned in time to see the retreating back of a man dressed in green.

It was your letter that he had brought over, your first letter after having been taken away, and the last letter you ever wrote in your life. In that letter you said many things that seem so funny to me now. Things like, "We must test our mettle in the blazing fires of the Cultural Revolution," and "The road taken by the rebels has always been the correct one." Then you copied out passages from Mao's "Quotations," word for word. But it was the last sentence you wrote that moved me and has been indelibly etched upon my heart; you said: "You must be strong!"

Yes, I needed to be strong. Lanlan, who was twelve, and eight-year-old Wangwang needed a strong mother. The family needed a strong homemaker. You, with your future so unpredictable, needed a strong wife who could come to your aid like someone traveling in the same boat. The Party, which was temporarily in a state of disarray and low morale, needed a strong member . . . I needed to be strong, that was for sure! It was then that my tears dried, and I steeled myself to meet the hard times ahead. Dear Weiming, it has been like that for twelve years, right up to this very day.

I waited impatiently for your letters and I waited impatiently for his visits. For the first time in my life I understood the loftiness and greatness of the poetic expression "man in green." But this particular "man in green," our postman, also brought me disappointment. He came at 10:30 sharp every day, knocked softly at my door and, without stepping inside, placed the day's newspaper, with its huge photograph and red-lettered headlines, on the table beside the door. When he saw the expectant look on my face he lowered his head remorsefully, as though it were his fault that there was no letter.

But the day finally came when he showed up before ten o'clock; he rushed in, his face flushed with excitement. I, too, was overcome with excitement as I took the letter from him, but I saw at once that it was Yang Lili's handwriting on the envelope—you remember her, don't you, my best friend at nursing school? She was the beautiful, slim girl who followed her heart, asking to be transferred from the provincial capital to a mountain region to be with the man she loved. She sent me her warmest regards and cautioned me not to be too anxious, saying that the "liberation of the Party Secretary" was just around the corner. She also invited me to visit her "peaceful little county town," where I could forget my cares. I'm sure I must have smiled when I read that. He was still standing in the doorway, unwilling to leave, looking greatly relieved; his buckteeth gave him an engaging smile.

"Thank you. Won't you come in and sit for a moment?" I asked him.

He just shook his head and walked off.

But his smile lingered long after he had left.

Ah, that smile! During that red reign of terror, throughout those many months when everyone seemed to have donned masks, when the Party Secretary's wife became "the stinking old lady of a traitor" overnight, how precious and dear that sincere, friendly smile was!

Even to this very day, a sincere, friendly smile has not reappeared on the faces of all our friends. Recently, in fact, the smile on the face of our future in-law, Lao Shi, has had a stifling effect on me . . .

Dear Weiming! I still remember your smile during those early days. It was filled with such self-confidence and charisma. When Director Li told me that you were the youngest and most promising Deputy Secretary in the municipal committee—only 35 years old—that your wife had recently died, and that you were living a bachelor's life, I immediately sensed the emotions hidden in that smile of yours. But I didn't have the time to mull it over, or look closely, or, for that matter, even to hesitate, for you won me over, deftly and with ease. You were like a mischievous child who wins out over a weak little kitten. Our courtship—if it can be called that—lasted only three months before the wedding arrangements were made. And you, afterwards you laughed at me and said, "What's wrong, don't you think three months was long enough?"

Ah, but the feelings between him and me developed over a period of agonizingly long months!

Lanlan was sent down to the countryside the year after you died. She's a bright, mature girl who grew up fast during those chaotic years. But she's really only a girl, barely sixteen! I almost wept aloud when I read her first letter from the farming village.

"How is Lanlan? Is she homesick? Does she need anything? If not, why not scribble an answer to her right now? Or send a parcel. I'll take it with me, and it'll get out in today's mail . . ."

He was watching me with a look of deep concern on his face. He stood off to one side wringing his hands, not knowing what he could do to help me.

Weiming, you never once had a look like that on your face. All the help you ever gave me was of a totally different kind. My application for Party membership was approved a month before we were married. When I was pregnant with Lanlan I was transferred from the hospital ward and assigned clerical duties at the Secretariat Division. Later on I was sent to the Propaganda Section, where I was promoted from a clerical worker to a Deputy Division Head. After the first round of the "Four Cleanups" campaign came to an end, I was appointed Assistant Director of the Municipal Party Secretariat Office. From start to finish I fought to be strong and to perform my duties conscientiously, so that I would never bring shame upon you. Naively I thought that all my promotions came as a result of my own efforts. It wasn't until I entered the hospital in 1965, where I met my classmate Xiao Zhang—she was still a duty nurse, and she deferentially called me "Director Zhou"—that it hit me like a bolt out of the blue: my steady advancement up the ladder was a perfect example of that ancient saying, "The husband's nobility brings glory to the wife"!

"Don't talk nonsense!" I can almost hear that annoyed drawl of yours. "I was just helping you get ahead!" That's right, where politics were concerned, you were very demanding with me. You often talked to me of the spirit and intentions of your superiors and instructed me in how to avoid making mistakes. "That's all I did for you?" you might ask. No, that's not all. You were also a good husband: you knew I loved flowers, so you had the gardener bring me some orchids; you knew I loved books, so you had the people at the bookstore bring the new arrivals over for me to select the ones I wanted; you knew I liked to look nice, so you allowed me to buy a few pretty outfits that were selected only after long, careful thought; and you knew I loved you, so you frequently took the time to be affectionate with me, showing me the attentiveness and tenderness that only a husband can offer—all of this you called love. But love like this is anything but equal! Those are only the sorts of kindnesses bestowed upon someone by a superior!

The minor spat we had the first time I accompanied you to a dinner party is something I won't forget for as long as I live. Being in the presence of that senior official who was the city's representative on the Provincial Party Committee and his wife so terrified me that I didn't know what to do. When it was my turn to offer a toast, not knowing the proper flattering remarks made me look like an awkward fool. The wives were twittering about my being a "little nurse," and their condescending looks put me on pins and needles the entire night. I would have given anything to sprout a pair of wings that would allow me to fly right out of that splendid dining hall. But when I looked at you for help, you pointedly turned your face away, a sure sign of your displeasure at my lack of social graces.

That night I cried into my pillow. I hated myself for bringing you shame! After that I made every effort to learn how to socialize like the rest of those smug wives with their superior attitudes, even though I loathed them with all my heart. And you rewarded my efforts by praising me: "You're learning." That, of course, was a result of your "help"!

But he—a lowly "man in green"—what help could he give me? He delivered and picked up my mail; occasionally he delivered parcels and money orders; he took the children to the doctor on his bicycle; on his days off he made repairs to the roof; . . . and that's about it. Everything was so commonplace, as commonplace as water. But isn't there a difference between the water that rushes out through an open faucet and that which bubbles up from a spring in an endless stretch of desert?

Was it only sympathy? Was it only friendship? No, for glowing in the depths of that sympathy and friendship were sincere, kindhearted, magnificent embers. Admittedly they were weak, but they were strong enough to illuminate a faith in life. Look: sincerity exists, kindheartedness and ideals exist, which must mean that truth exists as well. And not behind us, either, but directly in front of us . . .

Dear Weiming, last autumn, after you had lain in the ground for years, your case was finally "cleared up." As a result, my days of "standing off to the side," my long period of enforced idleness, also came to an end. When I told him that I would be going back to work, he let out a sigh of relief and his face lit up with that toothy smile of his. He broke precedent by staying over to eat that day. "A toast to your new life!" He drained his glass of wine. Just before he left he gazed out at the orchids in front of the window, and his eyes suddenly grew sad.

Oh, those orchids. Wasn't that the pot you had the gardener bring over to me? It died long ago, the same year you left us. I couldn't bear to throw the dead branches away, and I often stared at the yellow, waxen leaves until I was nearly spellbound, almost as though I was expecting the arrival of the spring that would breathe life back into them. He was aware of all this. Actually, he understood my heart better than I myself. One night toward the end of spring he brought over a pot of fresh orchids, which he placed on the table beside the door. "I planted it myself. . . ." He smiled shyly, then looked at me searchingly. "You . . . won't refuse it, will you?" I was so touched that I didn't dare look at him, for fear that tears would flow against my will. My eyes remained fixed on those tender green leaves so full of life . . .

I returned to my job at the Municipal Party Headquarters. Everything there was both familiar and strange to me. Problems and difficulties had accumulated: there were three times as many complaints, much more idle talk, laziness and irresponsibility.

I returned home every day, my heart weighted down with worries, which included an anguish that I was unable to face: I wouldn't be able to see him every day anymore.

On that first Sunday I was up bright and early to await his arrival. I wanted to talk to him for ten or fifteen minutes, when it wouldn't interfere with his work, of my feelings about the previous week. Finally I heard the familiar sound of a bicycle bell. "Newspaper!" The crisp voice carrying across the courtyard belonged to a young woman. "What's wrong? Where is he? Is he sick?" I asked as I rushed downstairs.

"You mean the regular postman? He swapped mail routes with me. He's working in North City . . . ."

Ah, Weiming! When I had sunk to the level of an "untouchable" and had to struggle against the lashing storms, without any fanfare he brought me news of my family, and he brought me warmth, brightness, and fragrance. Now that I had regained my position as Assistant Director, the Housing Section Chief enthusiastically offered to assign me to new housing; the manager of the hardware outlet stubbornly insisted on sending me a hard-to-get Honeybee sewing machine; the head of the aquatic products retail department brought freshly caught fish "on his way by"; the Director of the Women's Federation, as "representative of all the women in the city," nominated me for Deputy Director . . . As all of this was happening he quietly removed himself from the scene.

Ah, when the water faucet has been reconnected, so that for twenty cents a cubic meter you can use filtered water to your heart's content, the spring water in the desert flows back into the earth! . . .

I recall asking him once why he never got married. "My family background is no good," he had said with a forced smile.

"That doesn't make any difference these days."

"But who could ever take a fancy to a 38-year-old postman who earns thirty-eight *yuan* a month?"

I tried to comfort him by saying that a person's worth can't be measured by his family background, his position, or his salary. There will always be some nice young woman who could love a decent man like him (I said this with all sincerity, but I was stopped by the mocking expression on his face). Then one day I discovered that the person who had fallen in love with him was not just any nice young woman, but me!

Dear Weiming, I was terrified and I was bewildered. I denied my feelings vehemently, and I berated myself for having them. No, no! It's not possible! It's not practical! It's not normal! It's not right! I'm already 43 years old! My children are already grown! I'm a Party member! I'm the widow of the Municipal Party Secretary! I must treasure my good name and that of my departed husband! I stood in front of your photograph, silently begging your forgiveness.

You were looking at me with smiling eyes. "You must be strong!" you were saying.

Yes, I had to be strong. I had to overcome these improper feelings of mine. I had to throw all my energy into my work. I voluntarily took on the job of reassessing the office of Assistant Director, which any number of cadres had avoided like poison. And so my life was filled with receptions, explanations, examinations, discussions, disputes, sympathy, anger, anxieties, urgings, and reproaches. I offended many of my superiors, many of our closest friends—yours and mine. I used this as a burden to weigh myself down so hard that I could barely breathe.

As I ran into one obstacle after another in my reassessment work, Lao Shi was my staunchest supporter. He was still the Deputy Secretary in charge of organizational work. He frequently praised me in various situations as being a strong woman. But he couldn't keep from linking me with you. "She has proved herself worthy of her position as wife of Comrade Weiming, our old Party Secretary!" This heartfelt praise made me feel guilty, because every time I had a moment's peace, the image that floated into my mind was that of his smile, with those prominent buckteeth of his, the smile that had given me courage during those trying days. I was powerless to drive it away.

Dear Weiming! When I was young I once heard a tale of the agony of widowhood: in order to overcome her feelings of emptiness and loneliness, a widow tossed a hundred coins onto the floor every night, then turned out the light and groped around on the floor picking them up one by one. By the time they were all back in her purse she was finally tired enough to go to bed and fall asleep. And that's how she spent her nights right up till the day she died, letting a hundred coins, shiny from being rubbed countless times, stand as proof of her bitterly attained virtue. She died with a clear conscience and a sense of pride.

Now that our children have left their mother's embrace, the moonlight shines dimly onto the head of my bed, the subtle fragrance of orchids gathers at the window, loneliness and solitude gnaw away at my heart, and I am reminded of that ancient tale. Am I, too, expected to turn out the light and grope around on the floor for the "coins of chastity" stained by blood and tears? No! Let those widows die with their clear consciences and their pride. I need love, I need a husband, not a fading photograph, but a living, breathing man! I ask myself angrily: Why is that impossible? Why is it impractical? Why is it abnormal? Why shouldn't I? After all, I'm only 43 years old. Why should a Party member take pride in scrupulously abiding by feudal moral standards instead of doing away with them? Why must my happiness be locked up in a casket in order to gain the respect of others?

The pains of love filled me with courage. One day, as I was investigating a misjudged case at the Post and Telecommunications Office, I asked for and easily obtained his address. Then when the weekend arrived, I washed my hair and changed my clothes in the late afternoon, giving myself a once-over in the mirror. Yes, I was still young. There was even a youthful blush to my cheeks. Just as I was leaving I slyly splashed on a few drops of our daughter's cologne—ah! Please forgive me, dear Weiming! Look how shameless I've become!

I located the crude and simple room that he shared with his aging mother. Not having the nerve to even glance at the look of pleasant surprise on his face, I forced myself to tell him matter-of-factly that I just happened to be in the neighborhood and dropped by to say hello. I casually asked him why he no longer came by to pass the time of day and why he still hadn't resolved his "personal matter." All in all, I conducted myself rather foolishly and could feel my cheeks begin to burn. I knew that he was watching me attentively and could see right through my deception, not that it was all that clever in the first place. Beginning to feel extremely restless, I hastily said I had to be going.

He walked me out onto the secluded narrow street. My heart was refreshed by the early-summer evening breeze, making it feel younger, happier, and more sensitive than ever. I was waiting for him to speak, knowing that I'd be moved by anything he said. But his mood seemed gloomy, and he didn't say a word, seemingly lost in thought.

Suddenly, he let out a short, bitter laugh and said:

"I can't figure out why you're paying me this call. You're now the Director . . . if it's kindness you're giving, I don't need it."

I was stunned. Kindness! The word was like a dagger! Could it be that the change in my professional status automatically brought with it a change in the nature of my emotions? I was powerless to defend myself, and could only stare dumbly at him, as I began to feel cold all over. In that brief moment I felt that the ground between us had suddenly opened up and we were quickly being driven apart, separated by a fathomless chasm.

Had he misunderstood my actions? Had I been wronged? Was I disappointed? . . . No, Weiming! For someone deeply in love, this meant very little. In fact, his masculine reticence and personal self-esteem hit me like a bolt of lightning. He was even more worthy of respect than I had imagined, more precious and more admirable. Oh, I knew I had to break down his misconceptions about me, even if I had to abandon my most fundamental self-respect in the process. Had we been separated by a real chasm, I still wouldn't have hesitated to cross over.

Early the next morning I showed up again on his doorstep. No one was home, so he must have already left for work. I turned around dejectedly to leave. Suddenly I was stopped by a familiar and friendly subtle aroma. Oh, it was orchids. The delicate, dew-laden petals and green leaves were smiling at me! The aroma's silent explanation was so detailed, so moving!

Weiming! He and I fell quietly in love. But our love was beset by so many hardships! We didn't dare to be seen taking walks together, or going to a movie together, or being alone behind closed doors; we didn't even dare to take the slightest liberties when we talked. It goes without saying that we didn't have the nerve to squeeze one another's hand when we were in darkened corner of a stairwell where the lightbulb had been stolen. We had none of the freedoms to express our love that young people have, nor did we dare to strive to get them. All we could do was exchange ardent looks and listen to the happy beating of our hearts.

And even that was to be denied us!

Two weeks later, Lao Shi gave me a warning during a casual chat. First he expressed concern over my predicament, then praised me for being a model wife and mother, telling me how much I was respected by all the office cadres for safeguarding the reputation of "Secretary Weiming." He even used phrases like "upholding one's integrity in one's later years," which he intended as a clever pun. Finally he smiled and said, "There's talk about a postman who is five years younger than you . . . of course, it's just a rumor, and I trust you . . . "

That phony, sanctimonious grin of his nearly suffocated me.

Weiming, do you remember how sincere his smile was at our wedding, when the widowed Deputy Secretary of the Municipal Party Committee took as his wife a young nurse who was fifteen years his junior? For that matter, who didn't feel that ours was a marriage made in Heaven?

I didn't try to mask my irritation. Before he had even finished, I got to my feet and walked off. After work that day I made my way home very slowly, trying to figure out how to deal with them. I was surprised to find someone waiting for me at home—it was my old classmate, Yang Lili.

She had hardly changed at all. She was still slim and pretty and straightforward. Her warm embrace drove the unhappiness right out of my heart. How I had longed for a close friend to whom I could pour out my innermost feelings!

"What, you're still a widow? Are you trying to earn a memorial arch to commemorate your Confucian chastity, or is your heart really as dead as an ancient well, never again to be stirred by love?" She looked me over very affectionately. "You're not old," she said, "not old at all. That sort of foolishness is a waste of time, Lianghui! Weren't you the cleverest one among us back then? Back in the fifties we were mired in all those traditional concepts, dreaming about pure, true love, while you sneaked off and married a Party Secretary! Boy, in those days you were *the* topic of conversation! But afterwards we realized that you were the clever one, that yours had been the right way."

"No, Lili, no!" I hastily disputed her. "I believed then and I still believe today that pure, true love does exist!"

"*Sure* it does!" she said with a mocking laugh. "I've seen right through all that 'I pledge my eternal love, till death do us part' stuff!"

"What? You and that doctor you fell head-over-heels in love with aren't having troubles, are you?"

"We're divorced! He has the kids. And since I'm still young, I've found myself another one."

This took me completely by surprise. Just then I heard the sound of a car pulling up outside, followed by the deferential shout of a driver: "Comrade Yang! . . . "

"Coming, coming!" She glanced at her wristwatch. "I have to run. The old guy can't get along without me for a minute. Remember, if you feel like talking, you can call me long distance—just ask for Deputy Political Commissar Wang's home at the Provincial Military District switchboard. Lianghui, use your head. You don't have to coop yourself up here all the time. Take a trip over to the provincial capital and leave your cares at home. Your municipal guesthouse isn't as comfortable as my place!" She picked up her fancy purse, turned, and strode briskly out the door, the sound of her milky white high-heeled shoes tapping out a sense of contentment. I accompanied her down the stairs. "He's twenty years older than I," she said as she put her arm around my shoulder, "and his eldest daughter is just my age. But he's still physically fit. Why, he . . . " She fixed her eyes on me and whispered in my ear a couple of anatomical terms in Latin, then laughed raucously.

My face flamed with embarrassment, and I couldn't laugh at all—I wanted to cry. I had genuine doubts as to whether the silhouette of the woman slipping so easily into the back seat of the car really belonged to Yang Lili, my old classmate.

Weiming, I want you to know that the day after Lao Shi came by to talk to me, my romance was the topic of the day all over the Municipal Party Headquarters. News of it quickly spread in the halls, in the cafeteria, in the bathrooms, in the offices, even in conference rooms where they were discussing "practical standards." It traveled from ears to lips and back to ears, and even in that short distance the plot thickened and grew in true creative fashion. Legitimate love was thus transformed into an obscene scandal. That very day, as I was walking past the office of the Women's Federation, I overheard them loudly discussing "that loose woman," and the Director, the "representative of all the women in the city," was laughing louder than any of the others.

The Organization Bureau's reaction to this incident was swift. They asked me in for a talk, saying that in light of the citywide prestige enjoyed by the late Party Secretary, they were transferring me to the Municipal Political Consultative Conference as its eleventh Deputy Director (I don't know if this was Lao Shi's idea or not, but I'm sure he approved). It was obvious that they felt that the dignity of the entire Municipal Party Headquarters would suffer if I continued working there. Their sensitivity, concern, and decisiveness in this matter was at least thirty times greater than one of their official responses to an obviously misjudged case.

But I had not suffered through the ten-year calamity in vain. If I was able to endure being labeled the "stinking old lady of a traitor," why should I worry myself over the slanderous gossip everyone was spreading behind my back! In fact, it had the opposite effect on our love: the rumors, the reproaches, and the pressures brought to bear on us had the same effect as trying to douse a fire with alcohol. Before I had a chance to finish expressing my outrage to him, he rushed over to me, hugged me tightly, and said in a trembling voice:

"Let's get married! . . . "

"The sooner the better!" My voice was also trembling.

We kissed passionately, our hot tears running down our tightly pressed cheeks and mingling together.

Was this then the second time I had fallen in love? No, Weiming, it was the first! This is what love was supposed to be. Nothing else could be called love! All this "office director," "eleventh Deputy Director," department rankings, new houses and all the other fringe benefits, including, of course, that most glorious title of all—Communist Party member (which people these days have laughingly taken to calling a "Party meal ticket"!)—all of these things that I really have no right to claim, things that were bestowed upon me because of your position when you were alive or your posthumous influence—please take it all back! Allow me to return to my humble situation as a nurse. That's the only thing that will free me once and all from the humiliating fetters of "The husband's nobility brings glory to the wife!" and allow me to recapture my independence, my self-respect as a woman, and the right to love!

I wanted to shout this out boldly. In the Organization Bureau. In Lao Shi's face!

But, Weiming, when my prospective mother-in-law came over with a tear-streaked face and talked to me about something that was very painful to her, what did I have to shout about?

"Director . . . Zhou, you and I are both ill-fated women! I come from a poor, simple family, and when I was studying at a girls' trade school, I caught the eye of a military officer who took me as his mistress. He died on the eve of Liberation, leaving me and my only son. I don't have to tell you what our lives were like after that, you know perfectly well . . . Just knowing that you think highly of us, that you have shown us your kindness, is a debt of gratitude we—mother and son—can never repay. You've been a widow for many years, and as someone who has had the same experience, I know only too well how hard it's been for you. But the worst is over now, since your children are grown, and you should enjoy the years you have left to you. That child of mine has no sense. He can't have what he wants, but he won't settle for less—he's almost forty, yet he still acts like a little boy! How could he ever aspire to Director Zhou's heights? *Ai!* He's not really worthy . . ."

I looked at her silver strands and listened without saying a word. I understood only too well. She didn't want her son to marry a widow with children of her own. A widow was impure. A widow was unlucky. There was no honor in marrying a widow. And that, even though she herself had suffered through thirty years of widowhood!

I bit my lip, for my heart was screaming out, "No, no, I *am* pure! I *can* bring good luck! I want to fight for, create, and enjoy love and happiness, without a shred of shame! I'll have nothing to do with the widows' 'chastity coins' of your generation, venerable old mother!"

The moral codes of her generation had to die away. I was unafraid!

What does frighten me is the younger generation. Weiming, I am truly frightened by my own dear children!

Lanlan, with her young lady's sensitivity, was the first to detect it. Many times she looked searchingly at me with doubt in her eyes. One evening, as he and I were in the room sitting across from each other at the round table and listening to Schubert's "Serenade," Lanlan rushed in through the open door.

"It's already nine o'clock!" She snapped the radio off. "Mama, you need your rest."

Her face was deathly pale and her eyes sparkled with a cold, threatening light.

She had rudely chased off this "uncle" whom she had once affectionately snuggled up against. She had forgotten that it was this "uncle" who had ridden her over to the hospital on his bicycle when she had an acute lung infection, and had spent the entire night beside the makeshift bed they had set up for her in the corridor, until her condition had improved slightly; that it was this "uncle" who had mailed every parcel that was sent to her when she was working in the rural production team, and who had always included an expression of good wishes of the kind only a family member would send; that he had delivered every one of her letters to me with his own sweaty hand, bringing with them his heartfelt concern . . .

Now neither she nor Wangwang calls him "uncle." They refer to him as "that guy."

Unavoidably, the rumors eventually reached the children's ears. When I returned home from work one day, I heard Wangwang shout emotionally, "I refuse to believe it! Mama couldn't possibly be that shameless!"

Lanlan was sobbing loudly.

"If . . . if that really happened," Wangwang said, cracking his tender knuckles loudly, "I'll kill that guy!"

My heart froze. I supported myself on the door frame with trembling hands, unable to find the courage to enter the room.

From that day on, whenever Lanlan saw me, she turned a reproachful back to me. Either that or she'd avoid me by staying in her room and keeping the door tightly shut. As for Wangwang, he claimed that since he had to prepare for exams, he might as well stay at the home of a classmate.

I suffered the children's ostracism in silence. I wanted to take them aside so many times and have a heart-to-heart talk with them. I wanted them to understand and forgive their mother. Your mother doesn't want to stand in the way of your happiness, but she's a living, breathing human being who, like you, wants to find her own happiness! I went over and over what I wanted to tell them, but when I was face-to-face with them, the words wouldn't come. I couldn't muster up the courage. I was so afraid! . . . Oh, Weiming! A single child's tear is enough to extinguish a mother's ardent love, the lone sigh of a son or daughter is enough to dissipate a mother's resolve to fight for happiness!

Late last night Lanlan came into my bedroom, barefoot and with mussed hair, threw herself down beside me like a girl possessed, and sobbed, "Mama, why are you doing this? Why, Mama?" Her red and swollen eyes bored into me. "Are you afraid there'll be no one to take care of you? No one to be with you? No one to look after you? You have us! We'll take care of you, and be with you, and look after you. Dear Mama, please reconsider. Your own daughter is about to be married, so how can you remarry now? How could you stand all the talk? How could your daughter, your son-in-law, your own son face society? Mama, won't you even think about us? Dear Mama, your Lanlan is begging you, I'm begging you! Please do as I ask! . . . Mama, this is the last time I'll ask. If you really go through with . . ." Her choking sobs tore at my heart.

Oh God, dear God! Why are you so brutal, so cruel to an unfortunate widow, to a vulnerable, middle-aged woman, to a devout seeker of love, to an innocent child who has just barely become conscious of the dignity of human life!

I don't have the strength to go on. I've been bent over my desk writing since dusk—an entire night—shedding bitter tears and looking at your photograph. To whom can I pour out these feelings of mine? No one but you, Weiming! And you are beyond knowing, beyond feeling, and cannot answer me. Who knows, maybe I'm able to bare my soul to you without holding back precisely because you are beyond knowing, beyond feeling, and, except for smiling warmly, cannot answer me!

Dawn is about to break, for I can see the darkness begin to give way. The orchids are eagerly sending me their fragrance. Not to console me, but because it is their nature to greet the sun's rays. And me, how am I to greet my tomorrows?

I hope that another world exists there in the regions of darkness, and that somehow you will see this confusing letter of mine. In that world there should be no prestige associated with the Municipal Party Secretary and no charity bestowed to the low by those on high. In that case, answer me as an equal, as a friend; I'll be waiting here for you to enlighten me in my dreams!

Lianghui

Originally published in *Wenhui yuekan*, no. 1, 1981.

Translated by Howard Goldblatt and Ellen L. Yeung

The Tolling of a Distant Bell

by Zhang Kangkang and Mei Jin

Photo by Saundra Sturdevant

Twelve O'Clock

The great clock on the customs house struck. Its oppressive tolling collided with the cold winter night and resounded over the broad avenues.

"One, two, three, . . . ten, eleven." In the darkness, Ji Yuan opened her eyes and counted. The sound was vague and yet distinct. Once the ringing stopped, there was utter stillness again in all directions.

Yes, it was eleven, and her son Ji Dongping was still not home.

She reached out and turned on the little lamp at the head of the bed. Sitting up, she pulled a wrap over her shoulders and rested her back against the wall as she gazed out the window, as though this might make her wait seem shorter. She picked up the first book that came to hand and began to read, but after a few pages she still had no idea what it was about. Was it only because she was waiting for her son that she didn't feel like sleeping, weary as she was after teaching for a full day? She smiled wryly. Perhaps it was just habit. How many times had she waited like this a few years back, bitterly longing through the lonely nights for her son to suddenly come home from the Farm in Heilongjiang and never leave her. And yet that had been a blind and pitiful fantasy. For ten whole years, her son had left after every visit. During those years, other people's children managed to move back for all sorts of reasons, whether by special permission or because of some hardship. But Dongping had not. He had almost no qualification for returning to the city, only the fact that twenty-seven years ago his mother had divorced his father, an officer in the old army. Of course this didn't elicit sympathy from anyone—who asked him to be born the son of an officer in the old army? But she had gone on hoping, hoping in her dreams deep in the night, to the point that she often mistook the striking of the great clock on the customs house by the riverside not far away for the sound of her son knocking at the door. And yet, the great clock had finally been the bringer of good news. Not long ago, in the early winter of the second year after the fall of the "Gang of Four," her son had finally managed to come back, though only on sick leave, not to take over a job. But he wasn't sick at all, thank the stars, and even luckier, he hadn't been back in the city for a month when he got a job in a factory. The whole process took place with such amazing speed that people didn't dare believe it. It seemed as though some god were secretly helping this orphan boy and his widowed mother, who had been through every sort of hardship. Ji Yuan summed the whole thing up as "wise government." The times were different; government policy had changed, that was all. What was there to be suspicious about? She hoped that henceforth she would not hear the great clock ring again in the midst of her sound and peaceful sleep.

"Dong . . ." The sonorous stroke of the clock came through the night air.

It was eleven-thirty, and her son had still not come home.

But really, why did she have to go on waiting in such anxiety that her stomach churned, she asked herself. That a young fellow in his late twenties should go out to meet his girlfriend in the evening was a perfectly normal thing; why should his mother be so concerned? But no, life was not as simple as that. For the whole point of her son's meeting tonight was to break up with his girlfriend, to completely break off relations with her. Her son had almost wept when he agreed to do so. Ever since Ji Yuan had learned that the girl's cadre father was dead set against their engagement she had been forcing this decision on her son. She was a woman no less proud for her unfortunate station, and she had never gone with bowed head to beg from anyone.

She turned away from the darkened window lattice, shifting her attention to the room. Perhaps a dozen square yards in area, the little room was dark and cramped, and gave off a damp and moldy smell. The entire family property consisted of two beds, a square table, a dresser, and a few stools. She could hear the regular breathing of her daughter, sound asleep beside her. But who knew the bitter course over which she had dragged and carried her children these past few years? It seemed that Fate had decreed that she should always be waiting for something with deep longing.

She was vaguely aware that the clock had begun to strike again, twelve times. But no, it was the sound of rubber soles on the uneven planks in the hallway, those footsteps that she knew so well.

"Mother!" her son called out happily as he rushed in, bringing with him a blast of cold night air. His face was red from the cold, but his eyes sparkled with happiness.

"Mother, haven't you gone to sleep yet? Were you waiting for me? I've kept you up so late!" He threw off his cotton-padded overcoat in a rush and tossed his hat and muffler wherever they might land, at the same time saying emotionally, "I shouldn't have done it; several times I thought of saying to her, 'I'd better be going; I've got to go home!' But I couldn't get the words out of my mouth. We walked and walked along the river, until it seemed that we would walk until dawn and still not finish with all we had to talk about . . . Oh, Mother! Why are you looking at me like that?" He stopped suddenly, and stood there blankly.

Ji Yuan had prepared some words of consolation for her son in advance, and had them already formed in her throat, but not a word could she use. Her son was in such a joyful mood, not at all sad and depressed as she had imagined. She guessed why, and at once her heart shrank within her.

"Did you discuss it?" she asked coldly.

"What? Did we . . ." Her son stole a glance at her.

"You know very well what I mean."

There was nothing in the room but the ticking of the alarm clock.

Dongping stood in the center of the floor, one hand toying with the corner of his jacket, his face suffused with red, looking as though he had done something bad. His other hand he kept in his pocket, as though there were something precious inside. He lowered his head and stared at the tip of his shoe without saying a word.

"Dongping, raise your head and take a look at this house of ours," Ji Yuan said, speaking as tactfully as she could, though feeling her heart on fire. "Surely then you will understand why I want you and her . . ."

"No, Mother," Dongping said in sudden apprehension, "Mother, you can't be like this, you mustn't talk this way again. Ye Meng and I talked everything over tonight, everything, and she doesn't agree. She loves me; she loves me! Why do you want to force us apart? Why . . . ?"

For a moment Ji Yuan felt herself turn ice-cold inside. Now she understood—her son had repudiated their agreement. The promise that his mother's love and power had forced from him a few hours ago had come to nothing, submerged by the limitless tenderness of the person he loved. And in fact Ji Yuan had anticipated that this might happen. Didn't she understand the fiery love and snow-pure friendship that existed between these two young people? Why did she want to stand in their way after all? Why play an inglorious part so contrary to her own desires? But the situation was clear; if she didn't manage to work it all out as a mother truly should, the consequences would not bear thinking about. Ye Meng's father had been transferred back from a cadre school only last year, but in view of all the injustices he had suffered during the "Gang of Four" period, he had been made Chief of the Intermediate People's Court in one jump. Ye Meng's elder sister was married to the son of a Vice-Secretary of a Provincial Party Committee; her elder brother had wed the darling daughter of a Vice-Minister. This was Ye Meng's family. From their standpoint, wasn't the son of an officer in the old army, an unskilled worker without even a rating, really too humble? It was difficult to imagine how she, an impoverished elementary school teacher, was to walk into that luxurious parlor and sit down with them. No, she was absolutely unwilling. But of course what compelled her opposition was not her own self-respect, but the son whose very survival was bound up with hers. Was she really willing to look on at all the cares and frustrations he'd have to bear as a result of this unequal marriage? Once she had heard the attitude of Ye Meng's parents, she told her son in the most definite terms that Ye Meng would no longer be welcome in their home. Yes, she had taken the initiative in breaking off relations . . .

"You've made me wait for you for nothing," she said, heaving a deep sigh.

This remark actually made Ji Dongping, who had been standing aside for a long time, feel a sharp pang in his heart. He loved his mother and felt a twinge of remorse at having hurt her. His nose twitched, he bit hard on his lip and squatted down by the head of his mother's bed. Her hair had turned white at the temples, and wrinkles had spread like a spider's web over her forehead. And it was all from worrying too much for the sake of her two children. All the burdens that would be borne by the father in other families had been placed on her shoulders.

"Mother," he spoke softly, wanting to appear as considerate and gentle as possible, "Don't get angry now; let me finish what I have to say. Ye Meng isn't that kind of person, she's not like other cadres' daughters. We have suffered so many years together, I understand her . . ."

Ji Yuan looked tenderly at her son, and nodded without realizing it.

"We talked about so many things tonight, about when we first met, about the years we spent on the Farm, and also about our families. Everything is so much better now; the worst is over; why should we separate now, of all times? Why should we create unhappiness for ourselves? We've decided," he paused for a moment, as though making up his mind, and then said decisively, "we've decided to go ahead with it, to get married!"

Ji Yuan trembled once, like the echoing stroke of a deep bell, and said nothing for a long time. In her confusion she hardly knew what to do, and only got out a question, "And the attitude of her family, has it changed at all?"

"Changed?" His lip curled in a look of disdain. "How could it change? Her brother and sister have already begun introducing her to suitable partners. A Secretary's son here, the scion of a Chairman there, a whole string of them, all waiting to get on the scales to be weighed. Whichever one can raise her up, that's the one they want!" He muttered angrily, and then suddenly threw has arms sadly around Ji Yuan's neck, pressing his cold forehead against her chest, and murmured, "Mother, won't you let us get married!"

Ji Yuan said nothing. There was something thick and bitter trickling down her throat into her heart.

"Mother, dearest Mother, won't you agree!" He half knelt beside her bed, as he had when he was a little boy, begging her to let him go for a winter swim in the river. "If you don't agree, who will stand behind us? I love Ye Meng, I love her!"

Ji Yuan covered her eyes with one arm.

"Mother . . ." He shook her shoulder.

Ji Yuan bent over and covered her ears with the corners of the quilt.

"Mother!" He seemed to flare up a little, and blurted out, "You, you have forgotten the reason for your own unhappiness!"

Ji Yuan whirled around and sat up, her face deathly pale. She bit her lips and gave her son a deeply accusing look.

Dongping knew that he was in for it and ducked his head in embarrassment, saying, "I . . ."

"Don't say anything more, I understand perfectly . . ." Ji Yuan stroked his hair sadly, slightly shaking her head.

"Look!" As though to lessen the tension and make his mother forget her sadness of a moment past, he reached into the pocket of his padded jacket, fished something out, and put it in front of her. "Ye Meng just gave this to me. She said that it represents her heart. It's that gold watch I told you about before, the one that I helped her hide ten years ago when her house was being searched at the beginning of the Movement. She says that she is leaving the watch here as a token of our friendship, which began then."

Dongping put the watch gently into his mother's hands, probably so that she could see it a little more clearly. Ji Yuan lowered her gaze and glanced at it, without much wanting to. Suddenly the loose flesh on her face twitched, and she stared intently at the delicate gleaming golden watch chain. She shivered a while, and then reached out with two fingers to turn the watch over. Her hands trembled violently.

"Dongping, the lamp, bring it . . . bring it a little closer!" She was so agitated that her voice shook.

Her son bent the hand-made table lamp a little lower, wondering at the sudden change in his mother.

Ji Yuan had found a tiny letter "J" on the back of the watch; her heart pounded, and she almost fainted away. She pressed hard against the pit of her stomach, gasping for breath, leaned against the bed-post, and said faintly, "Where did this watch actually come from?"

"Ye Meng gave it to me. It's the thing that her father is most fond of, and he didn't give it to her until she was leaving for Heilongjiang."

"Ye Meng's father? What . . . what is his name?"

"Ye Heng, I think; yes, his name is Ye Heng, the 'Heng' written with the 'jade' radical and *hang*."

The gold watch slipped from Ji Yuan's hand and would have fallen to the floor but for a lucky quick catch by Dongping. When he looked up and discovered the look of misery on his mother's deathly pale face, he began to feel frightened in spite of himself.

"Mother, what's the matter?"

"Nothing. Go to bed, you should get some sleep. You still have to go to work tomorrow . . ." She spoke with great effort, and then reached out a trembling hand and switched off the light.

From outside came the tolling of the ancient bell; it was midnight.

Five-thirty

"Have you forgotten the reason for your own unhappiness?"

In the darkness, her son's large flashing eyes, still a little childish in appearance, stared at her with anger and resentment. The angry words that he had blurted out seemed to stab at her heart like a needle.

How could she forget? Perhaps happiness could be forgotten; but the enormous hurt that she had suffered, her whole crushed and ruined life, these were carved on her bones and heart, were part of her very existence, wounds that would not close until that eternal night that was so slow in coming.

There was just such a gold watch among her painful and humiliating memories, one whose gleaming yellow case and brilliant golden chain anyone would have admired. It was a present that her father, the owner of a jewelry shop, had given to her in the year of her eighteenth birthday. But it had never occurred to her then that all the pain she would suffer later would seem to flow out of its perpetual ticking. It was now fully thirty-two years since she had lost it, but it had left her more nostalgic longings and bitter memories than she could tell. It seemed that it was always grief that was wound up with its spring. In thirty-two years her pain had never ceased; indeed, it had grown heavier with each passing day. She had thought that she would never see the watch again in this life, but like a substance endowed with intelligence it had suddenly reappeared before her, shedding its light in all directions, dazzling and confusing. How had it made its way back to her?

Her son turned over, snorted, and mumbled something, and then sank back deep into his dreams.

After thirty-two years, the bitter dream that she had reviewed almost daily during her still sleepless hours late at night seemed to be as clear as though it were yesterday.

She had met him in her last semester of high school. It was the second year after the end of the War of Resistance,* and at last it was possible to study in school without worrying. One day in late autumn, when the scent of bay trees floated on the air, she had gone to a pond behind the school to memorize classical poems. As she chanted them, she caught sight of a boy student concealed behind a rock, studying, his tattered cloth shoes exposed to view. He was so absorbed in what he was doing he hadn't even noticed that a crimson centipede was crawling up his back toward his neck. Ji Yuan saw it clearly, shouted in alarm, and brushed it off onto the ground with her own handkerchief. He looked at her, nodded gratefully, and then buried himself in his book again. Ji Yuan was thoroughly surprised. She wondered what book could be so absorbing, and when she snuck a look, she discovered that it was Serafimovich's *The Iron Flood*.**

"Is it interesting? What's it about?" she couldn't help asking.

His face reddened slightly. "Of course it's interesting. Do you want to read it?"

"Would you lend it to me?"

"Why shouldn't I? But take good care of it."

---

* It was 1947—ed.
** A. S. Serafimovich (1863–1949)'s principal work, *The Iron Flood*, was first published in 1924 and became a classic of Soviet literature. It is a novel of unstinting optimism that portrays the masses as the heroes of history. See Edward J. Brown, *Russian Literature Since the Revolution* (Cambridge, MA: Harvard University Press, 1982), pp. 122-125.

And so they got to know each other with a book as a go-between. Later, the bank of the pond on campus became their usual meeting place. As time went on, she learned that he was in the next class, and that his name was Zhao Yeheng. He was three years older than she; his father was a stevedore. He had had to drop out of school twice because of difficulties at home, but he had read quite a few books, mostly recently translated Soviet literary works. These he introduced to Ji Yuan, and henceforth a new world opened up before her. She had grown up in a feudal home in which money came before all else. It was probably in order to get a better price for her that her jeweler father had sent her to school. He hadn't foreseen that it would be books and school that would lead her to understand the inequalities of the world and make her wish to break free of her feudal family. Zhao Yeheng's friendship lent her greater courage to struggle with Fate. The callousness of her family increasingly pushed her into his arms. But their contacts were somehow disclosed to her father, and she received a vicious beating at home. Afterwards she snuck out to see the boy and told him what had happened as she wept on his shoulder. He embraced her tightly and said, "Yuan, let's go together to the liberated area in northern Jiangsu!" She was so deliriously happy that she wept, feeling that there really was hope for her life. Although she was not very politically aware at the time, and didn't know that Zhao Yeheng had long since become an underground Party member, her whole heart still longed for the equality and freedom of the Liberated Area. Their love could not be contained in a kingdom of darkness, but tended necessarily toward the world of light. They decided to leave and agreed to meet on a certain day beneath the clock tower of the customs house, at seven in the evening. She was so excited by the prospect of the two of them spreading their wings and flying off together that she couldn't sleep for several days running.

But she never dreamed that just as she was packing her little suitcase and set to leave within a few hours, her father would lock her in her room and shout abuse from outside the door. "Cheap little trash! Giving things away while you live off us! Just see if you can get away from me!" Nor did he pay any attention to her, no matter how desperate her pleading. Only then did she realize that the whole family had been spying on her all along. The agreed-upon time had almost come, but her room was upstairs, with only a narrow window on the high wall facing the courtyard; how could a weak young girl escape from such a cage? The clock on the customs house struck seven, eight, nine. She collapsed on her bed, almost faint from weeping. As the sky began to grow light the next day, she was startled awake by the sound of terrible shouting in the courtyard. She could just hear her father saying, "What makes you think you're a fit match? In marriage the parties must be of equal status; that has always been the rule!"

Ji Yuan knew that he had come, that in the end he couldn't bear not to force his way into the courtyard. Perhaps he had waited for her all night under the clock tower. She heard his voice arguing and shouting, that voice so dear to her. But what use was it? Young people's happiness was worth no money in the eyes of the jeweler. She wanted to shout, but couldn't make a sound; her legs grew weak and her hands numb. Her heart was about to break in pieces . . .

Her father's voice came again, "Here, take this money for your traveling expenses. We won't pay any attention to where you go. Just don't bother her any more . . ."

She could hear only a single furious word from Zhao Yeheng, "Shameless!" The thick red lacquer door shut heavily. She called his name out once as though her very heart would shatter, and collapsed on the floor in a faint.

Only half conscious, she felt someone gently picking her up. When she opened her eyes, she saw it was Mu, the maid servant who brought her meals upstairs. In her desperation, she fumbled for the gold watch that hung on her chest and said to Mu, "Quickly, quickly, follow him, and give this to him; it is my heart. Wish him, farewell . . ."

She had already given up hope for her own struggle, and only longed for him to get away quickly, to escape to the land of freedom. She was sure then that her father was planning to marry her to an army officer. When she heard Mu tell her that the watch was in his hands, a smile played across her wretched face.

She spent a full two months closed up in that gloomy little attic, and in the end submitted to her father's will. It was not that she wanted to go on living at any cost, but that among the countless times she had wished for death, there had been born a faint hope that she would again meet Zhao Yeheng. In a way, a wish that simple had actually sustained her through all the rest of her life.

On the night before her wedding, she stole out of the house and ran to the customs house clock tower. She knew that she would not find him there, but it seemed as though the deep tolling of the bell sustained the love buried in her heart and poured out all her longing for him. It was in the depth of winter, and a heavy snow filled the air; the clock tower loomed up in the dark lowering sky, groaning painfully. She seemed like a kite with a broken string, floating away one knew not where. He, someone who had once led her toward the light, had in the end abandoned her to this boundless black night, while he went away into the sunshine. Did this mean that she blamed him? No, she cherished her eternal love and longing for him all the same. Then did she blame herself? After careful thought, she felt that to do so would be unfair. Of course it was her merchant family and her heartless father that were to blame. But not entirely, for wasn't "equal status" the real principle behind this society? Parents who wanted to maintain appearances in this society naturally had to respect the unwritten law followed for thousands of years.

The great clock sounded, a distant tolling, as though sobbing or complaining. She went back home. The happiness that she had once dreamed of seemed like the fallen leaves swept up by the north wind and blown away into the muddy river.

Less than three years after her marriage to the army officer, the whole country was liberated. In response to the new age, her once dead soul began slowly to revive. Perhaps because of the single pitiful hope still cherished in her heart, she resolutely divorced her husband after two years, and began to raise her son and daughter on just the meager salary she earned as an elementary school teacher. She invested all her hopes in her children. She toiled for the sake of their future happiness. For her, the whole significance of this happiness would lie in equality and respect between people and in not repeating the tragedy of her era. At times, she herself felt that her narrow understanding of happiness was a little ridiculous. But she couldn't help it. The brand that suffering had left on her heart was too deep. Once lost, love is a thing not easily found again.

Ji Yuan gently brushed a few tear-drops from her cheeks.

She heard the customs house clock sound, but didn't know what time it was. Perhaps it was getting towards daybreak; with her frail nerves, the slightest occasion was enough to bring before her eyes each and every old score accumulated over the years.

But what had raked up these painful memories tonight was really no slight occasion. The gold watch that had once carried away all the happiness she had known in life had now reappeared as though by a miracle. It brought with it the hopes of her lost thirty-two years.

Was it really her watch? She did not dare believe it. And yet the letter engraved on it was real.

Then was Ye Meng really his daughter? Was Ye Heng really him, Zhao Yeheng? She pondered and speculated, turning over in bed unable to fall asleep.

She suddenly remembered how, in the first year of the Cultural Revolution, after the disturbances over the "Four Olds"* had passed and the attack had been turned towards the "Capitalist Roaders," she had come home from school one day and noticed that the battered trunk in the attic had been moved. Full of concern, she questioned her son about it. Most mothers were concerned in those days. Although the dangerous period of suspicion that her family had incurred because of the "reactionary army officer" was already past, she still lived each day with her heart in her mouth.

"Nothing important, Mother. I . . . just hid something," her son replied calmly. He was already grown up, grown into a handsome young fellow with a pair of penetrating eyes that flashed beneath his thick black hair. He had shown intelligence from early childhood, and his marks in school were always outstanding. At the time he had just turned sixteen.

"Hid something? What was it?"

"Just . . . a watch. It belongs to one of my fellow students. She was afraid that it might be confiscated in a house search, and the only thing she could do was leave it with me."

She didn't blame her son; he was honest and sincere, and after all, had she herself ever failed to sympathize with people in difficulty? She sat down quietly, then suddenly asked, as though just remembering something that had been on her mind, "A fellow student? Is she a good friend of yours?"

"No, not really. Her whole family moved here from the North at the beginning of eighth grade. She was really stuck up and looked down on every one. We shared a desk, but she didn't say a word to me for a whole semester." He went on talking enthusiastically, always eager and earnest in telling his mother about things in his class. "One time she got sick and didn't come to school for quite a few days. When she got better, a car brought her to school, and that's how we found out that her father was actually some kind of big official. Whew! She was just like a little lady. She was awfully upset about having fallen behind, and it was only after I helped her catch up that she started talking to me. But you know what some students said? They said that I was making up to her."

"Dongping!" Ji Yuan cried out. She felt as though her heart had been injured. She had heard those words before, twenty years ago, when her fellow students abused Zhao Yeheng. At first she had thought that the wounds suffered by her generation could no longer exist in the new society, and yet during the past ten years there had never been a moment when she was not aware of a kind of new pressure, as she perceived ever more clearly the gulf in status that stretched between her children and those of other people. Her heart ached. She asked, with a frown, "Then, why, why are you still helping her?"

"Well, Mother, afterwards the situation changed. After her father fell from power, no one in class would pay any more attention to her. The class held a meeting to criticize her, and I was the only one who didn't speak. What could I say? She hadn't done anything wrong herself."

Ji Yuan didn't hear what he said after that. Her thoughts wandered off far, far away. Women are prone to feel sympathy in cases similar to their own, even if the similarity is only slight and uncertain. Could she say that her son had done the wrong thing? When his fellow student ran into bad luck, he had extended a friendly hand to her. Well, after all, wasn't he just taking after his mother?

After the storm had passed, Dongping brought his fellow student home to visit. She was a delicate young girl wearing a blue corduroy jacket and black cloth shoes, looking very simple and tasteful. Her eyes were full of wonder as she walked into the room; she was extremely interested in the little attic, chuckling as she scrambled up into it. Ji Yuan had taken a great liking to her from the first time she saw her, but she found an excuse to leave. She was afraid that a mother's inappropriate warmth of interest might arouse needless complications in the children's pure friendship. She was also very much aware of the distinction in status and circumstances between her son and a cadre family. This kind of distinction was almost as rigid and unchangeable as twenty years before.

If she had only known that the watch her son had hidden was linked to her in a matter of life and death! Why hadn't she taken a look at it? She couldn't have dreamed that a thing that she yearned for day and night, something she couldn't have found by searching even if she had worn through a pair of iron shoes, was actually slipping away under her very nose. That mistake alone had cost twelve years. Her son had grown up, and she had become an old woman.

The great clock sounded again, "Dong . . . dong . . . ," seeming to break up the heavy darkness and let a little light in. Ah, it was five o'clock. The window had turned faintly grey, and the noise of the first tram could be heard as it rolled past on the street, with the faint sound of talk and laughter from the early shift of street cleaners.

As for what had happened later, she couldn't explain it very clearly. Her son had never talked about how he and Ye Meng had become close during those twelve years. At the least, they had gone off to Heilongjiang together, and had often come back together to visit their families. Ye Meng sometimes came to their little room to help her with a few chores. She had become very proficient. Ye Meng spoke very little about her father; Ji Yuan knew only that he was still at cadre school. This could hardly fail to make her feel a measure of sympathetic affection for the girl. One time she couldn't help asking Ye Meng, "Is Dongping really so good?" The girl opened her eyes wide and said very seriously, "Of course he is. He is good-hearted, happy to help other people, and never indulges in idle talk. On the Farm he drives an 'East is Red' and fixes it himself whenever it breaks down." Her face suddenly reddened and she gave a little snort through her nose, "Mrs.

---

* The "Four Olds"—old ideas, old culture, old customs, old habits—were among the principal targets of the Cultural Revolution.

Ji, do you think I could like one of those little gentlemen from our circle? I saw right through them a long time ago." Ji Yuan walked away, her eyes brimming with tears. The girl had a mind of her own, but then the two of them were still in Heilongjiang. At the beginning of 1977, everything changed. Ye Meng's father returned to the city and took up his old post again, and Ye Meng was transferred back soon after. But they remained in love. As proof of her unchanged feeling for Dongping, Ye Meng often came to visit Ji Yuan, but Ji Yuan seemed to have already recognized the latent peril, and the change that was about to take place. She forced herself to treat the girl with an attitude that would keep her at a distance. Finally Ye Ming stopped coming. But her heart remained unchanged. Her letters reported to Dongping the wrong she suffered and the prejudice his eccentric mother had against her. Ji Yuan knew all this.

But, what really had linked the fates of these two young people? In fact they should not have been brought together. Ji Yuan kept asking herself this in the midst of her sharp mental conflicts. Had she not been thrown from her cosy little nest by that great upheaval, the young lady might never have had occasion to come into their humble little room. Once her father came on hard times, she fell into difficulties after him. She had gotten to know Dongping in the midst of her troubles, and had seen his pure heart. She hadn't been able to see it at first, and hadn't needed to.

That glowing golden watch once more appeared before her, and suddenly she felt as though she were suffocating. Was it possible that they, the young people of different status joined thirty-two years before by no more than a copy of *The Iron Flood* could only bridge the gulf between them in the sixties, through a great revolution soaked in bloodshed and ten years of upheaval and hardship? And yet, once the disaster was over, high walls rose again where there had been level ground, and the Heavenly River in the human world went on flowing as before, just like the one that divides the Herd Boy and Weaving Maid stars in the sky.* Didn't Ye Meng's father, her family, the stories of what had happened to the children of various cadres, didn't they all make that plain?

"No!" Ji Yuan cried out, "It isn't him, it can't be!"

Her son rolled over; had she awakened him? She calmed down.

"No, Ye Meng's father absolutely could not be Zhao Yeheng. The golden watch absolutely could not be his. Perhaps it had come into someone else's hands during the war years," Ji Yuan comforted herself. It wasn't that she didn't believe that such a coincidence could occur, but that she was positive of this much; the Zhao Yeheng who had personally suffered persecution from the feudal concepts of power and family influence could never under any circumstances come to embrace the concept of "equal status" as some cadres did. She would die rather than believe that.

She seemed to be feeling a little better and lay down for a while. But eventually she couldn't restrain herself and got up quietly, walked to her son's bed, and nudged him gently, "Dongping, Dongping . . ."

---

* The Herd Boy and the Weaving Maid are Chinese constellations that symbolize both love and longing; they are only seen together around the seventh day of the seventh lunar month.

Her son grunted several times and opened his eyes, still heavy with sleep.

"Get up and write a letter, a letter to Ye Meng." She spoke urgently, unable to control her agitation. "Arrange for her to come out this evening, and ask about her family in detail, ask about her father's background, whether he ever used a different name . . ."

Her son opened his mouth in puzzlement.

"Be a good boy; write quickly and send it by the morning mail truck. You know, I was too hasty before; if you inquire carefully, perhaps, perhaps I may reconsider your problem."

"Really?" Her son jumped up at once.

"Dong . . . " the great clock struck; five-thirty. Dawn would be breaking soon.

Seven O'clock

JI Yuan passed the entire day in a state of restless impatience. When she read the text out loud in her language class, she actually read several words incorrectly, something that had never ever happened in the past. Never had she so greedily longed to hear the sound of the customs house bell.

The north wind was blowing through the sparse bare branches of the tall phoenix trees, whipping the last snow into her face head-on. It was already midwinter, and where winter plum blossoms thrust themselves up from behind a high courtyard wall, they seemed like frozen stars on a curtain of night.

From far away, Ji Yuan caught sight of the lamp burning in the window of her home. Her daughter was on the middle shift today and couldn't be home yet. Her son's factory was far away; he never came home before it was pitch dark. He must have come back quite early today because he had his meeting with Ye Meng on his mind. She hastened her steps, and hurried up the stairway. As soon as she pushed open the door, she saw Dongping washing his face.

"What time are you meeting?" she asked anxiously.

"Seven o'clock, sharp."

"Oh, OK," she said, in a monotone, "You don't need to go."

"What?"

"I'll go. There are a few things that you wouldn't be able to get clear answers about."

She had been planning to do this for some time already; why not go and question the girl on her own? Everything could be settled very quickly. Seeing her son standing there blankly, his face a picture of doubt, she smiled and said soothingly, "Don't worry. I won't give her any trouble. Where are you to meet?"

"Under the bell tower of the customs house clock."

Ji Yuan's face went white. She turned quickly away. Always, without meaning to, life touches the sore spot in a person's heart.

She looked up and saw the little alarm clock read five after six. She hurried to get some dinner together for her son, but couldn't swallow a bite herself. Her heart pounded continuously, and her hands trembled uncontrollably. "What's wrong with me?" she asked herself. Why did she want to go meet Ye Meng in her son's place after all? Just because it was beneath the customs house clock tower, a secret and remote place deeply hidden in her heart?

She put on her overcoat and made up her mind to take a

look at herself in the little old cracked mirror. She had certainly grown old; her hair was white and her face haggard and colorless. Those eyes that had once been clear as an autumn stream were now tired and lifeless. The passage of time is so pitiless to people.

She shook her head slightly, but just as she reached the door, suddenly stood still.

"Dongping, give it to me," she said softly.

"What?"

"That watch."

He got the watch from beneath his pillow and put it gently in his mother's hand. The icy feeling of the metal made her shiver suddenly, as though in premonition of something unfortunate. She put the watch quickly into an inner pocket and left without saying anything. Why did she want to take it with her? What was it she wanted to ask Ye Meng? She herself didn't know.

The customs house clock tower was not too far from her house, two bus stops at most. She walked very quickly, with her head lowered, looking as though her heart were filled with some pain that so weighed her down she could not straighten her back. She suddenly began to regret that she had come. The cold wind on a winter night, the clock tower, seven o'clock sharp . . . All aroused the recollection of so many bitter bygone things. But what grieved her most was that thirty-two years before it was from here that she had not been able to fly away with her lover; and thirty-two years later, she was taking this road to accept the same sort of pain for her son.

The looming black shape of the clock tower rose up under the dark sky, gloomy and silent. The grey river showed pale blue shimmers of ripples as it flowed murmuring to the east. In the strong wind under a dark sky, the avenue so bustling in daylight was now silent and deserted. She rushed toward the tower, having already seen the shape of someone pacing back and forth below it. She crossed the road and called out, for the sake of courtesy, "Ye Meng, I've kept you waiting!"

The shape stopped moving. But it didn't come happily forward in welcome as she had imagined. He turned slowly, and only after the street lamp shone directly on his dark blue embossed woolen greatcoat, gleaming leather shoes, and well-preserved face wrapped in a thick, woolen muffler did Ji Yuan realize that she had mistaken him for someone else. This was a man of middle age, no, perhaps a little more than middle age. He was probably a senior cadre; there was a car parked not far away . . . oh no, no . . .

In a panic, Ji Yuan clutched a telephone pole beside her and rubbed her eyes. For a moment it seemed that her mind had played a trick on her; what had she seen? No, no this was something that couldn't possibly be true.

"You are . . ." The man stepped forward graciously with a charming, friendly smile. He extended his hand to her.

She saw him clearly now—the square face, the firm straight nose, the black mole amid his slightly drooping brows. Yes, it was he, he for whom she had longed through thirty-two bitter years. The hardships of the years and months had really not left that much of a mark on his face; his hair was still black, and the outline of his face still plump and full. What had changed was that his slightly smiling eyes seemed so cold and distant.

"You are . . . ," he said again. Yes, it was his voice, completely unchanged, rich and gentle, as it had been thirty-two years before. Yes, he was Ye Meng's father.

She leaned her entire weight against the telephone pole and said in a weak, almost inaudible voice, "I am . . . Ji Dongping's mother; he . . . is sick."

She stared directly into his eyes, sought his gaze, hoping that he would recognize her.

But he wasn't looking at her at all. His eyes, stern and solemn, were on the lights on the opposite bank. No, he hadn't recognized her; perhaps she had changed too much. He coughed once, rubbed his hands, and said mildly, "It's all right, your coming makes no difference. Mm . . . I've been meaning to look your son up and have a chat with him for a long time now, but our Meng . . . well, when Ji Dongping's letter arrived today at nightfall, she happened not to have come home yet, so I thought . . . well, that this would be a good time for me to come and talk with him."

Ji Yuan felt her heart sinking lower and lower, the blood in her veins turning cold, until it seemed as though it would freeze. Her whole body felt cold, and her teeth began to chatter.

"It seems to me, well, perhaps you and your son have not recognized the fact for a long time, but really, well, our household is really not a suitable one for him and Ye Meng to go on maintaining this sort of relationship. Naturally the reasons are many and various, and we needn't spell them out." He spoke with assurance and warmth, without ever looking at her. "Of course, the responsibility lies chiefly with us, with Ye Meng."

The last faint ember of flame in her heart went out. The world lay pitch black before her eyes. She buried her face in her hands, wanting to weep, but unable to. It was not that she was hurt by the destruction of some fond hope for a lucky bit of charity from Ye Meng's father, but because the man saying these things to her was none other than the Zhao Yeheng whom she had loved so deeply thirty-two years before.

"You mustn't get the wrong idea about us." He pulled out a handkerchief and dabbed at his nose, showing that he too was somewhat distressed. "You really shouldn't get the wrong idea. We are certainly not the sort of people to be unreasonable." He stopped for a moment, and seemed to be choosing his words carefully, "You and Dongping may not be aware of it, but the procedures for his return to the city and the arrangements for his job were all taken care of with our help. Our Meng knows this, but she hasn't been willing to tell you, so it has been left to me to explain it now."

Ji Yuan uttered a faint "oh," stiff with fear.

He took a few steps with his hands behind his back, speaking as he had become accustomed to doing to his subordinates, "I've discussed all this with Meng's mother a number of times, and we believe that Dongping's sincere attachment to Meng is understandable. Therefore we want to do everything that lies within our power. That way, Ye Meng will be treating Dongping fairly, wouldn't you say? Now, go home and try to persuade your son not to come to see Ye Meng anymore."

Ji Yuan shuddered violently, so angry that her entire body shook. So he had actually come to clear his account with her. She suddenly had a feeling that she had heard these words somewhere before. Where had it been? She went on wondering absent-mindedly, but couldn't recall where.

"All right, let's leave it at this. Young people are governed by their feelings, but they may grow out of them slowly later. You are older, and should realize that the distinction between us has an objective existence."

There lept into her mind the words that she had heard her father say to the poor young man in the courtyard from her high window in that dusky morning thirty-two years before. Then he had left in anger at the insult he had received; how could he say this kind of thing now? Of course he didn't feel that he was insulting them, what he held in his hands were not jewels, but . . . but what was it? Something that money couldn't buy. God! How superior he was to that despicable jeweler! Ji Yuan hung her head in dejection, feeling the world spinning about her with a wave of nausea. She had lived for fifty-one years, and yet been so naive. She had hated her father all her life, hated his cruelty, unable really to understand why he had wanted to destroy the happiness of two young people. But now she suddenly understood. Her father had said, "The parties must be of equal status; that has always been the rule!" Was this really the answer that she had been unwilling to accept through thirty-two years of pain?

The car's horn suddenly gave a honk, and she awakened with a start. She saw Zhao Yeheng, no, Ye Meng's father, look at his watch and say to her with a very apologetic air, "Excuse me; I have another appointment at seven-thirty. Do you have anything more to say?"

Her lips moved once, but made no sound. Did she have anything more to say? Hadn't he said very clearly everything that needed to be said? She realized only now that she had made a serious mistake this morning at five-thirty. Of course this was a father who would not let his daughter receive Dongping's letter; that was something she hadn't thought of. Without intending to, she touched the ice-cold golden watch in her pocket, and her heart fluttered involuntarily. Perhaps she should bring out the watch and tell him who she was, tell him everything! What sort of scene would that lead to? Perhaps everything would change at once. Had she longed for him for so many years only to part like this? There was not much time left; if she let this opportunity slip, perhaps it would never come again. Tell him, not to change things, but to make him feel ashamed.

But she gave up these ideas at once. Across her worn and pallid face there flickered a trace of a proud smile. The watch had already been returned to its rightful owner along with all the love once conferred upon it; what need was there to disturb that carefree and complacent soul again? Stupid! Besides, the watch really was no longer hers; it had now become a symbol of the love between two faithful hearts, and no one had the right to dispose of it. It belonged in common to the son of a good mother and the daughter of a "well-intentioned" father.

She raised her head and straightened her muffler.

He asked, with a show of great concern, "Shall I have the car take you part way?"

"There's no need to," she replied, indifferently.

When she had taken only a few steps, she heard the car door slam heavily behind her. As the car sped past, he nodded to her politely from inside. A puff of black exhaust burst from behind it, and it drove quickly away.

Ji Yuan stood motionless in the cold wind for a long time, silently watching the car vanish into the endless darkness.

The stars had come out, and the vast Milky Way spread out across the breadth of the sky, cold and remote.

"After all, there is no Heavenly River to separate lovers in the human world!" she suddenly thought angrily, "Why do we still make our children suffer again the same unhappiness that we knew?"

She felt that she wanted to see Ye Meng, that decent and charming young girl, more than she ever had. She would take the girl into her home herself, ten square yards, it didn't matter, she and her daughter could sleep in the attic. For the sake of the happiness that she herself had once lost, she was willing to pay a higher price in her desolate old age than ever before. As for Ye Meng, that cadre's child "not like the others," how long she would stay in that simple little room, whether or not she would run back home, that was a problem for the young people themselves.

"Dong . . . dong . . . " The great clock on the customs house struck, the long reverberation dying slowly away in the air over the quiet city. Yes, seven o'clock, on the dot. The bell went on tolling and tolling in her ears, and as she listened it seemed to her just as thirty-two years before the sound of oppression, and of rage. ★

Originally published in *Shiyue (October)*, no. 3, 1980.

Translated by Daniel Bryant

THE SYSTEM

For me, the most splendid tribute to human dignity was something I saw on a mountain top in Peloponnesia. It was not a piece of sculpture or a flag, just the three Greek letters oxi *meaning "no."*
—Orianna Fallaci

        Living
A net
—Bei Dao

Hu Yaobang's speech at the 1980 Drama Forum contained a lengthy theoretical discussion of the correct way for writers to treat the twin problems of "bureaucratism and special privileges" (*guanliao zhuyi* and *teshuhua*). His position in brief was that these perennial evils of Chinese government could and should be criticized, but that such fictional criticisms should never imply that "bureaucratism" was a systemic problem or that the Chinese Communist Party represented some sort of specially privileged new class. Yet, two years later, at the Twelfth Congress, the Party leadership announced a new Rectification Campaign to purge the ranks of those Party members who cultivated their own personal interests rather than wholeheartedly serve the people.

The high tide of broadside attacks on cadre "special privileges" had gradually declined during 1980, but in 1981 and afterwards writers continued to produce rather more oblique critiques which were in fact sometimes much more successful as literature than some of the earlier exposés. The young, new writer Dai Qing's "No!" (*Bu!*) is a good example. The story never denies the good intentions of the "old revolutionary cadre" Liu Dayong, but the sad consequences of his thirty years of "perfect loyalty," of never saying "no!" to any Party directive however wrongheaded or cruel, is made abundantly clear through the revelation of his inner musings, recollections, and guilt. Dai seems to be telling us that this is a kind of unthinking loyalty that the Party can no longer afford to cultivate as it attempts to make China a truly modern nation.

Qiao Shi's "Providing a Meal" (*Guanfan*) gives another glimpse of how "the system" works and extends the neo-realist exposure of rural poverty from the Cultural Revolution all the way down to 1979. It seems to imply the complete failure of the Maoist revolution in the countryside through the weary Yan'an cadre's bitter words, "If our poor peasants are supposed to consider it their glory to be poor forever, then why did we need a revolution?" Earlier in 1979, the New China News Agency revealed that the average food grain allotment was less in 1977 than in 1957. This story provides a powerful image of those statistics in simple existential terms—eating coarse-grained porridge for thirty years.

Although she had authored two rather long and uninspiring

novels in 1974 and 1978, Shen Rong, now forty-nine, was catapulted to fame by her prize winning 1980 novella "Reaching Middle Age" (*Ren dao zhongnian*). It describes the unjust treatment of middle-aged professional cadres, who were branded "stinking intellectuals" during the Cultural Revolution, even though they were the backbone of China's modernization. Having pushed to the edge of political acceptability with that relatively critical story, she has subsequently written fiction whose critique is more subtle and reserved and whose denouements are more hopeful.

"Troubled Sunday" (*Fannao de xingqiri*) exemplifies another salient feature of her fiction—her ability to integrate personal and family life with the central social issues of the day. In this story the endemic problem of seeking special favors through personal "connections" (*guanxi*) or "going through the back door" (*zou houmen*) interferes with the leisurely Sunday routine of a leading cadre who happens to be the grandfather of a three-year-old who wants to go to the park. Once again, as in most works of critical realism, we are not offered any easy solution to the problem raised.*

★

---

* My thanks to the translator, Vivian Hsu, for her assistance with this passage on Shen Rong.

No!

by Dai Qing

Photo by Saundra Sturdevant

Night—still and silent, but a night on which the slightest sound could be heard: the tick-ticking of the clock, the humming of the watch by my pillow, the rustle of leaves outside the window, "krggt-ptt"—someone in the distance spitting into the night.

Liu Dayong was accustomed to waking at this hour. Was it midnight? One o'clock? The soft pillow, the soft bed, and this soft, light, fluffy eiderdown quilt. He didn't like it. It had no substance. It was like having no cover it all, yet it made his feet hot and clammy. He didn't like the feel of it when he turned over, the slippery, silky nylon rubbing against his shoulders, with an oily feel. It was no match at all for the thick, home-spun cotton quilt he remembered from his hometown days. Then there was the smoky smell of the adobe *kang** and the mats on it, browned from use. Ah! What perfect, unrestricted comfort.

The huge floor lamp cast a soft light on the deep-purple rug. The lampshade was a cross between red and blue, and Li Ying insisted on burning it through the night for him. On the day she installed it, he snored lightly pretending to sleep, but he overheard the entire discussion conducted in whispered tones. Li Ying wanted a light green one, but her young daughter-in-law protested that it clashed with the rug and insisted that it be exchanged.

"Huh! She thinks she will inherit it after I'm dead, the little hussy," Liu thought to himself, lying there with a gurgling sound in his throat as they haggled.

He felt out of sorts with Li Ying, this wife twelve years his junior. Catching sight of her sparse, thinning hair which she kept in little curls all over her head, he quickly turned his head away. For many years Li Ying had kneaded him in her hands with deliberate soft-spoken tones and a gentle, patient manner. Three meals a day turned into five. There was plain-woven silk in summer, cotton-padded silk in winter, a Simmons mattress, a rug, a lamp kept burning through the night, and a cabinet full of medicines. With respect to his body, which he thought of as a machine, the situation couldn't be more clear. His "machine," true enough, was still in operable condition, but it was too old, too worn; it had known too much wear and tear. A machine like this was beyond the point where it could be maintained merely by providing it with the best lubricant and keeping it touched up with a little shiny varnish. That would be the equivalent of replacing the gears regardless of the condition of the main drive-shaft or the motor. You just can't replace everything.

"When your time is up, it's up," he thought. His father had been more and more on his mind recently, a man who had never known disaster or illness. He died peacefully on the *kang* that served him as a bed all his life, without a trace of pain on his face. Death is something every man must come to terms with on his own, or at the very least leave to the hands of Old Man Heaven, but in his case it was all in Li Ying's hands. The cupboard was full of bottles of all sizes and colors—round ones, flat ones, tubes and liquids. Medicines of all types had gone down his throat year after year, but to no avail. What was the use, after all, of trying to sustain a body that would never have a second lease on life? For the glory of the medical profession? Not very likely. For the revolution? For work?

"Commissar Liu, we need you and so does the revolution . . . ," uttered the iron-legged Regimental Commander who made a special trip from distant Guizhou to visit him a year ago when this wretched ailment—cerebral thrombosis complicated by hemiplegia—suddenly flared up. Even the sun-scorched cheeks of this rare man of iron constitution, moved by some unknown emotion, were wet with tears. "Commissar Liu. . . ," Leopard called out in a hoarse voice, his contorted face exposing his snow-white teeth. He had been called

---

* A *kang* is a Northern Chinese bed made of adobe brick under which a fire can be built.

Leopard as a boy, and hearing that old familiar name again made a hotness flare inside him.

"I can't die yet," he thought, recalling all the physical examinations and medical treatments his old bones and flesh had endured on account of the bullet holes that had riddled his body. But that was a year ago. At present he was hardly so stupid as to believe the phrase "the revolution needs you."

Revolution! He was not yet twenty the first time he heard the word. The dirt floor of the village schoolhouse had been trod into hard little mounds by the muddy feet of the farm children. They sat in disorderly fashion around a crudely-constructed, unpainted table of poplar-wood, like flocks of sheep turned loose in the neighborhood. As the aged schoolmaster, clad in a long gown, raised his arm to write the word, his all-too-ample sleeves slid down all the way to the elbow, exposing those arms lined with blue veins. Revolution! The word entered my memory as my eyes traced those earthworm-like veins down the arm of this man in a long gown. Ah, almost half a century now!

Revolution! All those years—from the time he'd carried a sword, then a Hanyang rifle, then a pair of pistols on the hips, then a Browning automatic, following which came a pair of German-made binoculars and a gold-ringed Parker pen—right up to the present, when he kept reaching for his multi-function pocket calculator and punched away at it while squatting proudly at the corner of a table. During all these years not a day had passed when he wasn't preoccupied by the word revolution. But the strange fact was that the meaning of this word had changed over time. When the change began was no longer clear in his memory. It seemed the concept of revolution had expanded from being merely a substitute for fighting, reading documents, attending meetings and making business trips, to include ideals, personality, personal integrity, weddings and funerals, begetting and raising sons and daughters; and finally it even embraced the color of one's clothing and the style of one's cuisine. Meanwhile the burning hatred he used to feel for the Japanese, the warlords, and social corruption had come to seem alien to him.

"The revolution needs you." Ah, Leopard, this fiery phrase, this burning-hot title "Commissar Liu" by which you address me, retains its flavor and avoids clichés only when it comes from you. No wonder titles like "Miss Zhao" and "Mr. Liu" were penned on the envelopes of the letters that his son and his girlfriend wrote to each other. No wonder he sometimes became so angry when these letters came into his hands that he tore them to shreds. The son watched with a pale, ashen face as his father shredded the letters, but he made no effort to defend himself. No, no, he understood his son too well. The boy was fleeing something, not searching for it. But what was he fleeing? Could it be that his son was fleeing the concepts embraced by revolution? And by comrade? Yes! Yes! And how had he understood the boundless implications in these words? All he knew were the clichés that had been worn out on the lips of others.

How could the revolution get along without him? Anybody could lose touch with it, even our Chairman, our Premier, our ranking generals. Hadn't they all lost touch? Everyone does eventually, but Liu Dayong wanted the revolution to continue to need him.

Fatty Zhang, whose name always used to follow Liu's when it appeared in the newspapers, but who was later promoted internally by the Party Standing Committee to the position of Vice-Minister, spoke to him once when they were attending lectures by a visiting expert. "In an era when everyone is working hard for the Four Modernizations, if we don't push ourselves there is always the danger that we will fall behind," he said laughing, as he pulled out the big handkerchief he carried year in and year out, to mop the damp sweat from his bald spot.

Of course he was falling behind. It was a reality, and a clear warning that he no longer had the energy to keep pace. For the past year or more he had seen many official documents that were unfamiliar to him, large parts of which he couldn't understand at all. He was able to grasp the basic idea behind such phrases as "oceanographic radiation and ecology," and he had been informed that such words as "Cobol" and "Fortran" were neither English nor French, but machine-communication languages. With a little improvising here and there he was able to manage, but when he encountered such things as

$$\Sigma_F = \Delta X \cdot \Pi / \Delta \Pi \cdot X, \ \Delta X \cdot \Pi = \Sigma_F \Delta \Pi \cdot X \Xi \Sigma_F \Delta \Pi / \Pi \cdot (X \Pi)^*$$

or the ability of Litmus to absorb radon at zero degrees centigrade, he couldn't understand it at all. A few months ago when he still had a little resilience, he yelled at Li Ying, "I won't take any more; I won't read any more," as he pushed away the medicine bottles and documents heaped up on the bed. Li Ying's response was to part her lips slightly in a simple smile.

"Bad tempers are common among the sick," she explained to others. "He wants desperately to get well and go back to work." She had attended to so many things. After a year of illness he had everything he could ask for—a rug, a refrigerator, a soft bed . . . It wouldn't have bothered him so much had she confined her efforts to these few material things, but she even had the secretary deliver official documents to the house. On days when his condition allowed, she read them to him, haltingly.

"He hasn't been demoted to the position of advisor yet," he overheard her arguing with the confidential secretary when he failed to deliver two sections of documents. He could almost imagine the accommodating smile that was certain to be on the secretary's face.

"Things grow worse over there by the day. You just get your health back, old one, that's the important thing," she remarked, as she lightly rearranged his bedding, all the while sprinkling MAXAM perfume all around. This fussing all the time. Was it just to satisfy herself, this wife who understands everything yet understood nothing? He drew in his head, but there was no way to escape the depressing smell of perfume. Oh, if only he could escape to the adobe *kang*, where he could lie on a hard pillow and gaze through the window at the corn and red peppers hanging under the eaves . . .

When they married Li Ying was just fifteen. That was more than thirty years ago while he was still a Regimental Commander, stalwart and brave, with a stubble of black whiskers on his chin.

---

* The difficult formula given in the original at this point seems to be meaningless, perhaps because of faulty typesetting. An equally arcane formula concerning the economic problem of balance of payments in the United States (used in Theodore Roszak, *Where the Wasteland Ends* [New York: Doubleday Anchor, 1973], p. 48) has been substituted to make a similar point about the great difficulty of understanding modern social problems if one is not an expert in the field.

"Hey, old Liu, the new one in the cultural brigade isn't bad at all," teased his colleagues who were remarrying one by one after long years of bachelorhood.

"Don't be silly!" He thought of his first wife, five years his senior, who had been betrothed to him as a child. At the time they were separated by more than a hundred miles.

"I wonder if the baby has been born yet?" he often thought to himself.

"There's a regulation, you old feudalist, which says that if you have been apart for eight years, it's a legal separation." Their parents had arranged the match. They lived together scarcely more than a few days, but he could still recall her rosy, swelling cheeks and the black thickness of her hair.

"What a bright, handsome girl she is," they said, urging him on with smiles. In those days Li Ying was just like a freshly soaked, tender bean sprout, with her staring, anxious, intelligent eyes. But it seemed impossible. How could he ever justify it to his parents? On the other hand he hadn't seen her for ten years, and nearly everyone was in the same quandary. Tempted by them in this fashion, he felt desire rise in him, desire to be close to a woman. Precisely at this juncture, when he felt caught between conflicting emotions, he put her out of his mind once and for all, the wife who had suffered so many hardships.

He didn't know how she had been able to endure it. The local organization explained it all to her immediately after Liberation. He didn't dare reflect on it, nor did anyone else ever mention it again. The whole thing just dissolved from the face of the earth, like a dream, like a wisp of smoke. But not in his memory.

He saw her later on two occasions. Had it not been for the care with which the elder son led his mother by the arm, unmistakably indicating the relationship between them, he never would have recognized her. The son was taking her to see the doctor. He ran head-long into them at the entrance to the hospital, just as he was about to get into a car. Gone were the rosy cheeks and the thick, black hair but not the bound feet. He had paid no attention to them at the time of their marriage, but now they caught his eye. She obviously recognized him. Over the many years that had separated them she had not forgotten what he looked like. Probably she had seen many photographs of him over the past ten or more years since he renewed contact with his eldest son, but he had never seen any of her. Possibly she had never had her picture taken.

With lowered head the son walked quickly past, assisting his mother. His four-year-old son came running up, innocently calling, "Grandpa, Grandpa, I want to ride the little car." The fat little fellow stamped his feet like a spoiled child.

"Come back here," the usually mild-tempered man barked at his little son. Fully comprehending the situation, Li Ying cleverly thrust a packet of candy into the boy's hand and nudged him in the direction of his father.

The old lady cast a glance full of anger and sad resentment. Perhaps he had just imagined it—his son had never mentioned a word to him—but her look followed him. And it followed him today, right up to the sick bed where he now tossed and turned.

"Oh, my boyhood wife—." Recently, she had been in Liu Dayong's thoughts more and more. As Li Ying's fat, soft hands gave him the tremella which she had stewed into a thick gruel, he had the urge to knock it away in exchange for a freshly-baked corn muffin served by thin, coarse hands. Oh, how irresistible freshly ground grain smelled in his memory.

His son was just fourteen when he came to Peking from the village. He had a blue cloth bundle on his back and wore the same kind of cloth shoes Liu Dayong had once worn. It was under the old Scholar tree at the mouth of the village that she had thrust that pair of shoes at him, silently turning her back to wipe her eyes. More than ten years had sped by like a flash, and there in front of him stood the son. No need to look at the square chin or the small, bright, blinking eyes to know that this boy was his. He was the spitting image of his father. You had only to see the thick soles and the black uppers to know that one kick from these old mountain shoes was enough to send a man sprawling.

"Good," he said, patting the large-framed boy on the shoulder. Li Ying had arranged for him to attend a boarding school for children of ranking cadres. He was a headstrong boy. He made no friends at school and he rarely spoke while at home, which made Li Ying somewhat anxious for him. Liu Dayong wanted, over Li Ying's objections, to take him to the seashore during the summer vacation, but the boy declined, preferring to spend the summer at home with his mother. In 1959 the boy brought back unsettling news.

"Dad, the old folks in the village hope you can make a trip back home. If we keep blundering on the way we have been . . . "

"What are you talking about? Who put you up to this?" Even today he could still feel how his face had flushed as he berated his son. Actually, even as he bawled him out he knew that what the boy said was true. Yet old Party member Liu Dayong, the dialectical materialist who had always taught his son to speak up honestly and openly, yelled back at the voice of truth from the mouth of a child. And his opinion of the truth? Naturally he couldn't tell it to a mere boy. But at Party branch meetings, Party committee meetings, and meetings of the National Congress? He had never spoken up there, either. How could he?

How often he had awakened from nightmares, bathed in sweat, screaming "my conscience is clear." Actually, he had never been of two minds about the Party. Far from ever having spoken any doubts, he had never allowed himself to think such things before. Any reservations he had about Party policy could always be repressed by the simple, sincere query, "Do you think you are more brilliant than the Central Committee?" This never failed to provide him a safe haven from storms of doubt whenever they flashed into his mind.

He couldn't tolerate flippancy in the language of the younger generation, who always considered themselves to be right. On one occasion he simply lost control, and with a trembling hand, hurled a teacup at his son. But his strength was insufficient and the cup, which stood for his loyalty and indignation, fell to the ground and shattered, fully a third short of its mark.

"What did I do to deserve having to raise a counter-revolutionary?" he shouted, smacking the bed with his hand. Actually, when he wasn't angry, Liu Dayong loved his children very much. When they first moved to the city, it was his habit to lean over his young son's crib, which was festooned with magnolias and colorful toys, and run his hand through the boy's tousled hair. He loved to plant kisses on the chubby neck that reeked of mother's milk and urine. For the older son he reserved a more sober fatherly love. He couldn't control himself. Time after time he surveyed that sturdy physique and the brow deep in thought. It was as though his own life, his thoughts and aspirations, yes, even his love for griddle cakes flaked with green onions, would live forever in that same chin and that body with the same blood-type and chromosomes.

"Good boy," he thought warm-heartedly in his mind as he scrawled his signature on his son's report card. He came near tearing the thin paper every time. Only later did he realize how much this reticent boy loved literature. While still in his teens the boy secretly wrote reams of poetry about his family and scenes from his native village. Even today those poems had the power to tear Liu's heart out. But he had stubbornly insisted that the boy enter the College of Engineering.

"The nation needs engineering talent," he announced in dignified paternal tones. He thought he detected a flash in the small, deep-set eyes, so like his own, but the boy said nothing. A trace of fatherly tenderness swept over him. Had he been unfair to the boy? Was his personality being stifled? Nonsense! There were only the needs of the Party and the people. Nothing else.

His son spoke less and less as the years went by. He even seemed to diminish in physical stature. Only yesterday, at forty, he sat at his father's bedside in the home-made gray uniform he had worn for years and years. Its collar was bent and the pockets fixed too high. It looked like he had outgrown it.

"Elder sister-in-law's needlework," he overheard Li Ying and her son's wife whispering. "Actually she can't be saving much money that way." The worn edge of his cotton jersey showed inside the twisted collar. The son just sat there all evening without a word. The broken temple of his glasses had been tied with string and under the dim lamplight's glare the white, thick, bristling hair of a man at mid-life was transformed into a patch of eye dazzling brilliance, which sent a prickling sensation through his heart.

"Oh God!" Liu moaned, starting from a catnap. The son raised his head. There was no gleam of light under those eyelids tight from sleep, only weariness and wretchedness, and a string of saliva hanging at the corner of his mouth. Was this the son molded by his own hand? Was this the hope of generations to follow? His generation's successor? Son, pull yourself together. You have forgotten everything I taught you about struggling heroes and model workers, and all the revolutionary stories I told you since childhood. So this is how you have turned out? The older you get the more useless you become. Where has my ruddy-faced little fellow gone?

He lifted his down-filled quilt. The night beyond was the color of water. He loved it. He loved its gentle kindness, its tolerance, full of understanding and sympathy. Under night's thick curtain he could get everything off his chest, with nothing to hide. Not like under brilliant sunlight, when he couldn't raise his gaze and had to keep his eyes closed.

"Report your ideological progress at this stage," stated the secretary, opening his all-important notebook bound in red.

"We want an honest confession of your innermost thoughts," said the young commanders of the revolution, taking off their leather belts, immune to empathy with human suffering.

"Must everything come to light? Even tiffs between my wife's parents?"

Ah! The night! He wanted to sit up, but the bed was too soft, and there was nothing to prop himself up with. Slowly inching toward the edge of the bed he groped for his thornwood cane. By turning himself several times he was finally able to slide off the edge.

His strength declined daily. Several days ago he could still pick up his glasses, but now no matter how he tried, he couldn't reach the things he wanted. He decided not to tell the doctor or let Yi Ling know. He didn't need to. It was evident when he repeatedly dropped his porcelain spoon and couldn't cough up the soup caught in his windpipe. How could they fail to understand? But they kept repeating the same phrases, "After you're well again . . . , wait till you've regained your health," as though that day would come.

"That day" was constantly in his mind, but it was the day they would hold his memorial service. During the eulogy, of course, there would be the standard phrases: "Forever loyal . . . self-sacrifice for the good of all . . . for the Party and the people . . . ," but what good would that do him? How can a man's life be summarized in a standardized eulogy with time-worn slogans? Better to say nothing and allow the true images—the good and the bad—to rest in the memories of those who knew you best. Why must public opinion be molded to conform to one standard? I have seen enough uniformity in my lifetime.

He had attended all the meetings he ought to have attended. He had taken all the stands expected of him. The grey and olive-drab military uniforms, the Sun Yatsen jackets, the octagonal caps, the Liberation caps, the woolen caps, the round-topped shoes, the leather shoes, the gold star pens. The Hero pens . . . but what had he stood for? What had he ever opposed? Finer men than he had stood silent and had flowed with the current. What did he, Liu Dayong, count for? Ah, how much better to be like his father sleeping peacefully on the foothills, bathed in sunshine and wild flowers, the spot marked by a solidly erected stone tablet coarsely inscribed, "Communist Party member Liu Dayong."

He had wanted to achieve something in life but he had little to show for his efforts. He had been assigned work unsuited to his taste, but he had not dared to refuse it. If they begrudged him a burial plot, then they could just scatter his ashes over the clay soil of his hometown or among the drifting clouds in the blue sky. For God's sake don't have those ashes lie here in this room with the red rug, where every day he would see Li Ying oiling her hair and his daughter-in-law trying on clothes. That's how these women were. It was so easy to win a woman's attention. At the mention of fashion or hair styles, they forgot everything else.

Men, on the other hand . . . of course the time for spanking and cuffs to the head was long since past. It was fifteen years since he had last given his son a beating, and that was over a killing. With a group of fifteen- and sixteen-year-olds he had helped kill a woman said to have been the wife of an aging capitalist. Liu beat him mercilessly in the face, on his back, his buttocks, any place he could reach. The boy howled himself hoarse, finally dissolving into incessant sobbing. He beat and beat him as though he could drive away the well-deserved remorse that he felt himself. Is this what he had created? Liu Dayong could forgive neither his son nor himself, but the son forgave his father.

Several months later, while he was the target of struggle, the immature youth exhibited courage beyond his expectations. Countless times the son carried his father on his back from the courtyard to the cowshed, his temporary quarters. The full weight of his body in its prime crushed down on the boy's not yet fully developed shoulders. He could hear that tender, young heart beating courageously and sincerely through the boy's thin back.

"Even if I lose everything, I still have my son, who is full of the vitality of life," he wept. The two were so close then, father and son, like one mass of cells joined by skin and tissue and a single heart. But once the muscles began to swell in his arms, the son grew more distant from his father. While he was at the cadre school his son wanted everything his own way, since economic position determined everything. Recalling the principles of political economics that he studied years ago in the Party school, Liu Dayong could reconcile himself to the situation. Yes, there was nothing that escaped his son's attention, from housing repairs to face-to-face arguments with leaders of rebel factions, but after the Great Proletarian Cultural Revolution, the entire situation reversed itself. Liu Dayong was reinstated. The son had to rely on his father's influence to get transferred back from the countryside and secure a job, and he had to register as a member of his father's household. Liu's initial fears were that his son would rebel by wearing bell-bottomed trousers, or join the craze over the latest popular song idols, but Liu was sensible enough to realize that these fads were natural in young people and he believed he would be able to exercise reasonable control over his son. The problem was that the son became too serious, too severe. He seemed in hot pursuit of something, yet he stood on the sidelines with an air of aloofness.

Li Ying had worked in a cultural troop and was presently involved in propaganda work, so she liked listening to the daily, noontime fiction hour. For the past year he listened in a daze as she tuned in on the story of Li Zicheng.* The present episode was a woman reading the Tale of Perfect Loyalty in articulate, melodious tones:

Qin Gui sat in his room, his eyes rolling furtively. "Who can be appointed to interrogate Yue Fei?"

Not just her radio, but probably every set in Peking was blaring at once:

"Among the long-tailed dogs and short-tailed wolves, I, Yue Fei, will place myself at the disposal of my country. I'm a man of merit and have yet to be found at fault. Tai . . . ."

"Click!" The sound was abruptly cut short. Slowly opening his eyes, Liu Dayong's gaze fell on the flustered, exasperated face of his younger son. Not one to rebuke her son, Li Ying turned for help to the old man, who could do no more than utter a grunt.

"God-damned perfect loyalty! That brand of blind loyalty is China's undoing!"

"How dare you say such a thing?" Li Ying protested in alarm, bending a concerned face toward the bed. He closed his eyes. He felt as though he had been stabbed through the heart, but it was a joyous stabbing that made his stifled heart bleed.

---

* Li Zicheng (1606–1645) was a rebellious soldier who was instrumental in the downfall of the Ming dynasty. He captured Peking in 1644, then was overthrown by the Manchu founders of the Qing dynasty. His saga is being written in a multi-volume historical novel, *Li Zicheng*, by Yao Xueyin. Three volumes in eight parts have been completed so far.

Perhaps his son was right. He caught himself weighing the possibility over and over in his mind. No! These frivolous young people are not dependable. Recently he had heard that these half-baked kids were now engaged in finding devious ways of using the social system to their own advantage. These practices were certainly not to be found on the pages of *Das Kapital* or *The History of the Russian (Bolshevik) Communist Party*. He could ask, or have the secretary check the original works, but he didn't. All heresy! He wanted to curse but he just didn't have the strength. He had a vague feeling that he ought to be bidding farewell to his son, or to his life, or to all those tasks he was accustomed to handling with ease, whether he loved or hated them. But how could he do that?

He clutched the thick handle of his walking stick and with faltering steps made his way toward the door. This stick had been a gift from Zhao Shuanzi, a faithful orderly who had been with him since his teens. Ten years ago at forty, Zhao Shuanzi had been returned to his hometown, through an administrative directive signed and approved by Liu himself. This reliable and trustworthy administrative aid, flustered by God knows what, inadvertently omitted the word "not" in a document, making it read, "Regardless of the consequences, we should forget class struggle," instead of "we can never, under any circumstances, forget class struggle." At first Liu decided to help him out by having him write a confession and administering appropriate disciplinary action, letting the matter drop. Who could dream that in writing his confession the old boy would delete the word "forget" and write in bold, black letters, "Under no circumstances should we have class struggle." Poor naive Shuanzi, who under no circumstances would ever have advocated dispensing with class struggle, wept bitter tears, but he had to be sent back to the countryside where he came from for the crime of "evil attacks" on Party policy. This little, orphaned shepherd, who always brought him his wash water with his out-sized uniform trailing on the ground, stayed in Liu's memory. So did his chapped hands, split from exposure to the cold so that they revealed red, tender flesh. Shuanzi held no grudges against his old leader, even after he was sent home. He had even gone to the trouble of finding someone to bring this walking stick.

"Shuanzi, what have I done?" Leaning on his stick, Liu Dayong made his way to the window, the very window from which he later saw his first wife one last time. That was several years before he took sick. He noticed her standing at the base of the wall surrounding the compound of his three-story building. A sudden gust of wind churned up the dust. She turned away and beat the dust from her clothes with her handkerchief. Then from her bosom she extracted a cotton scarf. . . . He started, not knowing why she had. . . . He drew nearer to lean out the window, thinking to hail her, but he couldn't think what to say. . . . The old lady turned toward him, and her half-opened mouth appeared to be moving. . . , but had she really seen him? Another cloud of dust arose, and when he looked again she was gone. Then he heard a hesitant knock at the door. When he opened it, in walked Old Wang, stiff-legged, wearing a felt hat worn shiny, and a large cotton-padded jacket covered with dust.

"Auntie, she . . . Auntie said she had an errand to run; she told me to come right in . . . ," he said haltingly, taking some peanuts and red dates out of an old cotton sack flung over his shoulder.

"Old brother, you shouldn't have done this," said Liu,

coming forward to press his hand, which was coarse as tree bark. As he did, two cloudy tear drops fell from the old man's eyes, which were red and ringed by dark circles.

"Your nephew, he didn't mean to offend the commune . . . " It was yet another unjust case in which the farmer had no place to present his grievances. In the eyes of his fellow villagers Liu was a high-ranking official of the Party, a well-intentioned man whom they knew well. They had watched him grow up. In the end they knew that their only recourse was to come to him with their side of the story. Bringing the few peanuts and dates that they had sent so that Liu could enjoy them fresh, the old fellow had traveled over a hundred miles to find a sympathetic ear and justice. But could Liu do anything? He might write a letter to the provincial seat, but would it have any weight? Once he was passing through Xinhuamen district in Peking. Despite the speed with which his little Mercedes clipped through town, he could sense the people surging toward him, wrapped in mats and padded-cotton quilts. The effect of the glazed, wooden look in their eyes as they watched him go by was like saliva spit drop by drop into his face.

"Oh, Old Wang," he groaned and trembled, gazing through the window into the pitch-black night. After a while Liu Dayong didn't dare inquire about the fate of Old Wang's son, nor did he dare return to his hometown, although the yearning to do so these past years was tugging at his innards. He was afraid to see his fellow villagers, whom he had once protected, ask without a trace of resentment how he was getting on.

"Everyone on this year's production team was allotted more than five-hundred catties of grain, and we get more than fifty cents for a day's work," he read in a recent letter from Old Wang's grandson. "Granddad says that by year's end everyone will be able to afford some new clothes, thanks to the policies of the Party . . . Uncle Liu, be sure to take good care of yourself."

"I haven't the heart to face them." He pounded the floor with his walking stick, but it made no sound on the thick carpet. He felt inexpressibly depressed, as though he had spent his entire life in this small carpeted room filled with the opresive smell of perfume. He should have . . . but he hadn't. He was a leader, a strict father. He rode in automobiles and ate tremella. Was this the goal of life? True, he had achieved all these things, but he felt depressed. He had been depressed the whole last half of his life. Using the wall for support he had made his way toward the door. It was a moonless night, pitch-black.

Ah, fresh in his memory was the first violent uprising to eradicate traitors, which erupted on just such a night as this; and the first trip to inspect the huge dike project, also made on a night like this. With a sudden gesture he pulled the door open. The night wind swept across his face and blew a stack of documents off the table.

"I will go back home. I won't take any more medicine or sleep under an eiderdown quilt, and I'll ask my fellow villagers to forgive me," he said. Mustering all his strength he closed the door with a bang, a sound so resonant that it filled him with joy. "Life is for heroes." Falteringly, he stretched toward the door handle and pulled it open, letting in the wind. "Bang!" The door closed heavily again. "Bang . . . whack! Bang . . . whack!" In the still night this recurring sound elated him. It was like purging his life of many decades of grievances and depressions.

"*Ai*, old man, what are you doing up again?" Li Ying hurried out in her night dress.

"Dad bangs the door like that every night. It drives me crazy," he overheard his daughter-in-law complain.

"Will you get up and get Dad something to put on?" Li Ying called to her daughter-in-law, helping him lovingly by the arm.

"You are old, old, but you act like a child. What thrill is there in playing with the door? Quickly, get back into bed."

"No," he said, putting up a struggle all the while he was being pulled and bundled back into the soft-silky-smooth quilt. Quickly and quietly, Li Ying brought him a large handful of multi-colored tablets. The daughter-in-law with tip-tapping steps and Li Ying with plodding thuds padded back to their rooms. The lamp blazed away with a light somewhere between red and blue, and he could hear the tick-tick-tick of the desk clock.

"No!" Liu Dayong called out forcefully. But no sound came out at all.

"No! . . . No . . . "

Originally published in *Shiyue* (*October*), no. 3, 1981. This story was originally preceded by the quotation from Orianna Fallaci (without footnote) translated from the Chinese and used as the epigraph to this section.

Translated by Dale R. Johnson

Providing a Meal

Photo by Saundra Sturdevant

by Qiao Shi

Standing in the doorway, the Brigade Leader said with a snicker, "Third Mother, in the morning you're in charge of the food!"

Third Mother, who was sitting in the sun in the doorway spinning cotton, was surprised; the wheel, which had been humming along happily, came to a stop with a whine. She lifted her head, her eyes blinking, blinded by the sun. In a loud voice, she asked unbelievingly, "What? In charge of the food?"

"Right, in charge of the food!" The Brigade Leader answered with certainty.

When Third Mother heard it was for sure, she clearly was panic-stricken. Hastily throwing down the thread, she pushed the wheel aside and stood up.

"You want me to handle the food?"

"Right, I want you to handle it!"

"Good Lord, you want me to handle it?" Third Mother held out her palms, so agitated that even her voice was shaky. "I don't even have a cup of wheat flour!"

"It doesn't matter if you don't have any wheat flour." The Brigade Leader seemed to be comforting her, "Even corn flour is all right. Make coarse-grain porridge!"

"Coarse-grain porridge?" Third Mother could not seem to believe her ears. "Make coarse-grain porridge for a public official?"

"Right, coarse-grain porridge it is!" The Brigade Leader's answer was affirmative.

But Third Mother still shook her head, and stared at the Brigade Leader's face with doubting and uncertain eyes. She finally waved him away and, sitting down again by the spinning wheel on a brick made of grass and mud, stretched out her hand to grasp her cotton thread and wheel.

"Off with you! What kind of a joke is that, make coarse-grain porridge for a cadre!"

When the Brigade Leader saw that Third Mother really did not believe him, he quickly strode in through the door. "Really, Third Mother!"

As soon as Third Mother saw the Brigade Leader's expression, she knew this was for real. There was nothing she could do about it; she could only mumble, "Can't you send him somewhere else?"

The Brigade Leader said, "No, he specifically said he wanted to come to your house for coarse-grain porridge!"

When Third Mother heard this, her body unwittingly trembled, and her heart unwittingly sped up its thump-thump-thumping. The hand outstretched to grasp the thread and the wheel drew back again. She sat dumbly on the brick, her lips slightly trembling as if she were chewing on these words and measuring their weight. After a while, as if awakening from a nightmare, she asked, loudly, "Who? Who is it?"

"Who?" The Brigade Leader stared at Third Mother laughing. "It's a high official—the Prefectural Committee Secretary!"

The Brigade Leader had originally thought Third Mother would be happy that the Prefectural Committee Secretary specifically wanted to come to her house for coarse-grain porridge. He never imagined that when he said who it was, Third Mother would be as shocked as if she had been burned by fire. She yelled, "Good lord! The Prefectural Committee Secretary! *Aiya*, Brigade Leader, let Third Mother off! You want me to make coarse-grain porridge for the Prefectural Committee Secretary?"

The Brigade Leader panicked too; he knew this matter touched on Third Mother's sore spot. He quickly tried to explain and convince her.

"Uh, Third Mother, this time, it's him who wants to eat it, not you asking him to, and furthermore, one person is not the same as another; uh, uh, he also said, he wants the dumplings good and thick."

Actually, Third Mother used to enjoy having cadres to her house to eat; she regarded it as an honor. When she was young, she looked on the cadres who came to her house to eat as brothers who had come for a visit. Later, when she was a bit older, she looked on them as children returning from afar. What was worth celebrating was that ever since land reform, her home life was better than before. All the cadres who came to her house to eat, she felt, had been sent by Chairman Mao and the Communist Party to do good things for the people. They had turned their backs on their homes and bid farewell to their parents, and she would not feel right about it if she did not treat them well. So each time a cadre came to her house to eat she would go to great lengths to get something good for him to eat; rolls stuffed with vegetables, thick-cut noodles, fried pancakes, sesame cakes, soup noodles, and also stir-fried eggs and hot peppers. This was the best local fare, things you would prepare for your relatives. Third Mother would run around busily, not worrying about the smoke in her hair; as long as the cadres who came to her house got a lot of tasty food, she felt extremely satisfied.

But how could she have known that one year, when she was in charge of food, she would bring on a catastrophe and be deeply hurt. It was in the spring of 1975, right around February or March, when Commune Secretary Hou brought a group of people to get to know the place. On that day, it was her turn to be in charge of the food for Secretary Hou.

At that time, Third Mother's family were in such difficult straits that they could not even take the lid off the cooking pots. To say difficult straits did not mean there had been a natural catastrophe or that the crops had not been harvested. It was because this Secretary Hou had been saying for years: you cannot speak of who has more or less, only of your contributions; contribute more for your country, contribute more for the revolution; we must think of the whole four billion, and not complain about the watery rice in our own mouths; first country, then collective, then individual. So it was that, while the newspapers reported bumper harvests for years on end in this commune, making it famous throughout the province for its high-level, stable production and excellent contributions, Third Mother and her family went hungry for years on end. It was really true that "people should fear fame, like pigs fear growing fat!"

It seemed almost perverse that just exactly at that moment Secretary Hou was coming to her house to eat. There was a proverb that said a clever housewife could not make porridge without rice. Third Mother, who usually regretted being unable to dig out her own heart and liver for the cadres to eat, became extremely despondent. She held out her palms to her husband.

"Daddy, what shall we do?"

At that time, Third Mother's husband Li Santian was still alive. Li Santian sat on the edge of the *kang* sucking noisily on his waterpipe. He said slowly, "What shall we do? Whatever we eat, he eats!"

And what did her family eat? They couldn't even afford to steam a bun; for three days in a row, three meals a day, they ate alfalfa greens and rice dregs. Occasionally they made some corn-flour mush or steamed some corn-flour buns, and that was considered a great improvement. But Secretary Hou was the highest official in the commune; when he coughed, everyone else had to come down with a cold. Wouldn't it be just too embarrassing to make this sort of food for Secretary Hou? According to what people said, ever since Secretary Hou had been coming into town and taking turns eating at each house, everyone scrambled to think of ways to kiss up to him;

if we turn out to be "special," a level worse than everyone else . . . Third Mother stared dumbly at her old man, feeling things were especially difficult. "What are you staring at?" Li Santian chewed on his water pipe. "If he wants to eat dragon liver and phoenix wings, I have to have them first!"

Stumbling for words, Third Mother discussed the issue with her husband. "At least we should make some noodles for him!"

Li Santian said, "Go ahead and make them!"

Third Mother sighed and said, "And the wheat flour?"

Li Santian grimaced. "So! I thought you really were capable, and were going to make noodles without flour! Ha! That would be a rare thing!"

"Can't we borrow a little?" Third Mother said.

"And return it with what?" Li Santian asked.

"We can return it after the harvest," Third Mother said.

"It's still seventy days to harvest. What if they come ten times a week to get it?" It was true, this was a difficult problem. Third Mother, not knowing what to do, said, "Then what shall we do?"

Li Santian said, "I told you before; what we eat, he eats!"

Third Mother said, "But this is Secretary Hou!"

Li Santian tapped on his waterpipe as he said, "Isn't Secretary Hou a Communist Party cadre too? He's not a tiger in the mountains, or a god in the temple. He should share the thick and the thin with us poor- and lower-middle peasants. Do you mean to say he won't be able to forgive us for making him some coarse-grain porridge? You never know, he may even think it's something new!"

Third Mother thought about it and said, "That's true!"

Li Santian went on, "You've forgotten that year when you borrowed flour and made noodles for Brigade Leader Chen; not only did he not eat them, he criticized you good. Didn't he bring the bowl over and dish out the porridge himself?"

Third Mother could not help but smile and nod at this.

The Brigade Leader Chen whom her husband had mentioned was later District Committee Secretary, Chen Zhimin. At that time, Chen Zhimin was still the land reform Brigade Chief of this village. Although he later became District Committee Secretary, Third Mother still kept calling him Brigade Leader Chen; she was used to saying it, and couldn't change. What Li Santian was saying about Brigade Leader Chen dishing out coarse-grain porridge went this way: During land reform, Third Mother and her husband still lived in a broken-down old house that let in the wind on all sides. In the middle of the night they could view the stars, and at dawn they were frozen like two raw scallions. That day it was Third Mother's turn to handle the food, so she specially borrowed a pound of flour and made flat noodles for Brigade Leader Chen. For her own family, she only made coarse-grain porridge. To avoid stimulating the taste buds of her six-year-old daughter Yufeng, she sent her out behind by the chicken coop. Brigade Leader Chen wore a grey military uniform with a Mauser pistol in his shoulder holster. As soon as he saw Third Mother bring a bowl of noodles for him but not for the two of them, he immediately understood that they were playing a trick on him. Taking the bowl of noodles from her, he put it on the table and said, "Auntie, I'm not from this area. I don't like noodles!"

This really stumped Third Mother: "Well . . . "

The Brigade Leader pointed to the big ceramic pot on the chopping board and asked, "What's in there?"

"Coarse-grain porridge!" Third Mother replied with

difficulty. "Made with corn flour!"

Brigade Leader Chen slapped his thigh. "So! Coarse-grain porridge is my favorite!"

Without waiting for Third Mother or her husband to answer, Brigade Leader Chen walked right over to the chopping board; with one hand he picked up an old bowl, with the other a ladle, and dished himself up a bowl of porridge. He added a pinch of salt, poured on some vinegar and hot sauce, and slurped it up. When Third Mother and her husband saw him eating so greedily, they couldn't help laughing. As for that bowl of noodles, Brigade Leader Chen took it with his own hands and gave it to Yufeng, who was hiding by the chicken coop. The child had not tasted the flavor of wheat noodles for a long, long time, and wolfed them down so fast she choked. When Brigade Leader Chen first saw the way the child was eating, he laughed happily, but as he laughed, tears as big as beans welled up in his eyes. When Third Mother and her husband saw this, they could not help sobbing themselves.

When he was about to leave, Brigade Leader Chen criticized Third Mother, "Auntie, you took me for an outsider!"

Third Mother quickly disagreed, "No, no!"

Brigade Leader Chen said, "Then why did you borrow flour to make noodles for me? If you're going to be like this, I won't come to your house anymore. We are cadres of the Communist Party, not ward bosses of the KMT!"

It had already been twenty years, but this incident was especially clear in Third Mother's memory. Every time it was brought up, it seemed to be right in front of her eyes. In Third Mother's mind, Brigade Leader Chen was a yardstick; she used this yardstick to measure the cadres of the Communist Party. So today, when her husband Li Santian brought up this incident, Third Mother naturally thought that having Secretary Hou eat coarse-grain porridge was probably all right. Maybe, like Brigade Leader Chen, he would find it quite tasty!

That morning, Third Mother took special care with this batch of porridge; she mixed it a long time and got the fire exactly right. Needless to say, the fish-shaped dumplings were firm, shiny, and long. Third Mother was quite satisfied with her product.

Who could have known that Secretary Hou, who was very happy when he arrived and sat down at the table, would knit up his eyebrows in a flash when he saw that porridge brought out. He didn't say a word, but slowly picked up the bowl, and slowly used his chopsticks to slide the stringy dumplings strip by strip into his mouth. Once those shiny, long, fish-like dumplings entered his mouth, they seemed to become as gritty as sand. His expression was not that of someone eating food, but of someone taking a bitter and astringent Chinese medicine. Even a famous painter would have had a hard time accurately recording that strange face.

When she saw how uncomfortable Secretary Hou looked eating, Third Mother felt very uncomfortable herself. She looked at this "true dragon prince" of the commune with eyes full of trepidation, as if she owed him a debt. Her lips trembling, she wanted to explain a little, but in the end nothing came out, and all she could do was roll her eyes at her husband. Only now did Li Santian understand that although this Secretary Hou had broadcast his desire to "share the thick and thin" with the people, and had announced that he "liked coarse-grain porridge and iron-thread pancakes* best of all," this was really nothing but a gold lettered signboard, not something he planned to put into practice. Of course he saw the whites of his wife's eyes, but Li Santian pretended he saw nothing, and continued without expression to eat his cold porridge.

The situation was awkward, the atmosphere heavy, and all was silent in that small room.

Secretary Hou conquered the huge and difficult hardship: with incomparably tenacious revolutionary spirit, heroic bearing that took heed neither of misery nor death, and dauntless fighting spirit, he finished his coarse-grain porridge, put down the bowl, and got up and left without a word.

"Are you finished, Secretary Hou?" Third Mother asked quickly.

"I'm full!" Secretary Hou said as he walked away.

Secretary Hou . . . ," Third Mother said apologetically, "Ah, we have no good . . . "

Before Third Mother could finish what she was saying, Secretary Hou dashed out of the door and disappeared without a trace.

"What are you saying?" Li Santian threw a glance at his wife. "His teeth have been softened by steamed white buns and juicy meat. What's the use of saying such ridiculous things?"

Third Mother laughed bitterly and said no more.

After a few days, somehow everyone in the village was talking about it. Some admired Third Mother, saying she had "taken" Secretary Hou's "rook," and had "given him a taste of something new"; others were worried that her treatment of Secretary Hou would invite the "guillotine." Just at that time, all of the big shots were talking about the law, so who was not afraid! When Third Mother heard about these reactions, she could not help panicking; she blamed her husband Li Santian.

"Just look, I told you we should make him some noodles. . . ."

Li Santian, on the other hand, was still unperturbed. He said laughing, "Each family has fifteen, seven mouths and eight tongues, so let them say what they want! Eating a bowl of coarse-grain porridge is like celebrating New Years for us now; didn't we give him a treat? If we had sharkfins and sea cucumbers, don't you think I would bring them out?"

"But he's the Secretary of the commune!" Third Mother said argumentatively.

"Then he should know about the misery of the common people too!" Li Santian explained to Third Mother, "Can he cause trouble for us just because of one meal? And moreover, is his rank higher than Brigade Leader Chen's?"

When he put it this way, Third Mother calmed down a bit, but she did not feel entirely secure. For many years, she had felt things were slightly different than before, but she didn't want to say anything and could not really say anything anyway. As time went by, this incident also became part of the past.

Who could have known that when it came time to estimate wheat production, this bowl of old, stale grain, eaten but undigested in the stomach, would suddenly start to sprout?

On that day, Secretary Hou led some cadres from the large and small brigades to the wheat fields to estimate production. Li Santian was the representative of the poor peasants in the large brigade, so naturally he was called on to participate as well. This piece of communal land, everyone said, could

---

* Corn-flour pancakes.

produce three hundred, but Secretary Hou said no, three hundred and fifty; everyone said that this piece of land could produce four hundred and thirty, but Secretary Hou said no, five hundred and ten. There was, of course, no arguing with Secretary Hou; this naturally became an ironclad production estimate that no one could change. Everyone could see what was going on, but they still said Secretary Hou had rich experience and had estimated accurately. Li Santian, always too honest, got the worst of things. He thought to himself, if we go on like this won't we all have to go hungry? He sighed lightly and mumbled: "What a way to estimate! How can grain that's not in the ground show up on the scales?"

As luck would have it, not only was Secretary Hou's sense of taste extremely sensitive, but his hearing was highly developed as well. Just as Li Santian's words hit their mark, Secretary Hou whirled around, opened his eyes wide, and said sneeringly: "If it doesn't show up on the scales, how can it end up in your mouth?"

Li Santian was stunned and said nothing.

Everyone said that Secretary Hou's face looked as if it had been covered by a layer of black clouds, dark, cold, and stormy. The rays that shot from his eyes pierced like lightning.

"I figured out a long time ago that you are a trouble-making devil up to no good! You have been dissatisfied with the Party for a long while!"

If you said anything else about this old poor peasant Li Santian, he would never say a word. True or false, he wouldn't argue or hold a grudge. But, if you said something about his feelings for the Party, that really was like digging out his heart with a knife. He had been pierced to the core, and could not help opening his eyes wide in amazement: "Me?"

"Yes, you!" Secretary Hou stared at him angrily, his lips wide open like a pair of scissors. "You are just like a pig, staring at the food in your trough! You are against planting more grain, contributing more for the revolution! You run around in other villages borrowing grain just for the purpose of giving socialism a bad name! You drink corn broth just to make a point before the commune leaders! From words to actions, what is the difference between you and a rightist?"

Li Santian would never in the farthest reaches of his imagination have thought that Secretary Hou would treat him like this. He felt so terrible, he just stood there like an idiot.

No one had imagined, either, that on the first field of production estimation, this raging storm would suddenly appear. From Secretary Hou's words, everyone also clearly discerned that this was that meal of coarse-grain porridge unleashing its tremendous power. But with Secretary Hou's anger so extreme, he had to be placated. Who could have known that the reasonableness of their pleas would only add fuel to the fire?

"Hey, old poor peasant!" Secretary Hou's nostrils flared, "You've shed your skin and metamorphosed! Class relationships have sparked another change! The old poor peasant of before now becomes a turncoat, an opponent of the revolution! Li Santian is a living example!"

No matter what was said, Secretary Hou would not withdraw his criticism. That evening, Li Santian was pushed up front during the general criticism and struggle meeting of the entire commune. His head hanging, bent at the waist and with tears in his eyes, he was a target of their barbs for three hours.

Late that night, he went home with his breast full of humiliation and rage; he lay by his wife's side, so miserable that he shook all over.

Tears were also flowing down Third Mother's face. She said sobbing, "Oh, if only we had made some noodles for him! Look what we've done just to save a handful of flour!"

Now Li Santian understood that Third Mother had been right all along. After all, as soon as Secretary Hou stepped out of his door, he walked right in through Li Sangui's gate. And as for the first meal Li Sangui prepared for Secretary Hou, everyone in the village knew he had bought Western Phoenix Wine, made juicy meat, stir-fried some eggs, made meat dumplings, brewed chrysanthemum tea, and bought Peony Cigarettes. After that time, Secretary Hou became a frequent guest at Li Sangui's. And this Li Sangui, who was known throughout the village for his stench of dog shit, who racketeered in cloth-ration tickets, grain tickets, chemical fertilizers, and wood, who profiteered all day on this conscienceless money, within a short time became Secretary Hou's pet. Even that son of his, who had graduated from high school and been back home just a few days, was "recommended" to a university with a word from Secretary Hou.

"The world still belongs to those with money and power!" Third Mother went on, so hurt and angry.

Li Santian said nothing. He was thinking: was it really true that what the chopsticks picked up could mean so much? What sort of mystery was hidden in this cold, harsh reality?

"If you have money you can hire devils to grind the grain for you, if you don't people just kick you!" Third Mother was still complaining angrily. "Huh, all your life you have only known the hoe and plow, worked for the revolution farming the land, farming, farming, farming; why didn't you learn a little from Li Sangui?"

His wife's words made Li Santian mad. "We're farmers, old poor peasants; we're poor, but we're poor and decent, we're poor but we've got our pride."

Third Mother didn't care if he was angry. She rebutted him right away, "Oh, you're poor? Poverty is just a gold lettered sign board. Who pities you for being poor? You're so poor you've become an opponent of the revolution, and you're still bragging!"

Li Santian suddenly turned over and lay facing Third Mother: "You're wrong! Brigade Leader Chen said poverty is an honor, we are the pillars of the revolution!"

Third Mother laughed coldly. "Why try to go by a torn old calendar of bygone years? Secretary Hou is right before our eyes, not Brigade Leader Chen! The world has changed!"

Li Santian could not help but give a cold shudder. The world had changed? He had no way to counter his wife's argument, so he might just as well sigh and say nothing. After a long, long time he said, "I just won't believe that the world will always be this way!"

Third Mother asked, "Then when will it finally change?"

Li Santian didn't answer, but just opened his desolate eyes and stared dumbly at the stars in the sky outside.

Now, her old companion Li Santian was no longer in this world. He had died. Taking his humiliation, and taking his beautiful hopes, he had gone to another world.

Today if someone just mentioned providing a meal, especially making coarse-grain porridge, Third Mother unwittingly thought of her husband, and the wounds deep in her heart secretly bled.

Ai! Sighing, she got up from the spinning wheel and

mumbled, "In charge of the food, in charge of the food! Coarse-grain porridge, coarse-grain porridge! What monster is coming this time!"

But she still scooped up half a ladle of corn, and quickly but not too quickly went over to the electric grinder; she ground it into fine, white, new corn flour, brought it back, lit up the stove, and started to work.

Everything was ready. Once again she sat at the spinning wheel in the door, slowly and sadly turning the wheel and thinking; who was it? Who specifically said he wanted to come to my house to eat, and even specifically said he wanted coarse-grain porridge? Ha, what a joke! Are there such cadres today? This must be another trick! She shook her head slowly, wondering if this would turn out to be fortune or misfortune.

Just at this moment, she saw someone wearing a grey uniform come bouncing in, striding with one step through the door, laughing happily, staring at her, shaking a head of pepper-white hair.

"Elder Sister, do you still recognize me?"

Third Mother couldn't say a word. She squinted her old eyes and looked at this stranger. For the last several years, no one who had eaten here had called her "Big Sister" or "Elder Sister." When they came they wanted all kinds of offerings, but when they sat down at the table and had a bowl and another bowl, finished and wiped off their mouths, you could hardly get a few polite words out of them. But today, she hadn't even invited this person; he had found her door by himself, and as soon as he opened his mouth out came "Elder Sister." This was really something new! She couldn't help but warm up to him. She wondered who he was, and at the same time answered haltingly, "Yes, I recognize you, I recognize you!"

This person looked at her, laughing, and shook his head. "You're fooling me! You've forgotten, you don't recognize me."

Third Mother had allowed him to see right through her, so she might as well honestly admit it. "*Ai*, yes, it's true." Laughing with embarrassment, she said, "I'm old, my memory is not so good any more!"

This person laughed, ran over to the chopping board, grabbed an old bowl, grabbed a ladle, and dished up a bowl of fish shaped dumplings, saying, "Hey, do you remember now?"

Third Mother, laughing so hard the tears flowed down her face, rubbed her hands over and over on her apron.

"Ha ha, Old Chen, Brigade Leader Chen!"

Old Chen pinched some salt into the bowl, poured on some vinegar, added some hot sauce, and laughed happily.

"I was just wondering if Elder Sister could forget me! It's certainly an honor for me to be able to eat your coarse-grain porridge!"

Third Mother couldn't stop herself from lifting up her apron, wiping her eyes, and putting on an angry manner.

"So you've become a high official and forgotten our poor family!"

Old Chen laughed, "Poor family? Ha ha, isn't this poor family a cornerstone of the revolution?"

"Cornerstone, cornerstone," Third Mother found herself so angry her eyes turned red. "We've already become the opponents of the revolution, and you still call us cornerstones!"

Old Chen put down the chopsticks in his hands, and looking with moist eyes at Third Mother, said heavily, "Elder Sister, I know, I know everything!"

The room fell silent.

Third Mother suddenly felt that it had been almost twenty years since she had seen Old Chen, so she really had no reason to cry or get angry. She quickly wiped her eyes dry with her apron, and laughed, "*Ai*! Hurry and eat! It's just that I haven't anything good, otherwise I wouldn't make you eat this coarse-grain porridge!"

Old Chen said laughing, "This coarse-grain porridge of yours is the only thing I like. It's better than the meat noodles in the restaurants!"

Third Mother said laughing, "Ha ha, I simply don't believe you!"

Old Chen said, "You may not believe it, but I do!"

Third Mother said, "How come your hair is white too? I remember you're over ten years younger than me!"

Old Chen, chewing on his porridge dumplings, said, "I ran into catastrophe, a flood and a drought!"

Third Mother could not help giggling, "Then was your hair drowned or scorched?"

Old Chen said laughing, "Both drowned and scorched, and with the locusts, it's a wonder it wasn't chewed off!" When he was done laughing, his expression became serious again, and he said, "Otherwise, how could I eat your coarse-grain porridge today? This is the good fortune these catastrophes have brought me!"

Third Mother saw the slight quavering of the muscles in Old Chen's face, the raging sadness shining in his eyes, and the pain in the corners of his mouth. It seemed something was eating away at his heart.

"If our poor peasants are supposed to consider it their glory to be poor forever, then why did we need a revolution?"

Old Chen spoke with agitation, the chopsticks in his hands falling on the ground with a clack.

Third Mother was shocked and said nothing. Quickly picking up the chopsticks from the floor, she wiped them off and said, "Old Chen!"

After Old Chen had gone, Third Mother felt extremely uneasy. She leaned against the door for a long time, gazing in the direction Old Chen had gone, gazing, gazing. The brilliant sun beat down on the spring land. The wheat sprouts were a swath of jade green. A few branches of peach blossoms stretched over the wall. Swallows were flitting among the willow leaves. Third Mother picked up her apron, wiped her eyes, and thought, *Ai*, if only my old husband Li Santian were still alive and could see Old Chen taking up that old bowl to eat coarse-grain porridge!

Originally published in *Shanghai wenxue*, no. 5, 1979.

Translated by Wendy Larson

Troubled Sunday

Photo by Saundra Sturdevant

by Shen Rong

It was a Sunday morning in early May 1979. Mu Zhijian, the Party Branch Secretary at a certain university, sat on the living room sofa browsing through the newspapers. His work kept him so busy that during the week he could only glance at the headlines. It was not until Sunday that he had time to search out and read the important articles from the week's papers. This had been his habit for many years.

Ganggang, his three-year-old grandson, leaned against the side of the sofa and pulled his grandpa's arm with his chubby little hands. Twisting his body coyly, he asked, "Are we going, are we going?"

"Yes, yes, we're going," Mu promised. His mouth uttered the words, but his body didn't budge, and his eyes were still glued to the newspaper.

"You promised to take him to the park and ride the airplane," interceded Wang Lei, his wife of many years, poking her head out. "So hurry up and go!"

"Okay, let's go. Let's go right now!" Mu Zhijian finally put down the newspaper and shuffled to the front window in his slippers. On this clear, sunny day, the air was filled with the gaiety of spring. The tall poplars were dressed in emerald green, and pairs of birds flitted among the branches chirping endlessly. Mu Zhijian stretched and muttered to himself with a smile, "Such a beautiful day. We really should take a walk in the park!"

Before the Cultural Revolution, Mu Zhijian was already the Party Branch Secretary of this university. He was not even fifty at the time. Rich in experience and ability, and extremely energetic, he was regarded as a leading cadre with a bright future in higher education. Now, ten years later, his hair grey at the temples, he had returned to take up the responsibility of his office again. Fortunately, he was still in good health and full of energy, and confident that he could do a good job.

"Ah, Grandpa's taking me to the park!" Ganggang cried out joyfully. Mu Zhijian turned around, picked up Ganggang, and held him up. Looking directly into his happy face, he tapped Ganggang's forehead to his own. Then, putting him down, he said in a commanding voice, "Go get Grandpa's cloth shoes. We'll get going right away! Do you know how to get them?"

"Of course!" Before he finished answering, he got his sturdy little legs moving and ran into Grandpa's bedroom. He crawled bravely under the bed and pulled the shoes out one by one. Then he picked himself up, with a big shoe in each hand, and ran back with a *"deng deng deng"* into the living room.

Just then there was a light tapping heard in the hallway.

Mu Zhijjian put Ganggang aside and went to open the door. The visitor was a tall, thin, bespectacled man of about sixty.

Seeing Mu Zhijian, the visitor bowed with hands clasped and greeted his old friend. "It's been too long, honorable Mu!"

"Aya, it's Old Dai! Come in, come in. It's been years since I've seen you." Mu Zhijian stepped forward and warmly clasped his guest's hand. With delight he led the guest into the living room.

Ganggang didn't feel the least inclined to welcome this uninvited guest. He had a premonition that the fine prospects for going to the park would burst like a bubble. First he pouted, then tears began to sparkle in his eyes.

Mu Zhijian had no choice but to momentarily leave his

guest aside to console his little grandson. "Ganggang, be a good boy and go play with Grandma a little while."

"No, I won't . . ."

"Be nice. Grandpa is going to talk with our guest for just a little while. Then I'll take you to the park, I promise."

The name of this Old Dai was Dai Jiyao. He used to teach at this university and was quite a scholar of Ming history. During the Cultural Revolution, he was ousted from his post. Now he was ensconced in the History Research Institute. Perhaps because historians are so steeped in ancient times and pay no attention to the present, or perhaps because Dai really had something on his mind he seemed oblivious to the existence and change in humor of his young host, and proceeded to sit down on the sofa.

Mu Zhijian handed the unhappy Ganggang over to Wang Lei. He brewed a cup of Dragon Well tea and handed it to the guest. Smiling, he asked, "Old Dai, what breeze brought you here?"

"A devious breeze," Dai replied as he bowed to receive the tea. There was no trace of a smile on his face, but rather a look of sullen vexation.

Mu and Dai had not seen each other for more than ten years. Through their contacts in the past, Mu had formed a certain impression of the historian. He was a "scholar" who concentrated on his research and didn't even know what went on outside his window. People called him "master" to his face, but behind his back they called him "bookworm." Mu remembered that he rarely came to visit. One summer the roof of Dai's house leaked. He put a bucket under the leak to catch the rain rather than bother those in charge at the school. Mu had even made a self-criticism over this matter, faulting himself for not paying enough attention to the welfare of high-level intellectuals. Now, what devious breeze could have brought this "bookworm" to his door?

"I came to take advantage of a back door." Dai looked at the surprised Party Branch Secretary, and came out straightforwardly with his words. "I've always been buried in history and never even set foot out of my door. But now, what can I do? People force you to go through the back door. You've got to do it, whether you want to or not. It's really absurd, absolutely absurd."

Mu couldn't help laughing. This scholar who doesn't know how to go through the back door is truly not good at it, he thought. Just look at his indignant manner. There's not the least sense of seeking a favor.

Mu consoled his guest, saying, "It's okay, Old Dai, just say it. What is it?"

"There's a graduating student at your school named Ding Dazhi, isn't there?"

Mu thought for a moment, then nodded. "Yes, there is such a student."

"This person was originally from Peking, but was sent down to the countryside. In '76 he was admitted to the university through recommendation." Here Dai drew out his words slowly. "In the job assignments to graduates, I have heard that he is being assigned back to the province where he was before. His father became anxious and arranged for a job for him in Peking, through connections. He also worked it out at the other end, and they've agreed to let him go. Now, Honorable Mu, they've asked me to put in a word for them and ask the school to give him some special consideration and let him stay in Peking."

Dai talked with his head lowered and didn't look up to see how his listener was reacting to his words.

As he listened, Mu searched his recollections. That's right, in the graduating class there was indeed a student called Ding Dazhi, very good-looking, active in the school, had a wide-ranging social life outside of school. But not particularly good academically. Mu had the impression that he was quite a freewheeling student.

In 1977, when the university admission system was reformed, some students had put up a big-character poster, criticizing the fact that the so-called recommendation system of the Gang of Four benefitted those who went through the back door and was detrimental to academic merit. They gave an example of a student who said, in the entrance exam, that the reason the Paris Commune failed was that they didn't learn from Dazhai. Although the big-character poster didn't name the student, the whole school knew in no time that it was Ding Dazhi who had made such a fool of himself.

Two days later, Ding Dazhi himself put up a big-character poster, adamantly denying that he had gone through the back door. He claimed that he was admitted to the university by the recommendation of poor and middle peasants after thorough deliberations, and that it had been approved by his brigade, commune, and district. Furthermore, the documentation from all three levels was all there. Not only that, he even criticized the other big-character poster for turning the spearhead on the masses and distorting the great directives for the Cleaning-up-of-the-Ranks movement.

Two days after that, the students who had put up the first poster put up yet another one. This time they named the person directly, saying that the documentation for Ding Dazhi's "recommendation" was obtained by his father, Ding Qiliang, who had personally gone to where his son was sent and spent quite a sum of money for "manipulating expenses."

This made Ding really angry. In fact, the first challenge that Mu Zhijian had to face after he was reinstated was to calm down this furor. He spent a whole week holding a series of meetings and mobilizing many cadres from the university and the department to work on the case. Finally, both sides agreed to call it quits and to concentrate their animosity on the "Gang of Four."

Now, in order to get a job assignment in Peking, this Ding Dazhi and his parents had shown remarkable cleverness. Not only were they able to make connections with a receiving unit in Peking, but they also worked through their contacts in the other province to get them to "agree to relinquish him." They even enlisted this stolidly honest Dai Jiyao to go through the back door! This Ding Dazhi, what did his family do anyway? How come they could maneuver so well?

There was dead silence in the living room. Having done what he came to do, Dai couldn't think of anything else to say. Mu Zhijian puffed continually on his cigarette and wracked his brains for quite a while before he spoke.

"Old Dai, this student you're talking about doesn't have a very good reputation at our school. He went through the back door to get admitted."

"Is that right? I didn't know that!" Dai leaned back just a bit, took out a handkerchief, and wiped his nose vigorously. He didn't know what to say next.

"Now on this job assignment, he's going through the back door again. Is that right or not?" Mu looked hard at Dai, and subconsciously raised his voice. "Old Dai, you've been teaching a good many years. Before the Cultural Revolution, how many graduates contested their job assignments? Those were rare and extremely special cases. Now? Some people have publicly announced the slogan: 'Tian-Nan-Hai-Bei,* or nothing!"

"What's this Tian-Nan-Hai-Bei?" Dai didn't understand.

Mu laughed, squinted his eyes, and explained, "Tian stands for Tianjin, Nan is Nanjing, Hai is Shanghai, and Bei is Beijing."

"I never thought there were such students," Dai said, as he kept shaking his head.

"Old Dai, you are a historian. Now is the time we must follow the example of the Han Emperor Gaozu, and uproot this chaotic world and set it right again. Only then will we bring peace and order to the world!" Mu became a bit overexcited. He stood up, poured himself a glass of water, took a couple of gulps, and went on. "This time when I was reinstated in my job, I stated several times at Party Branch meetings that in order to rectify the atmosphere of the school, we must grab hold of the two ends—one being student enrollment, the other being job assignments. We've got to get hold of these two strategic points—entrance and exit. Then there's hope. If we are not selective at the entrance, how can the caliber of education be guaranteed? If at the exit people don't comply with the state's assignments, what's the point in cultivating talent?"

"What you say is absolutely right," Dai said, nodding several times.

Mu sighed and continued. "The trouble is, determination on the part of the university is not enough to grab hold of the two strategic points. There's too much of a push from society at large."

"My taking the liberty to come to see you today can also be counted as being pushy," Dai said very apologetically. "But Honorable Mu, don't mind me. I've only come as a favor to someone else. Whether or not it would work out rests entirely on the two sides. Don't let yourself be put on the spot, by any means!"

Hearing this, Mu's curiosity was piqued. "What connection do you have with Ding Dazhi's family, Old Dai?"

"We're not relatives, not old friends, nothing really." Dai shook his head, and then went on. "About this Ding Dazhi —how tall he is, what he looks like, what kind of person he is—I know absolutely nothing. And I know even less about what sort of person his father is."

"Then who was it that asked this favor of you?" Mu thought this was becoming very peculiar.

"This is all the fine work of that Minister of Internal Affairs I have back home. Actually, she doesn't know this Ding family either. She has a cousin who knows Ding Dazhi's father. They say his father is in some kind of business. Now Honorable Mu, I don't have any vices, except Duke Ouyang's fondness for the cup.** I've got to have a couple of ounces of good wine every day. Now, I don't know if Ding's father probed and found out about this love of mine, or if my wife went through her cousin to get Ding's father to get me some. In any case, for the past couple of years, I've never been without good wine. *Hai!* It's all my fault for loving the cup and causing all this trouble. And now they've come to ask this favor. My wife's cousin came to our place several days ago and used all her wiles on me. She said that since I'm a good friend of yours, and since you're in control of job assignments, I should help out on this. Honorable Mu, this kind of thing is really hard for me to bring up, but what can I do? It's really exasperating, truly exasperating." As he became a little excited, he pounded his right fist into his left palm.

"Old Dai, you don't need to be upset either," Mu said with an ironic smile. "It's not been just eight or ten people who have come to me about this sort of thing. In the right drawer of my office desk I've got a list of thirty-eight graduates' names on it, all requests from people who have come to me. Some even came with official documents asking for special consideration in job assignments. Your visit just adds one more name to the list."

"What are you going to do?" Dai asked.

"What to do? There are only two approaches to the problem," Mu said with a slight smile. "One is not to be afraid of offending people or of losing one's post; stick by the rules and don't make any exceptions except for those that require special consideration as stipulated by official policy. The other approach is to keep one eye open and one eye shut, exercising one's prerogative to expedite matters for oneself or for others. We're having a meeting this very afternoon to discuss the question of job allocation for these thirty-eight—or thirty-nine students."

"I'm really sorry to have made things difficult for you," Dai said. He truly felt from the bottom of his heart that he had done something he shouldn't have.

"Oh, it's nothing. We'll look into it and see."

"I'll be going then, Honorable Mu," said Dai, as he stood up. He walked to the door, then turned his head to say, "Honorable Mu, I'd like to apologize again. I've ruined a fun outing for you and your grandson."

After seeing the guest out, Mu paced back into the living room. The spring sunshine was just as enchanting as before and the birds in the trees were just as happy. But the joy of spring had slipped away from him. Those thirty-eight—no, thirty-nine—names were spinning in his head. Behind each name there was a whole set of connections. Those connections were like a spider's web that had him ensnared in its center, making it impossible for him to move.

He recalled the time two years ago when those students had exposed Ding Dazhi's admission through the back door. As the story went, the brigade had originally recommended an educated girl who had been sent down to the countryside. The girl had done better than Ding. But Ding's father, by giving someone a Yongjiu (Everlasting) bicycle, had gotten Ding placed ahead of the educated girl.

"Despicable, absolutely despicable," Mu thought as he paced back and forth in the living room. He had never seen this Ding Qiliang, but he had an image in his mind of someone nodding and bowing, and always affecting an obsequious smile. He even began to wonder if Ding Qiliang hadn't had an eye on him ever since he returned to his post at the university. This father had probably sized up Mu's social contacts early

---

* The phrase "Tian-Nan-Hai-Bei," literally "South of Heaven and north of the sea," should mean anywhere in the world but actually represents the cities of Tianjin, Nanjing, Shanghai, and Beijing (Peking), where most college students would prefer to be sent to work after graduation.

** Duke Ouyang is the Song dynasty scholar, official, and poet Ouyang Xiu (1007–1070), who styled himself the Drunken Old Man (*zuiweng*).

on to make sure his son stayed in Peking. Then he picked out Dai as the weak link. Employing that wine as his entry, that was using a long rope to make the connection—why, he must have spent two years plotting this back door maneuver.

"People like that must not be allowed to get their way," he thought. He stopped in his tracks. He had made up his mind, and a burden seemed lifted from his heart. Just then Ganggang pattered into the room, shouting at the top of his lungs, "Are we going or not? Grandpa, let's go."

"All right, let's go. We'll get going right away."

This time Ganggang didn't wait for Grandpa's order—he brought over the shoes by the door and watched Grandpa put them on. Mu finished changing his shoes, but before he could get up, he heard a woman's boisterous voice laughing and chatting in the hallway.

"Sister Wang, are you here?"

Wang Lei hurried to the door and welcomed her friend with a broad smile.

"Sister Li, come on in!"

Sister Li was one of the people who had lived on this street the longest. According to the story, way back when only members of royalty lived in this lane, the Li family had already built a little shanty in front of the lane. By the time Sister Li married into this family, they had already been here for umpteen generations. Sister Li herself grew up in a compound in Peking. She was very spunky and capable, spoke directly and had strong principles, never shying away from criticizing injustice or speaking her mind. When Mu Zhijian was under attack and the whole family was really down and out, when all their other friends had deserted them, Sister Li still continued to visit them as she always had. As she would say, "Everybody is weighed on the same scale. Whatever a person measures up to, people know in their hearts. You can't arbitrarily make it any more or any less." When Mu was sent down to labor camp, and his son was away, it was the warmhearted Sister Li who singlehandedly took care of the old and young ones left at home. The Mu family all had a great deal of respect for her. It was the older generation that called her Sister Li. The younger generation called her Mama Li, and the even younger ones called her Grandma Li.

When another visitor's voice was heard in the hallway, Ganggang's smiling face turned teary again. Mu Zhijian patted his little head, saying, "It's Grandma Li coming to see Grandma. We don't need to bother with them!"

Ganggang's tears broke off and he smiled. Mu stood up and took Ganggang's hand. Just as they were about to leave, Wang Lei brought Sister Li into the living room saying, "Old Mu, Sister Li has something she wants to talk over with you."

"Ahh," Mu stopped short, wondering what she wanted to talk to him about.

Ganggang was so upset he stamped his feet and cried.

Wang Lei picked up her squalling little grandson and carried him out of the room.

"Sister Li, sit down, sit down. What's on your mind? Tell me all about it," Mu said, brewing a cup of tea for her, as he did for all his guests.

Sister Li sat down, took the cup of tea, and then sighed before she began to speak.

"Old Comrade Mu, there's a family named Song at the east end of our lane. The old lady's name is Jin. Do you know her?"

Mu shook his head. He had lived here several decades, but still wasn't clear who all lived in this lane.

"*Ai*! It was Sister Jin who grumbled to me about this matter. When I heard about it, I felt sorry for them. I don't know if I ought to meddle, but I just didn't have the heart to stand by and not do something about it."

What could this be? Mu was really puzzled. Could she be trying to go through the back door too? But, on second thought, Sister Li was staunch and upright—never the type who would maneuver through a back door.

Then he heard Sister Li go on to say, "Well, on Sister Jin's mother's side of the family, there's a nephew . . . "

As Mu listened, everything sounded more and more far-fetched. Now in Mr. Song's household there was an old wife named Jin, and on her mother's side of the family there was a nephew—what kind of nonsense was this! He could hear Sister Li sighing and going on.

"This nephew of hers had the baby-name of Mallet—the surname is Ding."*

As soon as he heard the name Ding, Mu's mind jumped! Why, here's another one named Ding. He heard Sister Li spinning out the story.

"This kid's school name is Ding Dazhi, and he's a student at your school. Old Comrade Mu, do you by any chance know of this kid?"

Comrade Mu didn't know what to say. He just nodded.

"You've got such a good memory," Sister Li said with a smile. "There are hundreds and thousands of students, and you can still remember one so clearly."

"I may not remember the others, but I certainly do remember Ding Dazhi." He furrowed his brow for an instant, and smiled scornfully, but Sister Li didn't notice. She just went right on with her story.

"Getting him into college just about ruined his parents. They went broke and had all kinds of trials and tribulations."

Mu was startled. What was all this?

"*Ai*, Old Mu, of course you wouldn't know the whole story." Sister Li continued, "This Ding Qiliang is a low level cadre in the Bureau of Commerce. He doesn't make much money. His wife is just a housewife and she's never been in good health. They've never had it easy. Things have always been hard on them. They've got two kids. The older one is a girl who was born with some sort of heart ailment. So she stayed in Peking and was assigned to a factory. But she can't even put in two days' work out of every three. The second kid is this Ding Dazhi. He was sent down to the countryside in '69. When he first went, there were several dozen schoolmates with him in the same village. Within two years, all those who had influence had joined the army, got jobs, returned to the city, or got into school. Everybody left, leaving just a few kids who didn't have back doors to languish away in that mountain gully. Just imagine, watching everybody leave, being so far from home—how could a kid not get restless? The two old folks were worried too, so they sought out everybody they knew to help their son get transferred back. In '76, when colleges were enrolling students, they heard that the brigade was allocated one opening. But an opening is no use if you

---

* Ding is a homophone for a character meaning "nail," and thus the baby name is a play on the child's surname.

just stand by and watch. In those days, you had to be recommended—but who would ever recommend you?"

Sister Li stopped to catch her breath, took a sip of her tea, and then went on. "The two old folks talked it over thoroughly, and decided they had to do some hustling for their kid. They couldn't let this opportunity go by. So they sold the old man's watch, scraped up enough money for the trip, asked for a leave from work, and took a trip to where their son was to beg for the favor from the powers that be. There's an old saying—people's favors are bigger than the sky. You can't buy it if you don't have money and influence! Now things aren't supposed to work that way anymore, but there are still plenty of people who respond to money and influence, but not to principle! A petty cadre like Ding Qiliang—who would do him a favor? The old man sold his watch; they spent all their money and ran their legs to the bone. The only thing they didn't do was kneel and kowtow to the powers that be. They exhausted their resources and didn't accomplish a damned thing. *Ai*! Luckily, just as they were leaving, the Party Branch Secretary in charge at the village opened his golden mouth and let slip that he would let their son go if they could bring him a Yongjiu bicycle. There was no other way, so the old man went home and sold everything in the house that was worth anything. But that wasn't enough so they begged here and borrowed there, and finally managed to buy a Yongjiu bicycle. The old man himself lugged it there to the guy, and only then managed to get his son into college."

Mu just sat there stunned. What he heard put him into a daze. Never in a million years would he have suspected such a pitiful tragedy lay behind this absolutely despicable drama of going through the back door.

Sister Li crossed her hands over her heart and sighed endlessly as she went on. "Well, they managed to get their son back, but they incurred a pile of debts. This was too much for the old lady, and she became ill and bedridden. The old man had to keep up with his job and take care of his sick wife at home. On top of that, he had to eke out money to pay back the debts. What kind of a life do you think that's like? For the past couple of years they haven't even been able to light a stove in the dead of winter. And they never buy vegetables on the racks. They just pick up half-rotten stems and leaves from rubbish piles and steam them up in some dough. They can't even afford pickles. They've really had a hell of a time getting by. I heard Sister Jin say that this brother-in-law of hers is barely fifty, but that he's already bald, his teeth have fallen out, and his back is hunched. His legs even shake when he walks. Why, he's aged so that he looks more like a sixty- or seventy-year-old. Whatever for? Didn't it all come from going through the back door for the sake of their son? Now wouldn't you say that's just too much punishment to bring on oneself?"

The more Mu listened, the heavier his heart felt. He envisioned an old man so burdened from going through the back door that he couldn't even lift his head and straighten his back. This man was walking toward him, painfully, step by step. He seemed to hear this old man opening his toothless mouth and asking, "Have I committed a crime? What have I done to deserve this punishment?"

"Now, they're faced with another crisis." Sister Li's voice seemed to be coming from far away. "That wasn't the end of it. Now it's time for job assignments. They say that he's being sent back to the same place again. Isn't that practically asking them for their lives? The whole family is so upset, they've gone everywhere begging for help. This time they can be considered lucky. There's a factory in Peking that will take him, and the people at the other end agree to let him go. Now it's just a matter of getting permission from your school. I don't know how they found out that you and I are friends, but they sent Sister Jin to plead with me. When I heard about it, I told them that as long as Old Mu is in charge of this matter, they had nothing to worry about, that this guy Mu may be one of those higher-ups, but he's not stuck-up. He's congenial in his dealings with everybody and he's understanding and considerate. I told them that if I just told you the ins and outs of this story, you'd be sure to do what you could. Now, Old Comrade Mu, wouldn't you agree?"

Struck with that question, Mu was speechless. Sister Li put her cup on the table and went on with her own commentary.

"My old man kept trying to stop me, saying that this is tantamount to going through the back door, telling me I shouldn't get entangled in this. So I asked him—is there any justice left in this world? Oh, the sons and daughters of big cadres have it easy—they can breeze right through the back door. All they have to do is make a quick phone call, or drop a note, and it's all taken care of, while the kids of ordinary folks have to jump through hoops to get the littlest thing done and are frozen out. Now the whole Ding family has been ruined getting their son through the back door, and we shouldn't lend them a hand? I told my old man, I sure am going to meddle in this and he can just keep his patter to himself."

Mu didn't know what to say. Her story might be a rationalization, but it was the truth. The list with the thirty-eight names on it—didn't many of them get on it by just a phone call from a certain chief, or a note from a certain office? Of course, the fates of these thirty-eight hadn't been decided yet; they awaited the deliberations of this afternoon's meeting. But to get registered on this list was indeed no trouble at all for those "big guns." But for someone like Ding Qiliang, God only knew how much blood and tears he had to sweat. Looking at it that way, it was indeed unfair.

Sister Li stopped talking. She was waiting for an answer. Mu felt that an overwhelming weight was holding down his tongue and he was unable to speak. Finally he said in a weary, almost rude tone of voice, "Sister Li, you just go on home."

Sister Li looked up. She sensed that Old Mu was not his usual amiable self anymore. She stood up slowly.

After a pause, Mu added, "The matter you spoke of, we'll be discussing it at a meeting this afternoon."

As Sister Li said goodbye to Wang Lei, Mu just sat on the sofa; he didn't even stand up. He heard them murmuring something in the hallway. Then he couldn't hear them anymore. Visions of Ding Dazhi and Ding Qiliang alternated in his mind's eye. Now he suddenly felt that Ding Dazhi was not as free-wheeling as he had thought after all. Maybe free-wheeling was just another manifestation of vulnerability. When someone vulnerable is injured, he's got to be a bit free-wheeling in order to protect himself.

And yet, what could he do for this family and their son? Help them get what they want? But that was against the codes, and it went against the vow he made to himself when he resumed his post. Should he turn them down? That would be a heavy blow to the old folks. Moreover, if he was going to turn him down, he should turn down all thirty-nine who'd requested special consideration in being assigned to major cities. If he couldn't be even-handed, how could it possibly be fair?

"Grandpa, are we going or not? . . . " Ganggang was already standing in front of the sofa.

"We're going . . . " Mu's voice didn't sound so vibrant anymore. In fact he was a bit weary, as if he felt too tired to get up from the sofa.

From the hallway came the sound of another rapping on the door, followed by a very familiar man's voice. "Little Mu, are you here?"

From the familiar address, Mu knew right away that it was Deputy Minister Gao Chengzong. Gao was his first supervisor when he joined the revolution, and so could be considered his first mentor. A great deal of Mu's know-how and experience derived directly from him. Not only that, Mu's way of thinking, his work style, even some of his speech mannerisms and habits reflected shades of Gao Chengzong.

Mu got up and was about to get the door, but Wang Lei had already rushed up to open it.

"Minister Gao, how come Nini didn't come along?" asked Wang Lei as she led the guest in.

Nini was Minister Gao's only child. She always came along whenever he came to visit the Mus. There was an unspoken reason behind that; Minister Gao had hoped that Wang Lei would find a match for his daughter.

"Ha ha! Nini's got a match now, so she doesn't hang around her old dad anymore." Gao Chengzong laughed heartily. He shook Mu's hand while answering Wang Lei's question.

"Oh?" A trace of surprise flitted across Mu's face. Then he smiled and said, "That's wonderful! Congratulations!"

When Wang Lei went to make tea, Ganggang cuddled up to Gao and appealed to him. "Grandpa Gao, Grandpa promised to take me to the park, and now we're not going again."

"Ah, that's not right. We'll have to criticize him." Gao patted Ganggang's little cheeks. He said to Mu, "Little Mu, this thing with Nini happened so suddenly you must be a bit surprised, eh? Ha ha! Even I was surprised. Just think, this daughter of mine is already twenty-seven. You've got to admit she isn't exactly pretty. She's even said herself that she espoused the creed of singlehood. But, there was a real coincidence. Last Sunday I took her to Yunshui Cave. She ran into a high school classmate of hers there and the two of them hit it off right away. We came back on the bus together. Things developed very quickly, and both of them are very content. We ought to thank the God of Love for that. Ha ha!"

"That's wonderful!" Mu said, but in his heart he was feeling a bit suspicious. To describe Nini as "not exactly pretty" was an understatement. She was downright ugly. Besides which she was blind in her right eye. She herself had high expectations. They had asked all their friends to help, but nobody came up with anyone suitable. So how did she suddenly hit on such a match?

"Ah, Wang Lei, I can finally unload this rock that's been weighing on my heart," Gao said with glee. "Girls ought to marry when they grow up. I've had a hard time marrying her off. It really worried me to death. I've had my share of grief over it."

"When's the wedding feast," Mu asked with a smile.

"Soon," Gao laughed heartily. "What creed of singlehood! I saw through that. It couldn't stand up to a single assault, and caved in with the first onset."

Mu laughed with him.

"Oh! That's right, Little Mu, there's a matter that I need to have you take care of." Gao turned to Mu saying, "This future son-in-law of mine is in the graduating class of your school."

"Ah!" Mu was startled, and stammered, "What's his name?"

"The name is Ding Dazhi."

So it's Ding Dazhi again, he thought. The name hit him on the head like a sledge hammer. He leaned back against the sofa, utterly stupefied.

"I heard that Ding Dazhi was assigned to another province. Little Mu, under these circumstances, could you give him some special consideration and let him stay in Peking . . . ?"

Gao went on to say something else, but Mu couldn't hear another thing. He couldn't believe that there could be such a quick wedding in this world. Was it conspiracy, or was it really romance? Was it going through the back door, or was it a marriage? The images of Ding Dazhi and Ding Qiliang became blurred again in his mind. What kind of people were they anyway? Were they sharks at maneuvering, or were they pitiful worms completely oppressed by the burden of having to go through the back door? How could such people be pitiful worms?

"What's wrong? Is there some problem with Ding Dazhi?" asked Gao, noticing Mu's silence and the strained expression on his face.

"No, no," Mu said, shaking his head several times.

"In that case, would you please take care of it for me?" asked Gao as he turned to play with Ganggang. He felt that the conversation could just about be concluded.

Mu roused from his stupor. He would like to tell this old mentor of his everything that had happened in the visits from Dai Jiyao and Sister Li. He felt that it was his responsibility to do so, and yet, how could those contradictions provide a clear picture? And what would be accomplished by it? If Ding Dazhi turned out to be blameless, he might shatter the love between these two young people. And to Nini, this love was priceless. One might even say it was a once in a lifetime chance for her. But if it turned out to be a fraud, and he didn't warn them in time, what an awful blow it would be for both Nini and her father.

"Old Gao . . ." Mu finally asked complaisantly, "do you think Ding Dazhi really loves Nini?"

"I don't understand this thing called love. My own marriage was arranged by my parents." Gao suddenly seemed very sober.

"Mu!! What kind of a question is that," Wang Lei chided, as she tried to stop him.

Mu did not let Wang Lei deter him. "Old Gao," he asked again, "do you think Nini will be happy?"

Gao pondered a moment, and then answered, "Possibly in the time before I leave this earth, Nini will be happy."

"Old Mu, what's come over you today?" Wang Lei interceded peevishly.

"Little Mu is right," Gao said to Wang Lei, waving his hand. "What he's thinking of, I've thought of too. But I've also thought of some things he hasn't. All right, we'll just leave it at that. This matter about the job assignment, I'll leave it in your hands. Now I've got to go home and tell the young folks. They're waiting eagerly. Ha ha!"

Gao had recovered his crisp laugh, his brow was once again unfurrowed. The visitor left.

Mu leaned back on the sofa, his mind all ajumble. His images of Ding Dazhi and his father clashed in his mind—they were so despicable at times, so pitiable at other times. It was so confusing and elusive, there was no way to get a hold on it. Then visions and voices of the successive visitors replayed before his eyes and echoed in his ears—Old Dai's exasperated demeanor, Sister Li's righteous indignation, and Gao's ringing laugh. It seemed as though going through the back door had become an insurmountable tidal wave. It had engulfed so many comrades, stalwart comrades at that. This torrent was rushing up against him, and he felt he was already unable to withstand it . . .

"Grandpa, are we going or not?" Ganggang burst into the room, yelling as loud as he could.

But by the time this sound reached his ears, it was very faint, and was soon drowned out by that clamorous, chaotic back door stampede. No, I've got to hold firm, I can't fold up, Mu Zhijian resolved. That's right. It's not easy, but precisely for that reason, I've got to exert all my strength. He felt the eyes of all the teachers and students of the school fixed on him, watching to see if he could live up to the vow he made when he resumed office. In fact, he felt as though society at large was watching him, watching to see if this Party Branch Secretary could uphold the mission required of a Communist Party member and a prominent Party cadre.

"Grandpa, are we going or not?" Ganggang was practically wailing.

Mu stood up, patted his grandson's head, and said, "Come on, let's go. We'll go ride the airplane."

"There's not enough time, is there?" asked Wang Lei. "Don't you have a meeting this afternoon?"

Mu took his grandson by the hand and walked out, turning his head to say, "There's time enough. Right now we'll go to the park, get some fresh air, and perk up our spirits. Then, I'll go to the meeting." ★

Originally published in *Shen Rong xiaoshuo xuan* (*Selected Stories of Shen Rong*), Beijing: Beijing chubanshe, 1981.

Translated by Vivian Hsu

Marginal Lives

behind a small door
a hand draws the latch softly
as if pulling a rifle bolt

—Bei Dao

When you pass by my window,
Bless me, please,
For the light is still on.

—Shu Ting

Many of the problems and the compensations of life in China, as anywhere else, have little or nothing to do with politics. The alienation of big city life and cruelty toward the handicapped and deformed are aspects of life anywhere, as are a love as warm as a shared overcoat on a winter's night or as comforting as a desert oasis. Shi Tiesheng's sensitive story "One Winter's Evening" (*Yige dongtian de wanshang*) skillfully encompasses the elements of alienation, longing for a normal family life, fear of rejection, and mutually sustaining love that make up the lives of two people existing at the margin in China's capital city. Typical of Shi's richly imagistic style is the double encounter with the manhole cover; first to demonstrate the good-heartedness of the female protagonist, and finally to symbolize the true worth of these two gentle souls, kindred spirits who only appear crooked (deformed) from a distance, because no one takes the time to look closely enough.

In "Lunch Break" Shi Tiesheng takes us down into the "lower depths" of Chinese society, to witness the pitiful and ironic dreams of the much neglected lumpen proletariat. These are people who work in the small workshops of urban China and are not protected by the "safety net" of social welfare that secures the lives of workers in state-run enterprises. Not since Lu Xun's works have these people, warts and all, been portrayed in such a realistic manner. The story was reprinted in *Xinhua wenzhai* (*Literary Selections*) together with two critical comments, one quite favorable and one extremely opposed to writing about such things in socialist China. ★

One Winter's Evening

by Shi Tiesheng

Photo by Saundra Sturdevant

Ever since they got off the bus at four that afternoon the two of them had been wandering around the neighborhood looking for a certain lane.

"Are you sure you remembered it right?" asked the man.

"Quite sure," replied the woman. "Number 57, Moonlight Lane."

The whole area was a maze of lanes, which was unfortunate because the woman had lost her map with directions. The sun was already fast disappearing behind last night's heavy snowfall. The snow had melted slightly during the day and now was beginning to freeze hard again. Walking was difficult.

The couple were in their forties, with the man slightly the older of the two. The woman was tiny. In fact she was a midget. The man used a crutch and his face was covered with hideous burn scars.

It was quiet within the alleyways, but the wind was strong. People scurried past from time to time, no one looking anyone else in the eye, which was just fine by them.

The woman walked in front, hugging a large tin of cookies. She had tried several times without success to hold the tin under one arm to give the other a rest, but she was wearing too many layers of clothing and the tin was just too big. As the woman wrestled with the tin, the man walked on ahead and, breathing heavily, turned to look back at her.

"Serves you right," he said. "You almost managed to lose yourself too!"

She raised her face to smile up at him and took a couple of steps forward to catch up, still clutching the large tin.

The woman had lost her purse earlier when they were buying the child's tricycle. She was dithering back and forth, trying to choose the best one, when she discovered the loss. Losing a bit of money wasn't so important, but the map had been in that purse. Luckily, she could still remember the street name and number.

"It's very cold today," she said, stealing a glance up at her husband.

The man said nothing.

"Just think—we've been rushing around the whole day . . . ," she continued, looking up apologetically at the man, as if she were responsible for the day's bad luck.

With some effort the man continued on his way, his crutch under one arm, holding the tricycle in his other hand and dodging the patches of melted snow on the road, which were beginning to harden.

"Is your liver bothering you again?" asked the woman.

The man ignored her.

"It wouldn't look good if we didn't go—we told Mrs. Shi we would," she said in a small voice.

"There you go again, gabbling away and changing your mind. If you don't want to go we could have gone home long ago!" The man was very short-tempered.

The woman began walking faster, taking uneven strides forward. The cookie tin was too big, preventing her from seeing the ground beneath her.

"Your liver will get worse if you're unhappy like that all the time. What's more . . . " She swallowed whatever else she had been meaning to say. After walking a while longer she said, "Mrs. Shi has already arranged for us to see him. You can have a look at him first and if you don't want him we don't have to take him—it's not too late yet."

"I never said I didn't want him!" cried the man.

"In fact," commented the woman with a smile, "I don't think this child is at all bad—better-looking than that other one anyway." She spoke quickly, as if she had long been waiting for an opportunity to say this.

"Well, as long as you think he's fine, there's no problem, is there?"

"What are you saying that for? It's not just me . . . "

They went on in silence, examining the street-signs at the entrance to each lane. There were so many in this neighborhood.

"If you like him too, then we'll take him." The woman

was trying her hardest to ease the atmosphere slightly. "What's more, I ought to have another look too—I really only caught a glimpse of him on the bus that time."

The wind set a few courtyard doors banging.

Occasionally a flurry of snow would be blown off a shadowed roof-top and make its way down people's necks.

"I still think you should put on my scarf," said the woman. "I'm not at all cold and, what's more . . . " Her attention focused entirely on him, she almost tripped over a brick lying frozen in the road.

"I *told* you to give that tin to me," shouted the man.

"Well, I won't! Not unless you give me the tricycle to push!"

"That's not necessary—I can manage both of them." His voice had suddenly gone much lower.

A group of chattering, giggling girls turned out of the lane ahead and came in their direction. There was a silence as the girls walked towards them.

The man turned his face away, apparently studying the street-sign.

The girls walked on past and the couple continued without a sound. The woman wanted to go faster, but she was afraid the man would not be able to keep up. Some time passed before they heard the sound of laughter and voices again, going off into the distance.

"Give it to me!"

"Then give me the trike!"

"It's not necessary!"

"I know what you're afraid of," muttered the woman, holding on to the tin and walking steadfastly ahead.

"Me afraid? What have I got to be afraid of?"

The woman said nothing.

"If that's what you want, just go ahead and push it! What do I care?" The man was still shouting, but his tone had softened considerably.

And so the woman didn't take the tricycle after all. Whenever she got angry or felt aggrieved she would blink fiercely and not utter a word. She knew he was doing it for her sake, that he was afraid that she too . . . Well, being so small in the first place, and wheeling a child's tricycle too . . . But she still felt upset and angry with him. "Why didn't you find someone taller than me?" she asked silently.

"What if your leg had been fine and face not burned?"

"I don't know—my leg and face have been like this ever since I can remember."

"But just suppose . . . suppose your leg wasn't . . . "

"Just suppose?!" He flared up again and pulled up a weed which he twisted around his finger while looking off towards some lights in the distance. There was a small shed there belonging to the watchman at a construction site.

"If you don't want to talk about it, that's fine," she said. "But you mustn't be angry."

He turned his face fiercely towards her. "Just suppose I'd never existed in the first place, eh? Just suppose the world never existed?"

"What's the point in saying all this? I was talking about reality . . . "

"*I* know there's no point, so let's not talk about it. This is the way I am, and you're the way you are—*that's* reality for you."

They were sitting beside a pile of bricks by the roadside. The city moat's muddy water flowed on in the moonlight. Mosquitoes attacked their faces. Beyond, in the distance, lay the silent construction site.

"It'll be a real mess around here when those apartments are built," she commented.

He looked at the moon, saying nothing. The moon was so tiny and so far away. The moon that night, too, had seemed particularly small and remote.

"Reality's the only thing that matters—what's the point in talking about possibilities?" He continued looking at the moon as he said, almost to himself, "As soon as I saw you that day, I knew we should be together. That's reality for you."

"As soon as you saw me? When was that?"

"I've forgotten when it was exactly, but I was sitting in a bar near a bus-stop, watching you trying to squeeze your way onto a bus and never quite making it."

"Yes," she thought, "that's reality! So many years now." And she tried to catch his eye.

"I can carry it," she said. "Truly! It's only a cookie tin—I can manage it." She was deliberately pretending nothing had happened.

She continued, "Remember that time I got An-An? I managed to carry that big basket all the way back by myself, didn't I?" An-An was their cat.

Breathing hard, the man walked on, his crutch making a tapping sound as he went. She began to feel bad again as she remembered the loss of her purse.

"It was really strange losing that purse. You were standing right behind me when I was buying the cookies, weren't you?" She was trying to change the subject.

The man still said nothing, but did glance at her once.

"Why are you always so unhappy?" What she feared most was his getting angry, for as soon as that happened his liver began to give him trouble.

When she saw he still wasn't going to say anything she brought up the subject of the map once again.

"Mrs. Shi really took a lot of care over that map—she spent over half-an-hour drawing it!"

"And then you went and lost it." His tone was very mild. She laughed and said, "It would have been better if I'd given you the purse to carry!"

"Look out!" the man cried.

Startled, the woman avoided a small hole in the ground. She was always looking up at her husband, hoping he was happy, hoping he'd smile.

"Why do you keep on looking at me all the time?"

"How do you know I'm looking at you if you're not looking at me?"

"Well, what's the verdict? Better-looking than a baboon, eh?"

"Than what? Better-looking than who?"

"Haven't you ever been to the zoo?"

"Yes, when I was a little girl."

"Well, what do *you* think I look like?"

"Like a wooden lump that doesn't know how to laugh."

"If a wooden lump laughed there'd be an earthquake."

"What are you afraid of . . . there's no one else around."

"Aren't you afraid?"

"I'm really afraid when I see you unhappy all the time."

Then he smiled; he was really ugly; but she still hoped that their family could be just like other people's. . . . That night she told him for the first time that she really wanted a child; from a hospital, naturally, or someone else's. . . .

The sun had disappeared completely. They were still wandering around the same neighborhood, searching blindly everywhere. People were leaving work. It was cold, and they were hurrying homewards. The woman wanted to ask the way several times, but the man wouldn't let her.

"What's there to be afraid of?"

"Who said anything about being afraid?"

"I'll go and ask—you don't have to."

"No you won't!"

They continued onwards. The number of people going home now seemed to indicate a factory in the vicinity.

"Are you feeling tired?" asked the woman in a small voice as if she were afraid of startling someone. "Is your liver troubling you?" she asked again.

The man did not reply. He did not feel like talking.

"Oh, it's all my fault . . . What if you just sit here and rest a while and wait for me?"

The man rolled his eyes at her impatiently and continued walking.

They walked on silently through the tide of workers heading homewards, a gap sometimes appearing between them. A tall chimney in the distance spewed out black smoke which blew raggedly in the southeasterly wind. Some sparrows flew in a flurry onto a rooftop, then onto the bare branches of a jujube tree before flying off once again. An old woman wearing a white apron stood on a corner, crying, "Fresh hot meatballs! Just ready to eat!"

After some time they realized they had made their way back to the main road. Not far off stood the cinema where they got off the bus earlier that afternoon. There was nothing to do but turn back. Fewer people were on the streets now. The ruts in the road had turned into channels of ice and several children were sliding along them. The woman kept turning back to look at them.

"Are you coming or not?" The man had wanted to flare up at her again, but then he noticed that she was looking at the children.

A little flustered, she said, "I thought one of them was him."

"Which one?" The man stopped walking and looked at the children.

"It isn't him—he just looks a bit like that one over there, the smallest one."

They continued looking for a while. The children were having fun on the ice; all brightly colored, they looked like so many balls of wool.

"Let's get going," he said, nudging her with the tricycle. "Come on, let's go!" he said again.

"The little boy we're going to see is better-looking than that one over there—not that he's so bad himself." She was still turning back at intervals to look.

They passed two more lanes, neither of them the right one. The woman kept going on about the boy. "Why do you think everyone says illegitimate children are always good-looking and intelligent? His mother wants to get married—how else could anyone bear to give their own child away to someone else? That man must really be . . . "

"Look out where you're going!"

"The only thing is . . . I was thinking that maybe four-and-a-half is a bit too old."

"Well, whatever, it won't be like having one of your own."

"No, that's not what I was worrying about. What does worry me is . . . "

The man turned round fiercely to face her and she came to an abrupt halt, as if her own thoughts had scared her.

"You don't think he'll be afraid of us, do you? Do you think he'll understand? After all, he's only four-and-a-half . . ." She had finally managed to say it.

The wind had become even stronger. Somewhere an old iron pot was blown clattering to the ground. They walked on blindly, forgetting to check the street names.

In fact, this was not the first time either of them had thought of this, but for some reason neither of them had ever mentioned it. Perhaps they had thought that by avoiding mention of it, it would remain only a possibility; or perhaps they had meant to bring it up several times, but somehow the subject always changed . . .

"Do you think we should get a boy or a girl?" She sat on the bed, rewinding her precious yarn. Whenever she had some money, she loved to wander around the yarn shops, buying brightly-colored yarn which she never used and which lay piled up in a chest. That evening she had tipped it all out and was now rewinding it, ball by ball.

"It doesn't really matter which . . . boy or girl," he said. He had wanted to bring this up, but she had beat him to it.

"That's what I think, too. Girls and boys both wear bright colors nowadays." She was referring to the yarn.

He said nothing else, thinking that perhaps it wouldn't . . .

One night she was once again awakened by his shouts. He was always having nightmares. It was raining hard outside. He lit a cigarette. "If you want one, get one that's a bit older . . . ," he said suddenly. The red glow of his cigarette brightened and dimmed.

"Try to sleep some more—it's still early," she said. The street-lights were still on and the shadow of a tree wavered against the wall.

"That's all I ask—you can decide everything else."

"I'm afraid if he's too old he might . . ." She had wanted to talk about it then.

He came suddenly to lay his head on her breast. "People with cirrhosis of the liver don't live long you know. I think we should get an older kid—and then he can help you out when the time comes."

Lightning illuminated his tear-streaked face. She cradled his head and lay there, terrified, looking at the wavering tree-shadow on the wall. Later she cried, and forgot to talk about it.

And then there had been the evening they had sat enjoying the cool shade under the overpass. A young couple were playing hide-and-seek with their little girl at the head of the bridge. While the mother held her hands over the little girl's eyes, the father crept behind a tree to hide.

She watched them with rapt attention, leaned on his shoulders, and giggled, afraid to make a sound; then she stretched her neck out and laughed out loud anyway.

The young father tickled his daughter's face with his beard, so that she wriggled in his arms and chuckled loudly. . . .

He had thought of it again then and had been about to mention it when she once more interrupted his train of thought. She began talking about the little girl's bell-bottom pants.

"Just look how pretty those little pants are. The day before yesterday they were selling some just like that at our factory and lots of people were buying them . . ."

Later he thought of going somewhere else; seems as if he had thought of a remote-controlled toy car . . .

She remembered it again as she watched *Anna Karenina* serialized on television. Anna was persuading Alyosha to go to sleep, saying, "I'm a big, bad monster . . . ," but he wasn't home that time.

When they went to see *The Hunchback of Notre Dame*, a young child in the audience asked in a loud voice, "Why does that nasty bad man always keep ringing that bell?" Children always think ugly people are evil. That time they didn't say anything; didn't even talk the whole night long.

Today, when she suddenly came out with it he had not been prepared and neither, in fact, had she. Perhaps it was because she was unprepared that she did say it. But today of all days! But then, perhaps it was precisely because it was today. Once said, it could not be avoided—it had to be considered now. In some ways it was like removing a heavy stone from the heart, only to replace it with one even heavier.

They walked on in silence. The wind was still very strong. The tattered remnants of a paper kite hung on the power lines above.

Eventually they stopped in a spot sheltered from the wind. The man leaned against the wall and lit a cigarette. The woman put the cookie tin down on the ground and looked up helplessly at the man.

A flock of cawing crows flew crookedly against the grey sky and were buffeted southeastwards in the wind.

"All that's needed is for us to look after him properly," said the man. "I think if we look after him well enough . . ." He was looking at the tricycle which had a large-eyed dragonfly for its trademark. She was gazing up at the crows which had made a circle and were now flying back. . . . They wanted to rest on an old tree, but the wind was too strong.

The man repeated, "I think as long as we look after him really well . . . what do you say?" The hand holding his cigarette trembled incessantly.

The crows had finally succeeded in landing on the tree. The woman said, "How about getting a younger one? Perhaps there wouldn't be this problem if we got a baby."

"He's still going to grow up, isn't he?"

"But it's not the same—he'd be used to it from childhood."

The two of them stood there at the corner of the wall, protected from the wind, saying nothing more for a very long time.

The street lights came on. It must have been past six.

"Are you still tired?" asked the woman.

The man lit another cigarette. A village manure cart passed in front of them, its wheels clattering over a manhole cover. After it had gone by the woman noticed that the cover had not been properly closed.

She nudged the man and said, "Look at that manhole cover."

The man glanced at it.

"Look," she said, nudging him again. "The cover's not on properly."

"Will you keep quiet!" He gave her a strong shove.

"Well," she said defensively in a small voice, as if she had done something wrong, "the cover isn't on properly."

Ignoring her, the man poked with his crutch at some yellow earth in a hole in the wall. She stared worriedly at the manhole cover. After a while she began to walk towards it.

"Come back!" shouted the man.

"But it hasn't been closed properly," she objected, not daring, however, to go any farther forward.

"Come back here at once!" the man shouted again. The woman had to come back.

"Someone might fall down it," she said.

"Serves them right! Are you the only one who cares?"

She stood beside him, looking from him to the manhole, wanting to say something, but not daring. She was afraid to provoke him, with his cirrhosis and all.

The street lights and their shadows swayed in the wind. There was no one else in the lane.

"It's getting late, let's go," said the woman.

"Where to?"

"Mrs. Shi must be getting really impatient by now. Since we've come this far we really should go."

"I didn't want to come in the first place. I didn't want him in the first place."

"Let's go and have a look first, anyway, shall we?"

"We know already without having to take a look! It's not as if it were our own kid . . ."

The woman said nothing for a long time. Finally she swiftly picked up the tin and began walking rapidly forward. It was only then that the man realized she was crying. He grabbed the tricycle and followed. . . .

"Let's have one of our own instead!"

"No! No! I don't want to! You know very well . . ." She crawled onto the bed and cried.

"The doctor said that if only one side had it there was a chance it wouldn't be passed on . . ."

"And what else? What haven't you said? You haven't said that there's also the chance that it could be passed on! It can be hereditary. It's sure to be transmitted through me! I know—I've never been lucky!" She cried and shouted as if insane. . . .

He had never seen her like this before. Completely taken aback, he dared not continue.

"I didn't mean it, really . . . I meant . . . I didn't mean I wanted one of our own." He was trying hard to explain. "I really didn't mean that at all. I mean . . . I agree. We'll get whatever kind you want. If you really want a younger one, well then, I won't say no . . ." He was placating her, as if she were a child.

They walked on quite a distance, passing many small lanes and forgetting to check the names.

"We've already arranged it with Mrs. Shi," the woman sobbed. "We should at least go and take a look."

"Of course we'll go. After all, we don't want to have lost that purse for nothing, now do we?" He wanted to make a joke out of it, but only succeeded in sounding sarcastic.

"Anyhow," he hurried on, "you can eat those cookies, but I can't ride this tricycle!"

She smiled gratefully up at her husband. He gave her his

handkerchief. "Wipe your eyes. You can't go in looking like that."

For some reason she could not stop crying.

"Let's stop a bit for another rest," suggested the man.

There was a temporary vegetable stall with an awning set up by the roadside ahead. The sellers had already left for home and the stall was deserted, save for a few turnips nobody wanted that were piled up on a table. They went to stand in the shadows, away from the street lights. The woman continued wiping her eyes.

"Don't think so much. Really—don't spend so much time thinking . . . "

"I'm not, I'm not. I didn't want to cry."

"I just have a bad temper sometimes."

"No, you don't. It's me . . . I bring you bad luck."

"What a thing to say!"

"But just suppose if . . . "

" 'Just suppose' again! We've been together *ten years* now but you keep on saying, 'Just suppose . . . ' but, I tell you, those ten years of ours are the reality."

The moon was so tiny and so far away, just like on that other night. She leaned against him closely, afraid that all this was not real and that he was like that moon, so far away, so far away. . . .

"Let's go."

"All right."

Just at this point a door opened in a courtyard opposite and a young woman came out, leading a small child. A middle-aged couple followed to see her off, accompanying the mother and son to the end of the lane.

In a very displeased tone the mother said, "I must say I do think you arranged this badly . . . "

The middle-aged woman replied, "You can blame me if you like, but don't take it to heart."

The young woman said, "Actually, a professor wanted him but I couldn't bear to part with him. Otherwise—well, as it is, I'll just have to look after Mingming myself."

The voices slowly faded into the distance.

The woman stood completely immobile.

"Let's go, shall we? What's wrong?" asked the man.

The woman went back into the shadows, out of the street light's reach and leaned against the stall, staring wordlessly at the courtyard opposite. The man walked over to look at the door opposite. It was No. 57, Moonlight Lane. He came back to the vegetable stall and stood beside the woman, saying nothing. The middle-aged couple returned.

"You shouldn't have told her," said the middle-aged man. "I wouldn't want to give my kid away to a pair of cripples either."

"Well, I couldn't lie to her. I tell you what though—I won't have anything to do with this kind of thing any more," said the middle-aged woman.

"They'll be here in a while—what are we going to say to them?"

The gate slammed shut with a bang!

It was silent all around, as quiet as the desert. There was only the sound of the wind, making one think of a tiny boat caught in a deep valley between high, dark waves. The desert has its limits, the ocean comes to an end. If there were no oases, where could the camels go? If there were no harbors, where could a small boat shelter? There were times when neither of them could see the point of carrying on . . . times when they lay awake in the depths of the night. Perhaps he had had yet another nightmare, or she had dreamt of the hereafter, and then they talked of death.

"Do you think there's life after death?"

"I think there must be."

"You're just superstitious."

"Who can tell?"

"Have you thought about death?"

"Of course."

"Then why don't you die?"

"If I died, the loved ones I left behind would suffer too much. What about you?"

"The same."

This was their oasis, they looked to this as they walked through the desert. They were each other's harbor.

It was very late. Somewhere in the distance came the sound of the time signal. Eight o'clock or maybe nine. Probably eight.

They continued standing in the stall, their thoughts confused, saying nothing. The wind continued unabated—it would probably blow all night. The matting of the stall roof had blown open a crack and was flapping noisily against the roof beam, letting in a flurry of old snow which fell on them, unnoticed.

A long time later the woman said suddenly, "We haven't fed An-An yet." An-An was their cat. They kept a pet cat. The woman spoke almost dreamily.

He pulled her into his arms and wrapped her up inside his large padded coat. She felt as if the cold were all on the outside; let the wind blow—nothing could penetrate their overcoat.

"We haven't fed An-An," she said from inside the coat.

He caressed her face, her eyes.

"I'm fine now," she said.

"I'm fine too," he said.

"Shall we go home now?"

"Yes, let's."

"Let's go then."

They turned homewards, keeping close to each other. They had left the cookie tin and the tricycle behind in the vegetable stall. They were always losing things.

"Oh, yes! I forgot! That manhole cover," she exclaimed suddenly.

They retraced their steps to the first place they had stopped. They found the manhole, but the cover was tightly shut.

"Was this the one?" asked the man.

"I think so, or at least, this seems to be the only one around here."

The man banged his crutch down on the cover several times but it didn't budge—it was shut tight.

The woman went back to the corner where they had stood before.

"Oh, from here it looks as though it's not on properly because there's a bit of black showing through the snow, like a hole." ★

Originally published in *Chouxiaoya* (*Ugly Duckling*), no. 10, 1982

Translated by Alison Bailey

Lunch Break

by Shi Tiesheng

Photo by Saundra Sturdevant

All at once the whirring sewing-machines stopped and the world became quiet. Warm sunlight filtered lazily through small windows set at odd angles, and particles of dust hung suspended in the air. One by one people began stretching, yawning, and looking around; tired, expressionless faces sagging and blurring as hints of half-smiles appeared at the corners of their eyes and mouths. It was time for their lunch break, time for a breather, time for a good laugh. Every day it arrived as regular as clockwork, the way April Fool's Day makes its appearance in the West every year.

The luckiest people are those born with the ability to do as they please.

"Luck? I'll tell you what luck is—it's whatever you fucking well want it to be, that's what luck is!"

The expounder of this theory was Old Bai, the presser, chewing away at his ripe-smelling, pickled-bean-curd-stuffed *mantou*.* Exactly who had been responsible for propagating this theory no one was quite sure, but they were all completely convinced by it. It might be thought that this theory was rather similar to Ah Q's philosophy of life,** but none of the eight-and-a-half people present (there was a young man paralyzed from the waist down who could only be counted as half) had any notion of who Ah Q was, even if some of them had heard of Lu Xun. In fact, just the day before they had been debating whether or not he lived in Zhongnanhai like all the other bigwigs. In the end only the young cripple had dissented, while everyone else had come down in favor of Old Bai's opinion—after all, what else could you expect with someone as famous as that?

Enamel mugs clinked and the low, old room was full of the pungent smell of garlic.

"How much meat have you got in there?"

"Meat? I'd have to bite my own tongue off if I wanted to taste any meat!"

And then it was quiet once again—but don't worry, it was just that no one had yet found the right topic to start the ball rolling. The sound of brakes squealing came suddenly through the back window. Everyone stopped in mid-chew and pricked up their ears.

"You tired of living or something?"

Obviously no one was hurt. The engine soon started up again and the car drove off, leaving the stage free for the next act.

"Yesterday, after work . . . ," began old Mother Xia, narrowing her eyes and stretching out her neck in an effort to swallow a piece of dry pancake. "Yesterday, after work . . . ," she gulped down some water before taking a deep breath. "Yesterday, after work, I almost died of fright! There I was just walking along, when all of a sudden there was a noise behind me just like that one a moment ago."

"The hell! I thought you'd choke to death first!" Madame "Little Feet" sitting opposite broke off a piece of her vegetable stuffed *baozi** and popped it into her mouth before continuing, "The way you were carrying on I thought at least you were going to tell us you'd found a diamond or something . . ." She grimaced and turned away, sitting with her right leg crossed over her left and her four-and-a-half-inch bound foot swinging

---

*A *mantou* is a kind of steamed bun eaten in northern China.

**A PRC urbanite who does not know what Ah Q stands for or who Lu Xun was is culturally deprived in the extreme. The protagonist of Lu Xun's novella, *Ah Q zhengzhuan* (The True Story of Ah Q), is the best known fictional character in modern China. He is the epitome of what Lu Xun regarded as the debased national character of the Chinese people. It is rather difficult to see what his "philosophy of life" has to do with Old Bai's remarks about luck; that is probably part of the author's characterization of these unlettered people.

---

*A *baozi* is another form of steamed bun which is usually filled with meat or vegetables.

proudly in the air.

The young cripple clicked away at his abacus as he ate. "Mother Xia, you've had half a day off this month for personal matters and half a day's sick-leave—that means 92 cents less this month."

"I turned round to look," continued Mother Xia. "The alley was so narrow and the car so wide, just where do you think I was supposed to get? So I started running as fast as I could . . . if it had been you with your precious little feet you'd have never made it; you'd have ended up as a wheel-block instead." She got her revenge on Little Feet.

"When I reached the end of the alley the car was just able to get past. Some schoolkids said it was a 'Red Flag.' I've heard of them, of course, but I wouldn't know what one looked like, would you?" She slapped her leg in apparent exasperation at missing the chance to get a really good look at one.

Everyone looked solemn at the mention of the "Red Flag," except for Old Bai who let out a grunt and said, "Well, you have led a poor life, haven't you! I'll tell you what a 'Red Flag' 's like—big and really fancy with bullet-proof windows. Made in Germany they are. That's what a 'Red Flag' 's like." His eyes met those of the young cripple, whereupon he added, "Of course, China's got the know-how to make them herself now, too . . . only bigwigs get to ride in cars like that. Why, years ago, Ma Lianliang* used to . . . ," Old Bai stopped in some confusion when he heard the cripple laughing to himself.

Just then Little Feet broke out into a prolonged cackle of laughter. The more the others called her a crazy old woman the harder she rocked with laughter.

"Quick! Send for an ambulance! We've got a nutcase on our hands!" Apparently in deadly earnest, Old Bai rushed towards the door. "I thought there was something funny about the way she looked this morning . . . as if she couldn't tell her arse from her elbow . . . "

"Mr. Bai, you've had one day off for personal reasons and two half-days off sick—that makes one *yuan* 85 cents off." The cripple was still doing his accounts.

"Take it, take it! There'll be less for a thief to take if you do!" said Old Bai breezily as he squatted by the door, his eyes fixed on Little Feet and a self-satisfied, crafty smile on his face.

Little Feet finally stopped laughing, only to begin hiccoughing instead.

"Hic! That old bitch was getting at me," and she stabbed her finger in Mother Xia's direction. "Hic! So you think I'll end up as a wheelblock, do you? Hic! Well, let me tell you, it would be fucking good luck for me if I did, hic! I'd lie there stretched out in the road, all comfortable, no cares in the world, with the car-owner's two bodyguards to look after me and lots of good things to eat and drink . . . hic!"

"Are you sure you wouldn't like something to smoke as well while you're at it?" Old Bai peered closely at her, a sycophantic look on his face.

"Naturally!" Little Feet swept him a glance and assumed a stern expression. "Listen to me, old man! When it happens, you can be sure I won't need you around any more! Go on out, old man, and buy a couple of Zhonghua filtertips!"**

Old Bai snorted in reply and grabbed Little Feet's wrist, applying himself to the task of taking her pulse. "Is Madame awake then?"

Little Feet gave him a violent push. "And why not? I was knocked down, after all, wasn't I?" From the way she said this it seemed as though her fate was not so bad after all.

"So they'd hit your poor old bag of bones, would they? And then you'd just lie down there all nice and quiet, would you? You'd lie down in a quiet mortuary or a crematorium!"

Old Bai broke a match in two and unhurriedly began picking at his yellow teeth.

Round-eyed, Little Feet looked all around, feeling vexed and having nothing to say, but then all at once she brightened up and announced, "Well, even if I do get killed by the car there's still my son!"

"And when he dies there'll be your grandson, and his son and grandson, and so on and so on . . . You might only be able to dig away a little piece of the mountain yourself, but all that's needed is time and it'll all disappear.* Three times seven is twenty-one. Three from five leaves two." The young crippled intoned all this to himself as if reading a sutra, his head down, his eyes looking neither right nor left, straightening his accounts while holding a half-eaten wheat pancake in his hand.

"Well, what about your son, then?" someone enquired curiously.

"The car owner would have to give my son somewhere to live so that he could get married at last. Just think—he's thirty-two already and his girlfriend's twenty-nine!" Little Feet's eyes had brightened up considerably and her forgotten vegetable *baozi* rolled to the floor as she spoke. "That way we could hurry things up a bit. We wouldn't even have to bother with the lousy room the housing people gave us. Why, we should fucking well be given an apartment in a block with a kitchen and an inside toilet. My son and his wife could live in one room and I'd have the other . . . "

Old Bai poked her. "I can see I'll have to wake you up again! You've already been killed off by this car of yours or had you forgotten? But that doesn't matter! I'll take over the room for you instead and in the future I can do a bit of baby-sitting and such-like for your son and his wife." He wrinkled his nose as though he could easily cry. "If you do a good deed like that you'll be sure of being born into a good family next time round!"

People were on the point of laughing when another old woman joined in the conversation. "Old woman" is not very accurate. She wasn't all that old, but she didn't have a single tooth in her head and she wheezed a bit. A whistling noise issued from her throat as she spoke, "You're right there! Mind you, it can be good or bad being run over by a car, depending on your luck. The year of the earthquake my old man was knocked down by a hand-tractor and broke his leg; but the driver had hardly a penny to his name so there was no way of claiming anything for it. What a mess! But then there was a simple girl back in our old village who got knocked down and

---

*The identity of Ma Lianliang is not known.
**These are fairly expensive cigarettes.

*The young cripple is making light of Mao Zedong's favorite story, "The Foolish Old Man Who Removed the Mountain." Although he could do very little with a pick and shovel in his lifetime, his sons and grandsons could continue the job and someday it would be finished. The story was required reading during the Cultural Revolution.

killed by a 'Shanghai' model car, and guess what her family got? One thousand *RMB*! One thousand! And that was just a 'Shanghai'."

Everyone's eyebrows shot up and their mouths fell open in astonishment. This was deadly serious. They all slowed down their chewing and seemed to be calculating something in their heads. For a while the old room was almost deathly silent and even Old Bai's face had lost its crafty smile.

"Aunty Luo—three days' sick-leave—that's two *yuan* 77 cents off." Only the young cripple continued as before.

"If I'd been hit," said the woman addressed as Aunty Luo, "I wouldn't want a thousand *RMB*. After all, however much money you get, it all gets spent in the end. No, what I'd do is to get them to find me a real job. Maybe I could work for the car owner's family as their nanny. I don't know what she did in her past life to deserve it, but one of my neighbors is a nanny in a bigwig's house. They're always throwing away all kinds of things, but they're all good enough for the likes of us. Of course, I wouldn't say no if I could get a regular worker's job instead."

Everyone's eyebrows relaxed as if they had suddenly all seen the light.

"Isn't that why we can say life's better these days?" queried old Granny Lu who did the button-holes, lifting up her one eye above the thick lens of her glasses to peer at everyone as she expressed her thoughts.

"In the old days my old man used to pull a rickshaw for the boss of a medicine shop. I remember going off to find him at work one cold winter's day carrying our eldest girl. He gave the little one a piece of New Year's cake from the boss' kitchen and got a real bawling out for it—just a little thing like that! What wouldn't I eat if I had the money? I'd eat . . . " She held out her hands as if cupping a large bowl between them. "I'd eat . . . I'd eat . . . ," just exactly what it was she wanted to eat never came out. Her one eye blinked repeatedly behind her thick glasses.

"My old man's been going on about the old days the last day or so . . . mm! I know! Green-haired turtles . . . or maybe the navy could get me some fresh prawns and the air force could deliver them. . . ."

"That's what Lin Biao did! You're getting yourself all mixed up!" said the cripple as he rested his cheeks in his hands and smirked at her.

Old Bai snorted and stood up with a grin. He took a few turns around his stool before sitting down once again and saying,

"Are you stupid or something? Lin Biao's turned into the boss of a pharmacy and you've been eating his New Year's cake! You're getting old and muddled—whatever will your kids think of you?"

Amidst the general laughter Granny Lu slowly drew in her outstretched hands, an embarrassed smile on her face. She said nothing more.

After that they returned to the original topic of discussion.

"If it were me, the least they would have to do would be to get the kids' dad moved back to Beijing. When they sent all the important industries into the interior for safety it was meant to be for only three years, but our little "safety token"* is thirteen years old already!"

A sigh came from someone in the corner.

Somebody lit a cigarette by the stove. "If I got hit it wouldn't be asking too much to get them to help get my son transferred back from Yunnan."

"Just getting allocated a job would be good enough!" A gob of spittle came from behind a pillar. "My kid's been back from Inner Mongolia for over two years now, but he still hasn't been given a job. Just think what would happen if a 'Red Flag' drove up to the factory and issued an order! The boss' arse would be way up in the air, bowing and scraping away he'd be! But . . ."

"Come on! Let's not get greedy here—just a little bit more in the pocket each week would suit us ladies fine!"

The low, old room was silent once more, but you couldn't say the silence of satisfaction after a good meal. Far from it. There was a strange light in everyone's eyes—yearning, perhaps, or joy or possibly a longing for some kind of fulfillment? Who can say? Whatever it was, it was a light rarely to be seen in this dilapidated old room and in these elderly eyes. They seemed like statues, gazing unmoving into the distance. Some fingered moles on their faces. Some plucked at the hair in their nostrils. Yet others had picked their nose and were now rolling something between their fingers . . . , it was as if they were all listening to something away up on high.

"Ice . . . Cream!" The chilly autumn breeze carried in the long-drawn out cry, wrenching everyone back from their world of forgetfulness.

"Yes, well, I don't fancy being knocked down and killed by a car, I can tell you!" Just who first came down to earth no-one knew, but all at once the small alley rang with the sound of laughter mixed with a barrage of curses.

With a whir the machines started up again and the world became frantic once more.

1980

---

*It was common during the Cultural Revolution for people to name their children after events of national importance taking place when they were born.

Originally published in *Xiaoshuo xuankan* (*Short Story Selections*), no. 1, 1981.

Translated by Alison Bailey

About the Translators

Alison Bailey is a graduate student in Asian Studies at the University of British Columbia where she is completing her M.A. thesis on Xu Dishan.

Daniel Bryant is Associate Professor of Chinese at the Centre for Pacific and Oriental Studies, University of Victoria. His main research interest is Chinese poetry of the Tang and Ming dynasties.

Susette Cooke studied at Beijing University for two years and is currently a postgraduate student in modern Chinese literature at the University of Sydney.

Michael S. Duke is Assistant Professor of Chinese at the University of British Columbia. His book, *Blooming and Contending: Chinese Literature in the Post-Mao Era*, will be published by Indiana University Press early in 1985.

Jeannette L. Faurot is Associate Professor of Chinese at the University of Texas at Austin and the editor of *Chinese Fiction from Taiwan*.

Howard Goldblatt is Associate Professor of Chinese at San Francisco State University, the author of *Hsiao Hung*, and founding editor of *The Journal of Modern Chinese Literature*.

Vivian Hsu teaches Chinese language and literature at Oberlin College, is the editor of *Born of the Same Roots: Stories of Modern Chinese Women*, and is currently working on post-Mao literature and post-1949 neologisms.

Dale R. Johnson teaches Chinese literature at Oberlin College and is the author of *Yuan Music Dramas* and several other books on the poetry and music of Yuan drama.

Richard King teaches Chinese language and literature at York University and has recently completed his doctoral dissertation (University of British Columbia) on literary theory and the novels of the Cultural Revolution period.

Wendy Larson is Assistant Professor of Chinese at Portland State University. Her doctoral dissertation (University of California, Berkeley) deals with the autobiographies of Guo Moruo, Lu Xun, Shen Congwen, and Hu Shi.

Winnie Lai-fong Louis is a doctoral candidate in Asian Studies at the University of British Columbia where she is completing a thesis on the images of youth in post-Mao literature.

Bonnie S. McDougall currently resides in Beijing. She has taught and published extensively on modern Chinese literature, especially poetry and literary criticism.

Saundra Sturdevant currently resides in Berkeley. She worked as Editor at The Foreign Languages Press, Beijing, 1981–82. The photos in this volume were taken in 1982 and are part of a larger photographic project.

Ping Yen is a graduate student in comparative literature at the University of California, Berkeley, where she specializes in English and Chinese literatures.

Ellen L. Yeung is an instructor in Chinese language at San Francisco State University and co-translator (with Howard Goldblatt) of Xiao Hong's *The Field of Life and Death*.

Shiao-ling Yu's doctoral dissertation (University of Wisconsin, Madison) provides a survey of post-Mao literature from 1977 to 1982. She was Visiting Assistant Professor at Ohio State University from 1983 to 1984.